Nov. 15, 2004

To Naomi —

God Bless You!
See you at the Rapture!

Best Always,

Steve Mamchak
&

Russ Scalzo

Beginning of Sorrows

A novel

by

Russ Scalzo and Steve Mamchak

Book One of the *"Chronicles of the End Times"* Series

authorHOUSE

1663 LIBERTY DRIVE, SUITE 200
BLOOMINGTON, INDIANA 47403
(800) 839-8640
www.authorhouse.com

First published by AuthorHouse 08/02/04

ISBN: 1-4184-4113-9 (e)
ISBN: 1-4184-4112-0 (sc)
ISBN: 1-4184-4111-2 (dj)

Printed in the United States of America
Bloomington, Indiana

This book is printed on acid-free paper.

"You shall hear of wars and rumors of wars: see that you be not troubled, for all these things must come to pass, but the end is not yet. For nation shall rise against nation, and kingdom against kingdom, and there shall be famines, and pestilence, and earthquakes in various places. All these are the *beginning of sorrows*." **Matthew 24:6-8**

DEDICATION:

"A wife of noble character…is worth
far more than rubies."
Proverbs 31:10

to Gail…
to Sue…

…beyond the edge of time…

BEGINNING OF SORROWS

by

Russ Scalzo and Steve Mamchak

TABLE OF CONTENTS

PROLOGUE:

Sorrow and the Silence

When he opened the seventh seal,

there was silence in heaven

for about half an hour.

Revelation 8:1

THEY WERE CREATORS OF SORROW AND SORROW'S SPAWN, all at once and both together. If there was light, they shunned it; preferring hard laughter in the shadows; the dull and twisted to the sharp and beautiful; the power that cruelty provided like a fire eating through their veins. Now that a part of the light they turned from had flickered and finally died, anticipation of the night made them all but giddy, ready for the exaltation brought by the copper scent of blood. Now, although they had neither the words nor the wit to express it, was their time, and instinctively, they knew it. They knew that it was dark and growing darker still.

The three men clothed in unkempt black garments and knitted black face-covering ski masks approached the house quickly, silently, making studied efforts that the crowbar would not swing against the blue-black barrels of the automatic rifles they carried and break the forced quiet of the evening.

Entry was effortless, two of them watching silently while the third worked a crowbar, snapping a simple lock on a simple door. They were inside as swiftly as they had come.

By agreement and without a word, they split up and began a swift, almost frenzied search of the rooms. Drawers tumbled recklessly from bureaus; bedside tables sprawled; mattresses thudded against walls.

One of them paused to scratch at the beard growing behind his mask. It was so easy, his lips relaxed enough to trace the pattern of a smile. There were wallets just left out in the open or on a chair or in the hall, and clothes left in curiously ordered piles on floor and bed and stairs -- with money inside! Not only here, in this place of shadows, but in every silent house they had 'visited' last night and the night before and the night before that. For one dizzying moment he held the vision of himself standing in a gold mine dark and deep within the belly of the earth, the gold ore crumbling and tumbling from the walls and rolling to a defined stop at his feet.

They met as planned at the bottom of the stairs, opposite the futile door they had forced just moments before. There was, in that darkness, only wasted slivers of light from the street, but they were used to the night, and they could see the rock-hard smiles leering through the mouth-holes of each other's masks.

That was when they heard the noise.

"Someone's here," one of them whispered, his eyes shifting between the two others.

The voice that invaded from the other side of the front door had age to it, but that was all. It lacked the crisp command of a voice used to authority, and the three of them knew that it was not the law, nor anyone who could offer greater pain than they could themselves inflict. The words were loud but somewhat slow, almost hesitant, edged with the weakness of uncertainty.

"Come out...come on, now...and put your hands over your head!"

There was a small silence that hung in the charged air and lasted a second, perhaps two. Then there was the slap and clash of flesh on the weapons and the three men turned in the general direction of the front door.

The blue-white flames from the muzzles of their automatic rifles illuminated the place they stood in a flickering strobe light that caught clenched teeth and wide eyes in a frozen, never-to-be-printed photograph, partly fear; partly fury; partly sheer joy. The sound roared in great, clamoring, deafening peals of thunder. The bullets reached the door and ripped it apart, tearing into it as a ravening beast might pull apart the doe it found cowering near its lair. Small and splintered fragments of wood flew everywhere; the acrid stench of gunpowder clung in shrouds on the walls.

The two neighborhood watchmen, volunteers in their sixties, residents three and five doors down the street, lay on the porch, each dead by a dozen wet, red wounds. Each grandfather was wearing the patch his group had jubilantly designed and bought months before, proclaiming the Neighborhood Watch motto of "Victory Through Vigilance." That phrase, however clever and catchy, could hardly be read now. It was swiftly being obliterated by the thick, dark blood that continued to ooze through the ragged, ravaged shirts of the two victims.

Inside, the creators of sorrow and lovers of the dark gathered what they had taken and ran through the splintered door and into the waiting night. One of them tripped across a dead man as he made his escape, leaving a half print of one black boot sole painted in dark red on one porch step.

On the street they paused. Wide, twitching eyes sought each other, and spontaneously they began to punctuate the evening with staccato laughter. They continued to laugh as they were absorbed into the velvet darkness.

Back on the porch of the dim and empty house, the deep red blood of one of the watchmen pooled quietly where he lay, finally reaching and being absorbed into the paper face of one of the myriad of newspapers that had not been taken in for many days.

The banner brazenly proclaimed the paper's name, *The Chronicle*, and the headline screamed:

DISAPPEARANCE OF MILLIONS STILL UNEXPLAINED

All else…

All else was quiet, almost tomb-like.

The silence and the sorrow had returned.

PART ONE:
Signs of the Times

*The Pharisees and Sadducees came to Jesus and tested him by
asking him to show them a sign from heaven. He replied,
"When evening comes, you say, 'It will be
fair weather, for the sky is red,' and in the morning, 'Today it will be stormy
for the sky is red and overcast.'
You know how to interpret the appearance
of the sky, but you cannot interpret the signs of the times."*

Matthew 16:1-3

CHAPTER ONE

Assignments in the Aftermath

JERRY WESTFIELD HIT THE KEYS that sent his copy to the compositor and let out a huge, deep breath. Rising from his computer, he stretched and ambled to the bank of windows that defined the street side of the newsroom, and he took up position there, staring out at the moving landscape before and several stories beneath him. Everything had the same gray and stoic look he remembered – the buildings, stark against the sky; the traffic weaving its mechanical snake dance a hundred feet below. Everything endured and moved and breathed in the same way it always had, yet the crawling in his stomach reminded him that nothing was the same -- nothing.

The combined noise of voice and machine in the newsroom became a more and more distant hum as one more time he played over the events that refused to leave his conscious mind at rest.

There wasn't much he hadn't seen in his lifetime. As a young reporter covering bush wars around the globe, he had existed, first hand, within the sorry shadow of the darkest side of mankind. He was in the frenzied, paranoid Washington of the Watergate hearings. For years afterward, he had covered the Mid-East, concentrating on Israel and terrorism and the Palestinian Problem, which was not as much a "problem" as an explosion looking for a place to devastate. His Pulitzer Prize, however, had come to him for his unbiased reporting of the Los Angeles riots of '92, a task that had nearly cost him his life.

He also was among those who predicted the revolution in Saudi Arabia, which led to the demise of King and Prime Minister FAHD bin Abd al-Aziz Al Saud and his family after the US pulled out of Iraq; an upheaval that saw the new right wing government demand and finally expel all US Armed Forces from their country.

There wasn't much he hadn't experienced; wasn't much he hadn't seen.

Until now.

It was something you might have read and dismissed as some sorry insanity or the most fantastic of science fiction or the worst sort of fevered dementia, had not so many people – regular, just-like-you-and-me, non-crazy people -- been witness to it; had not the impact of it been felt with a burning thud everywhere in the entire world. It simply…was, and the pain was too real. No one, philosopher to panhandler, found it easy to deal with in any way.

It played once more behind Jerry Westfield's eyes. Two weeks ago, millions of people, so many that it would take months even to accurately estimate, had disappeared from the face of the earth. There was no other way to state it. As far as anyone could tell, they were there, doing their jobs, watching TV, sleeping in bed, walking the dog – and then they weren't; then they were gone. The sorrow and panic was immediate, the inevitable theories were endless, and the stories ranged from the outrageously fantastic to the fanciful impossible.

The fact remained, however, that they were gone, and gone indeed. In a very short time, the world had become a different place, and it was more than just missing people. There had been a precipitous rise in theft, looting, murder, and every type of criminal activity. Police departments were overrun with calls, to the point where there was simply no way of keeping up. There were some who had said that it seemed as though Peace, itself, had been taken from the earth and Sorrow left in its stead.

His mind rebelled. He knew the power of words, certainly, but there was a part of Jerry Westfield which affirmed that there had to be – had to be – a logical reason for everything, and that included all of this. With eyes that looked out over the New York canyons and saw nothing of their grace and power, he allowed his mind to wonder about the copy he would write when he found the real story – what had really happened.

"Jerry! Hey, Jerry! Phone for you, man! On line three!"

It was Bill Foley who had shouted, bringing Jerry back into the clattering reality of *The Chronicle* newsroom. Bill, proven to be a reliable friend and travel buddy; was an acute photographer who had, more than once, driven home with his photos the grief and grinding reality Jerry had reported.

"Well?" Bill continued, "Are you going to pick it up or just look at it?"

4

"OK, wise guy," Jerry managed to smile, "I got it!" He picked up the receiver and intoned, "*Chronicle*, Jerry Westfield here."

"Yeah...ah...yeah," came the voice, so unsteady it created its own static, "Mr. Westfield, I know what happened, you know. To all those people, I mean. I mean, I seen it. I seen it come down and take them away."

"You saw what come down, sir?"

"You know!" and the intensity of the telephone voice levitated to a higher level, "It was the space ship! The Mother Ship! It just sucked them up! Right off the ground!"

Jerry drew a hand across his forehead and sat on the edge of his desk.

"You were there," he continued. "You saw this happen?"

"Yeah! Oh, yeah! It was unbelievable!"

"I'm sure it was, sir," Jerry sighed, succeeding in keeping all sarcasm from his voice. "Tell you what, sir, I'm going to connect you with my secretary, Mrs. Cortman. She'll take down your story, OK? Hold on, now."

But he couldn't resist, and he added, "She'll tell you what to do with your Mother Ship."

He pressed the right buttons and got his secretary. They were several desks apart, but they could see each other across the crowded newsroom even if they had to hear through the receivers.

"Mary," Jerry said, "I'm sorry, but I have another one for you. Pick up on line three...and thanks so much!"

Across the room, Mary rolled her eyes and said, "You know what, Jerry Westfield, that makes another one you owe me!"

Jerry kissed the air in her direction and hung up the phone. There had to have been...how many?... over 300 space ship stories this week alone.

That phone call, Jerry determined, would be the last "event" of his day. With his copy in and the morning edition well on its way to being "in bed," he reached for his lap top computer, put it and a few more items in his briefcase, gave a small salute to his desk and headed for the door.

"Leaving?" Bill Foley asked. "Me, too. Want to grab some dinner at Willoughby's?"

"Thanks, Bill, but I think I'm going to spend the night at Jeremy's."

Bill's forehead grew wrinkles. "How long are you going to keep this up, Jerry?"

"Look, Bill, the looting is – well, you know it's getting worse, and I just feel...well, someone has to be there. Besides, I keep thinking that maybe I'll find something...you know, something Jeremy and Kathy left behind."

"Sure, like a note saying, '*Have gone to Planet Mongo; please send chocolate chip cookies!*'"

Foley sighed, and his eyes grew soft for a moment. He placed a tentative hand on Jerry's arm, "If you need anything...hey, you know my number."

"That I do, friend," Jerry smiled, "that I do!"

And Jerry Westfield stepped into the elevator that would take him down into the deepening twilight.

*   *   *

Jeremy and Kathy Palmer lived about 15 miles from the city in a community most people would call a "good" neighborhood. Jerry had met the couple five years ago at a dinner party for a mutual friend. At that time, Jerry was going through a divorce laden with pain, anger and guilt, and he felt a desperate and gnawing need for someone to talk to. Jeremy, it turned out, was an excellent listener, and it was as simple as that. They became friends and the three of them spent a good deal of time together thereafter. Kathy even put up with Monday night football and the occasional golf game on Saturdays, but her main and compelling desire, it seemed, was to see Jerry Westfield get his life "back together."

The only day Jerry rarely visited was Sunday. That day the Palmers reserved for Church, followed by Adult Sunday School, followed by an evening service, all of which, to his amazement, they eagerly attended without coercion. They were very active in their church, he discovered, and often, they would try to get Jerry to go with them. Ordinarily, that would have been enough to start Jerry on a fast exit with a "nice-to-know-ya" finality. By then, however, he had come to know them personally... and he liked them. Far from the wild and austere "religious fanatic holy rollers" that TV and movies pictured; snake-handling psychotics about to shoot Santa Claus because God had told them to do so in a fiery vision, these were gentle, affable people, deeply in love with each other, fun to be with, who genuinely liked him and wanted to help. Therefore, when Kathy would suggest he join them at church, Jerry merely smiled and gently reminded them that he was Jewish.

"A convenient excuse," Kathy would smile, "considering you haven't seen the inside of a synagogue since you were a boy!"

Jerry set his thoughts aside and pulled off the road and into the driveway. Everything looked perfect and undisturbed. The lawn service was still keeping the grounds, and Jerry had personally made sure that the lights came on and off at the proper times. Kathy and Jeremy might not be here, but to a prospective invader, the house still looked occupied.

He turned off the car, locked it, and walked up the four steps to the front door, fishing in his pocket for the key the Palmers had kept hidden under a flowerpot that he had removed and taken with him several days ago.

Inside it was silent...and sad. It was not just quiet, with occasional outside noises muffling their way through walls and closed doors. Rather, this was a silence that hung in the air, dripped from the ceiling, pressed in upon you as you stood. This was a silence stuffed with sorrow that spoke of emptiness that might never be filled. Jerry coughed nervously, shook his head, and turned to his right.

In the living room, where they had spent so many hours talking and watching football, Jerry sat on the edge of the brown couch and, not knowing what else to do, pressed the TV remote to catch whatever might distract the scratch of happy memories whose sadness he would rather postpone.

The voice came first, the talking head on the news channel resolving slowly into focus.

"...the battle over Jerusalem continues. Today, the Mayor of Jerusalem declared that the city belongs to the Jewish people and should not be divided. Negotiations are at a critical point. Israel's Palestinian and Arab neighbors are calling for a 'Jihad,' a holy war, if Israel does not yield on its position."

"So, what else is new?" Jerry sarcastically asked the television set as he pushed the mute button.

He walked into the kitchen to get himself a Pepsi from the huge refrigerator he had restocked last week. The news reminded Jerry that Bob Lewis, the Managing Editor of *The Chronicle,* had talked about sending Jerry to Israel on assignment. Of course, that was before millions of people decided to shuffle off into nothingness world wide, leaving behind a sad and empty confusion that had commanded the front pages of newspapers ever since it happened. Now, Jerry wasn't sure what his next assignment would be. The stray thought wandered by that perhaps he'd be assigned to chasing after space ships!

As he returned to the living room, Jerry spotted Jeremy Palmer's Bible on a small table in the hallway. It was where it had been the day Jerry discovered that his young friends had "left" during the night, as had several million others. The Bible was large, its once-gold edges frayed and flecked from use, and its thin pages, Jerry knew, filled with a patchwork of notes, all written carefully and precisely in Jeremy's own hand.

Jerry paused and ran two fingers across the red leather cover of the book. Although many people – most people -- most semi-sane people -- attributed the disappearance to space ships or clandestine world-wide government experiments or even the mystic power of new-age meditations, he knew that there was yet another possibility. It was a possibility his missing friend had explained to an incredulous Jerry Westfield; explained in detail. It even had a name. It was called...the Rapture.

Jeremy had spoken with him about that topic just a few weeks before. He told Jerry how Jesus was going to take all His faithful followers home to heaven in an event called "The Rapture," and how this would mark the beginning of a time of trouble and testing for the rest of the world. When Jerry had listened to Jeremy, he had said nothing, keeping his face calm and relaxed, but the idea...the idea had seemed so...well... so crazy; so fanatic. Who could believe something as ridiculous? Now, it seemed to be one very logical explanation.

With a shake of his head, he drove his fist down on the Bible. No! It was only one possibility – one fantastic possibility -- among many, and that deep part of Jerry could not – would not – accept such a wild story.

Back in the living room, he switched on the volume in time to hear the TV anchor say, *"Rumblings from Russia; will Moscow get involved? That story and more when we come back."*

"You know," Jerry proclaimed aloud to the silent walls, "the world is insane, and I'm the paper boy making a delivery at the local asylum!"

He turned back toward the hall and paused at the table. Tentatively, he reached out and lifted Jeremy Palmer's Bible in his hands. He stared at it for a full minute before he tossed it under his arm and returned to the living room and slipped it into his black leather briefcase.

At that moment, the phone rang. Jerry jumped at the unexpected sound, fumbling for the phone, getting it on the third ring.

"Hello," he said quietly, making it almost a question.

"Jerry? It's Bill. Bill Foley."

"Bill, what's up? You hardly ever call me here."

"You were watching the news?"

"Yes...well, I heard some of it...a piece here and there. Why?"

"Our old buddies, the Russians, are getting more and more involved with the Mid-East situation. Our guys over there say it's more than just trash-talking. Bob Lewis wants a meeting first thing in the morning. Hey,

I'm sorry to call you at your friend's place, but he told me to find you, and you know..."

"No problem, Bill," Jerry interrupted. "I'll be there. Thanks."

Jerry hung up the phone. Slowly, he kicked off his shoes and arranged himself full-length on the comfortable sofa where he had spent more than one night, secure in the company of friends. A silent push on a button, and the TV faded and died.

In the silence, he could feel, if barely hear, the wind beginning to pick up. A storm was on the way, and Jerry smiled ruefully. Somehow, it seemed most fitting.

Oh, Lord, how he needed to talk! It was an ache that would not be sent to its room or dismissed in any manner. But there was no one, just the sad, empty rooms...and the memories. How he wished Jeremy and Kathy could be there now.

Right now.

*   *   *

Robert Lewis, a large man, large of body and will and mind, sat at his desk, his office door open, holding his red coffee mug with "BOSS" emblazoned on it in gold, his eyes peering over the rim of the cup, waiting. Not that waiting was new to him; he had waited before, for many things. As a young black man growing up in turbulent times, he felt he had waited, sometimes interminably, for such things as justice and equality, and he had waited with anticipation for his chance to make a difference. He attended Ohio State on a football scholarship, and, belying all the inane jokes about athletes and higher learning, he had graduated in the top ten percent of his class. Now in his fifties, he had worked his way up to Managing Editor of one of the largest newspapers in the country.

"Foley!" he shouted through the open door, "Where is Westfield?"

"Any minute, Mr. Lewis," Bill Foley answered with a false smile in his voice. "You know Jerry."

As the words were being spoken, Bob Lewis spotted Jerry Westfield entering the newsroom, black briefcase in hand.

"Westfield!" Lewis roared, "Get in here!"

"Good morning, Bob!" Jerry smiled, poking his head into the room. "How's the coffee? Has it quelled the beast within you yet?"

Bob Lewis didn't answer. Setting his private coffee mug firmly on the dark oak table that dominated one half of his office, he mumbled, "Close the door and sit down."

9

Jerry didn't have to force a smile. He and Bob Lewis had a fine relationship, professional as well as personal, and a call to the Managing Editor's office was hardly a novelty. In fact, Jerry looked forward to sharing coffee and pleasantries, even now, with so much…happening.

"Get yourself some coffee if you want to, Jerry, but don't get comfortable," Bob Lewis stated flatly. "Sorry, but this is too hot for small talk. Did Bill Foley tell you about what's going on?"

"Just the headlines," Jerry answered, and he leaned forward, giving the editor his full attention.

Lewis sank back in his massive leather chair and let out a long breath before he began.

"The Russians are moving a large contingent of troops and tanks along their southern border. Iran, Iraq, Syria – you name it! The whole Arab nation is stirring, and even Germany seems to be getting involved. Something big is about to happen, Jerry; our sources are confident of that."

"Have you seen any satellite photographs?" Jerry asked, suddenly all business.

"No, not yet."

"What's the word from Washington?"

"Nothing from the President," Lewis sighed, "but we do know that he has called an emergency meeting of the cabinet and some leaders of Congress for seven-thirty tonight. You'll have more than enough time to get there and get settled. Contact your regular sources and see what you can find out. Call me as soon as you have something."

"It's a good thing I didn't have any plans," Jerry quipped. "I'd hate to miss a good crisis."

"You won't." Lewis stated with a straight face. "You're very good at finding a crisis and getting the story on my desk. That's why we pay you…"

They finished the sentence together, "…the big bucks!"

"Precisely," Bob Lewis smiled. "Mary will fill you in on your arrangements. Good luck! Now, get out of my office and do something unusual, like get to work!"

Jerry smiled and nodded. Outside, he found Bill Foley waiting for him.

"What do you think, Jerry?"

"I think I could use a decent cup of coffee; Bob's is one step above swamp water!"

"OK, don't tell me," Bill laughed, "but if you need a tremendously talented photographer…" He let the sentence trail off as he smiled and returned to his cubicle.

When he was gone, Jerry snaked his way to the desk of Mary Cortman. Divorced and raising two children by herself, Mary had been a real help to Jerry during his own "unpleasantness," as he euphemistically called the debacle of his own divorce. They had become what the world might deny ever existed, a man and a woman who were, indeed, just good friends.

"So, Mary. What goodies do you have for me?"

"Okay, here it is," she answered, giving him one of her it's-not-that-bad smiles. "Your flight leaves at eleven fifteen. You arrive in Washington a couple minutes after noon. You'll be staying at the Hilton, as usual, room 315. I made arrangements for a car at the airport, if you want it. It's all here in the envelope!"

"Efficient as always. Thanks, I don't know how I'd get on without you."

"Are you sure you're not Irish?" she asked. "You have to be with all the blarney you manufacture! Come on! Leave!"

"But how can I pull myself away from your dazzling presence," Jerry intoned with rapidly fluttering eyelashes.

"By remembering one thing," Mary smiled back.

"And what would that be?"

"Just this, Bozo! You're already late for your flight!"

CHAPTER TWO

Beyond the Edge

A HARD, COLD DECEMBER RAIN was pelting Washington, DC, city of history and hysteria, and the traffic around the White House was picking up in bulk and volume. Inside the familiar building, the pressure was building as well, as individuals walked and talked their jobs with faces creased with concern and eyes that made only furtive contact with fellow workers. Since the elections in Russia, the new nationalist regime had been sharpening old sabers and rattling them very publicly, looking more like the old Soviet Union than what the West had hoped for years ago under the leadership of Boris Yeltsin. With the down-sizing of the United States Military and the increase in power and influence of the United Nations over the past several years, the US no longer wielded the military supremacy it once enjoyed, and the feeling on the Hill was one of great frustration verging on the edginess of impotence. That, plus the fact that "The Great Disappearance" had taken some key people in Congress, all added to the intensity of the crisis at hand.

In the Oval Office, the President was meeting informally with key members of his cabinet, a prelude to the formal meeting he had announced for later that evening. There was Chief of Staff, Benjamin Walls; Secretary of State, Philip Dresson; Robert Miller, the Secretary of Defense; and Harold Chambers, the Vice President. Various members of Congress joined the group as they arrived.

The President swiveled in his chair to face the Secretary of State.

"What have you got, Phil?"

"At this time, Mr. President, Moscow insists the troop movements are part of a routine, joint military exercise with Germany, similar to the ones they've been conducting for the last five years."

"Who are they kidding?" the President said as his eyebrows lowered. "The whole area is crawling with troops!"

"Mr. President!"

Heads turned to the man who had spoken. General Amos Weathersby stood firmly erect with a large envelope under one arm. The General had been a formidable opponent of the recent military down-scaling, calling it the "Dangerous Dismantling of America," and actively working against it. To many, even in this office, it was the General who was the danger, a very sophisticated bomb, but one that required very little prodding to explode.

"I've asked General Weathersby to join us," the President explained to the eyes that turned his way, all asking silently why the general was there at all. "He has the latest information from the Pentagon. General, if you would, please."

The General's clear, steel-blue eyes swept the gathering as he pulled himself up to his finest military bearing.

"What we have here, ladies and gentlemen," the General said, spilling the contents of the envelope on the dark surface of the table, "are satellite photographs taken early this morning. If you don't know what you're looking at, let me tell you that they show troop movements all along the Russian border. The Israeli government has already contacted us, expressing their concern, yet – ill-advisedly, I believe -- they feel that an invasion is unlikely. We, on the other hand, are hardly that confident. As you know, there has been growing unrest in Russia, resulting in near insurrection in many places with strong talk of revolution. At this time, a war would be just what they needed to restore a sense of unity to their country.

"As some of you may remember, in the Yom Kippur War of 1973, the Soviet Union supplied weapons, satellite photographs, and open support for Israel's enemies -- all in a losing effort. Well, this time it appears they are taking no chances. Right now, Russia has not only supplied the weapons, she seems poised to lead the attack."

There was general murmuring throughout the Oval Office, but it was Ray Jeffries, a staunch liberal senator from Massachusetts, whose voice broke through as other voices quieted for him to speak.

"General," he began, "am I not correct to say that this is your 'opinion?' We really don't know what their intentions are, do we?"

In that second, the General and the Senator locked eyes and positions, as they had a number of times before. Now, however, neither seemed ready to blink.

"Senator," the General said slowly, his voice determined and strong, "I believe you know their intentions, and I think a careful analysis of the facts will substantiate my…opinion."

John Sylvester, Senator from California and a prominent leader in the Republican Party, was on his feet.

"Personalities can wait until later, gentlemen," he stated, shifting his gaze between Weathersby and Jeffries, "Right here and now, if this is true, then we are at a supreme disadvantage. What are our options here? What can we do to prevent it? General, how about you going first?"

General Weathersby scanned the room, and several eyes dropped to avoid his stare. Almost everyone knew what was coming next.

"You are all aware, of course," the General intoned in a deep, crisp voice, "that some years ago I submitted a full report on the readiness of our Armed Forces after the second Gulf War. In that report, I outlined a scenario similar to this, establishing the need for a strong military presence outside the parameters of NATO and the United Nations. It was considered by many of you…" and the General paused just long enough to take in the Senator from Massachusetts, "…many of you to be ill-advised and out of step with the times. Therefore, with our current state of arms, we have very little choice. God help us, we have to leave it to the diplomats."

Senator Jeffries refused to even look at the General. Pressing his lips together, he swung around to face the figure that dominated the room.

"Mr. President, may I ask if the United Nations has released a statement yet? After all, sir, this really is *their* ball game, isn't it?"

"There has been no statement, Senator," the President replied. "A meeting of the Security Council has been scheduled for ten tomorrow morning. At that time, we will, of course, lodge a formal protest, which will do as much good as formal protests usually do."

Ann Shapiro was the President's Press Secretary, and she had been waiting for something – anything she could turn into a statement for the ravening press, who by now filled the briefing room in frenzied, rabid groups seeking desperately for anything that fell from the executive table.

Ann said, "Mr. President, if you will, sir…what should we say to the press?"

The president sighed.

"Tell them we are 'keeping an eye on the situation,' and maintaining an 'open dialogue with the United Nations.' That's no lie, since those are the only two things we can do right now. Tell them no further comment will be made until after the Security Council meeting tomorrow morning."

The President smiled weakly at her, and his voice grew soft for a moment. "I know it's not much, Ann, just a bunch of cliches, but it will have to do."

Ann Shapiro managed a smile of her own and a nod.

"That's all for now, ladies and gentlemen," the President stated in a much louder tone. "We have a long day ahead of us. As publicly announced, we meet here at seven thirty this evening. Please, be on time. Thank you."

All of them left swiftly, quietly, avoiding contact and small talk. There was much to do.

* * *

Ken Mailer sat in the plush lobby of the Hilton trying to read the *Washington Post*. He had called Jerry Westfield's office an hour ago, only to find that his old friend was on his way to DC. Ken was a high tech wonder, a 'techno-geek' who had worn that title like a war hero's medal, and he had known Jerry Westfield from their college days. Now, he worked for one of the largest communications companies in the world, and he was often privy to a great deal of behind-the-scenes information, information that he often secretly rejoiced in sharing with his college chum turned reporter.

He kept watching the entrance, not wanting to miss Jerry. He had some big news to tell his old college chum this time…big news.

Jerry walked in and headed for the front desk, shaking the rain from his coat, brushing back his damp hair.

"Jerry!"

Westfield spun around, and in less than a second, his face broke into a smile.

"Ken! Hey, man, it's good to see you!"

"Yeah," said Ken, "it's good to see you, too. Listen, Buddy, I…I hate to grab you like this the minute you come from the street and all that, but I really have to talk to you, OK?"

"No problem, Ken," Jerry smiled genuinely. "Give me a half hour, and I'll meet you in the coffee shop. I'll even let you buy me lunch!"

Ken laughed and firmly grasped Jerry's shoulder.

"Great!" Ken smiled. "I have a few phone calls I can make. The coffee shop in a half hour!"

"Good to see you, Ken."

"And you, Jerry. And you!"

* * *

The shower was very quick, but it did wonders for Jerry's morale, the hot water driving back the cold and gray of the street. Soon, he was headed to the coffee shop, where he found Ken Mailer waiting at a table off in a corner, studying the plastic-covered menu.

"There you are," Jerry laughed. "Hey, Ken, I think these are somewhat different surroundings than the last time we had lunch. Remember?"

Their last meeting had been in Paris, the 'City of Lights,' where they lunched at some fantastically expensive *bistro* on the *Rue de la*...something or other. They had met while Ken was speaking to a group of economists on *The Possibilities of a Cashless Society*, and Jerry had been covering a meeting of the Parliament of the European Community. They had renewed their college friendship as if it had never known a hiatus.

Both of them kept the conversation light until the waitress had disappeared with their order.

Now, Ken leaned a bit closer.

"Jerry, remember how many times I told you how close we are to becoming a cashless society?"

"Of course, that's all you've talked about in Paris, and ever since."

"That's why I'm in DC," Ken smiled and drew even closer. "I actually have a meeting with the President's top financial advisors...the top. We begin going over the preliminaries tomorrow.

"Jerry, it's unbelievable! I've been in meetings all over Europe; negotiations have been going on 36 hours a day! Yesterday, in Basil, Switzerland, I met with the World Bank's *biggest* players...I mean the *biggest!* I've been appointed to head up a panel of advisors, people who will help in the transition, to make certain it's smooth and painless for everybody."

Jerry leaned back in his chair and sighed.

"I've been hearing about this for years, not only from you, but others in the know as well" he reflected aloud, "but somehow I never really thought it would happen."

"Well," Ken explained as he consciously lowered his voice, "they couldn't let it become public for fear that panic would break out before they had answers for all the questions."

"OK, but how are they going to pull it off? Do you think people are just going to blindly accept a society where there's no such thing as real money?"

"Jerry," Ken said with a growing conviction in his voice, "we've run out of choices, Buddy. Look, last year, check frauds alone reached an unbelievable high of twenty-five billion dollars. That's *billions,* Jerry, *billions!* Credit card losses went through the roof years ago and are still climbing, and right here in the US of A, I'm certain you know that we can no longer pay the interest on the National Debt. Come on, Jerry, something has to happen."

Jerry met his friend eye to eye, and the professional in him reacted.

He said, "Should I consider this an exclusive interview for the record?"

"Not yet," Ken replied, "but you, Jerry, *you* will be the first. I'll see to it...I promise."

The waitress arrived, and conversation stopped as there occurred the usual banter about the need for food before they both starved on the spot and the server's assurance that she would be close by, waiting to attend to their slightest desires.

When she had finally left, and they had tasted the food, Jerry said, "OK, Ken, you have my attention, if you can compete with this turkey club."

"I'll certainly try," Ken smiled, and between mouthfuls of lunch, he continued.

"Within the last five years, information on every known individual in the Western World has been fed into a massive communications center in Bonn, Germany. Each person was then assigned a personal encryption number, which will enable that, and only that, human being to buy and sell on a worldwide scale, such as the World Wide Web. Think of it, there will be no need for foreign exchange of currency, because there will be only one value system for the whole world. Everything will be in the form of units. They'll be credited or deducted in your account much like money is now, except you'll never see it."

"Right," Jerry mused. "Then there will be no money to steal, no more bounced checks, no stolen credit cards. I can see that, and it's very neat and clean, but how would this...ID work?"

"The committee felt it better to move slowly in the beginning. When the system is introduced, everyone will be issued 'smart cards,' much like those used today for ATMs or checking accounts. But, this will only be temporary...only temporary. Soon afterward, individuals will receive their own PIN containing all of their personal data. It'll work like this: a small micro-chip, just an eighth of an inch long and just two millimeters thick will be painlessly implanted under the skin somewhere, probably on the back of the hand, because that would be the most convenient for scanning. And, even now, two of the world's leading research companies are experimenting with a new chemical that might enable us to merely stamp the information invisibly on the skin anywhere, on the hand, arm, chest, forehead. That part is still in the formulation stage."

Jerry listened to Ken, but deep in his mind, like something stirring the waters deep below the surface, he felt something move. What Ken was saying sounded personal…very familiar…as if he had heard…

Then Jerry closed his eyes, and he was sitting next to Jeremy and Kathy Palmer on the brown sofa as they read to him from the Bible, the one with the red cover. Jeremy was reading, *"…then he will issue a mark, so no one can buy or sell without the mark of the beast…"*

Suddenly, Jerry felt very cold, and he knew it had nothing to do with the December rain.

"Ken, isn't there something in the Bible about this? I mean something about placing a mark on the hand…"

"Don't tell me you're reading the Bible?" Ken asked, almost dropping his sandwich.

"No, I'm not, but I had a friend who read it all the time. He and his wife are gone now…"

"I'll tell you what," Ken said with a smile creeping across his face, "you start believing that crazy stuff, and I have a bridge to Brooklyn and some property at the bottom of the Atlantic that I'd like to sell you!" He laughed out loud.

Jerry was not laughing.

"Ken," he said, not really changing the subject, "what's your opinion of all these missing people."

"I don't really know for certain," Ken answered, looking up from his food. "I'll tell you this, however. Ever since the disappearance, things have been going better and much smoother toward the New World Order. No, that's an absolute fact! Look, Jerry, no offence if somebody you knew went…away, but as far as I can tell, it was only the troublemakers, fanatics, and those religious loonies who went. Really, I actually think it could be some radical kind of evolutionary cleansing to enable the rest of us to achieve a new and higher plain of society."

"Are you serious?" Jerry asked. He was incredulous.

"Absolutely! Among the leaders in Europe, there's a feeling that world unity is just around that little old corner now. You know, Mr.

Strapollos, one of the really great leaders over there, suggests that true global unity with one world leader now may be just a few years away —a few years!"

Jerry remembered that he had met this Mr. Strapollos before. He hadn't liked him then, Jerry recalled, and now, for a reason he only partially understood, he liked him even less. He stared at Ken.

"How can you or your Strapollos talk like that about world unity when the Russians and what appears to be the entire Arab world may be getting ready for war even as we consume the last French Fry on our plates?"

"Come on, Jerry. You have to know that Israel is the real problem here. They just won't yield; they're fanatics. You don't actually...I mean, you don't really believe there will be an invasion, do you? Believe me, my friend, peace is just beyond the horizon."

"Sure," Jerry intoned, "along with the Blue Bird of Happiness."

Jerry almost moaned as he looked at his watch. "Ken, I'm sorry, but I have to run – meeting at three. It was good seeing you, Pal, and you sure do know how to make dinner conversation. You have my number, right? So give me a call and keep me up to date on the progress. When that story's ready, I want it, and I want it first, agreed?"

"Absolutely!" Ken affirmed with a radiant smile.

The two men shook hands vigorously. Then they were off, both knowing that they were going in two very different directions.

*   *   *

The television that Jerry Westfield passed on his way out of the Hilton coffee shop vividly displayed Ann Shapiro, the President's Press Secretary, trying to cope with a voracious and somewhat petulant press corps. Jerry had been around for a long time, and even at a quick glance, he knew the story wasn't there on the screen. He knew it was behind the closed doors of the Oval Office and in a small country about the size of New Jersey.

A country called Israel.

CHAPTER THREE

Possibilities of Devastation

THE PRESIDENT OF THE UNITED STATES sat with both elbows on his desk, rubbing his temples in small, tight circles as he ran scenarios of sorrow through his mind. If the Russians were planning to invade Israel, the balance of power would shift so drastically, the world would never…could never be the same. Along with their Arab cohorts, the Russians would totally control Mid-East oil production, and the ramifications of that were…staggering. With Russia no longer dependent upon the benevolence of the West, a new and independent Russia would emerge – more powerful…and a great deal more dangerous.

"Mr. President," came the voice from the intercom, "Mr. Benjamin Walls to see you sir."

"Thank you," the President answered, sitting up straight and brushing back his hair with both hands, "Send him in."

The Chief of Staff was barely through the door before the President spoke.

"Ben, what do you have for me?"

"Mr. President," Chief Walls began, "These are the latest intelligence reports, taken just minutes ago, and they reveal heavy artillery units moving across the border into Iran. We're talking troop movements in the thousands."

"Have you heard anything from Israeli intelligence?"

"They've confirmed the reports, but they still feel that all their agreements will hold. They say this is just a scare tactic by the other Arab nations to bring more pressure on Syria and Jordan.

"And what do you think? Be honest, please."

"I don't like it. I never thought I would say this, sir, but I have to agree with General Weathersby. We're looking at an invasion the likes of which we haven't seen since World War II. I'm telling you, sir, Israel won't stand a chance. Right now, they need more than munitions, they need a miracle."

The President rose and came around his desk to stand face-to-face with his Chief of Staff.

"Why couldn't we see this coming, Ben?" the President asked. "We maintained a strong presence in the Mid-East for years, that position should have never changed."

Chief Walls took a deep breath and said, "Some things are out of our control Mr. President. Who could have predicted years ago that removing a mass murdered like Saddam Hussein from power would eventually help unify the Arab world in this way? And, we all knew a social revolution in Saudi Arabia was possible, we just hoped it would never happen.

Chief Walls looked directly at the President and said, shamefully, "And Mr. President, we all bowed to the rising public opinion against Israel."

The President lifted his eyes to the ceiling in disgust and replied, "All this talk about the 'New World Order' peace and military disarmament; we've been set up, big time. They have been waiting for this opportunity for years, and we opened the door and let them walk right in. I'm going to the UN myself; we have to put some pressure on Russia, perhaps through the EU, and get them to back off. Thanks for your time, Ben. I appreciate your candor and your friendship. I'll see you tonight, seven-thirty."

The door closed, and the President walked back to his desk and sat down. His headache was returning and had brought reinforcements.

How did this happen? At one time, he thought, this was the most powerful seat in the world.

At one time...

* * *

A few rain-soaked miles from the Oval Office, Jerry Westfield had made arrangements to meet with Sam Baskin, a Central Intelligence Agency operative who had spent a number of years in Russia and the Mid-East and who had been one of Jerry's most reliable sources for over a decade. Although Baskin never gave too much, it was enough for Jerry to get the journalistic jump on everyone else, and that was fine with him.

By this time, all the networks were busy breaking into soap operas and talk shows, reporting on the troop movements, and the news channels were trying, without much success, to elicit comments from various world leaders. What Jerry wanted was to share Sam's thoughts on what the Russians were thinking as well as doing. Was there a 'big' plan, *the master plan*, behind all this? What was it? What did they hope to accomplish? The flight from New York had given Jerry the time to get his questions in line and ready.

It had stopped raining, but the cold chill still drove inward, causing Jerry to pull his topcoat even tighter around his body that longed for that hot shower in the hotel room.

He spotted Sam Baskin's familiar form some distance away, and quickly moved toward him.

As the two men approached each other, Jerry was amazed to see the seriousness on Sam's face. He had never seen him so somber. Even during the times of gut-twisting reality that Washington can produce, Sam had never lost that sense of confidence and even smugness that Jerry had come to accept and expect.

"Sam! How's it going?"

"Hello, Jerry! Good to see you."

"Are you sure?' Jerry asked. "You look like…well, you don't look well, Sam."

Sam's eyes met Jerry's and the CIA agent said, "Things are getting bad…real bad."

Both men paused for a moment, and in a flash of clarity, Jerry realized that there was more to this than the crisis in the Middle East.

"Where do you want to talk?" Jerry finally asked.

"Not here," Baskin answered. "Just keep walking."

The two men walked towards the park. They were silent as they walked, and finally they came to a bench that didn't look too damp, and they sat. For more than a minute, Sam Baskin stared straight ahead, and Jerry began to feel uncomfortable, and he noticed that he was beginning to squirm.

At length, Sam said, "Jerry, do you know anything about the Bible?"

"The Bible? What kind of question is that?" Jerry asked, his voice rising. This was one of the last things he had expected to hear, and he was not prepared for it, not in the least.

"A friend of mine," Sam went on, "gave me a book. In this book, it talked about a great battle in which God miraculously helps Israel to defeat the invading armies."

"Do you believe that?" Jerry asked, and he understood that he was sounding as incredulous as Ken Mailer had less than an hour ago.

"I don't know, but it appears we're about to find out, doesn't it?"

Jerry moved an inch closer and asked, "You really think this is going to happen, then? Its not some sort of ploy; a military maneuver?"

"Oh, no. This is real. There's more fire power in that part of the world right now than there may ever have been before."

Jerry took a deep breath, forcing himself to remember that he was a reporter and had questions to ask.

"How big is this Russian Army?" Jerry continued.

"The official report shows about 2.3 million, but that's bull. Our latest intelligence report shows more like five million. Add to that the forces from Germany, Iraq, and Iran, and the numbers become overwhelming…beyond frightening and right to sheer terror."

Sam Baskin adjusted himself on the bench and looked straight at Jerry.

"I'll tell you something else at no charge," he said. "If the book I'm reading is right, and Israel wins this war, the worst is yet to come."

"What are you talking about, Sam? Don't we want Israel to stay sovereign; to keep the balance of power in the Mid-East?"

Sam seemed to have stopped breathing as he sat and returned to his act of staring into space. Jerry waited for him; he had little choice, and he knew Sam would speak when he wanted to…or could.

"The Antichrist," Sam said finally.

"What?" Jerry almost shouted, steadying himself lest he slip from the wet park bench. The word hit him harder than he himself understood.

"The Antichrist," Sam repeated, looking directly at Jerry with deep, unblinking eyes. "Ever heard of him?"

"Sure…well, I mean everybody's heard the term, right? What are you saying; he's a real person?"

"I'm not saying he is or isn't. I am saying that if this book is accurate, then after Israel wins, the man who signs a seven year peace treaty with Israel will be …him -- the Antichrist."

In spite of the cold, Jerry's hands had begun to sweat. He was beginning to feel physically ill, the turkey club sandwich sitting hard on his stomach. As Sam spoke, Jerry again had a flash of Jeremy holding that red-covered Bible and warning, *"I'm telling you, Jerry, you don't want to be here when the Antichrist comes. It will be awful for those still on earth…"*

Jerry felt the nervousness clawing at his spine, and when he spoke, there was a noticeable change in the tone of his voice.

"I don't get it, Sam. Why are you saying all this? I never heard you talk like this before, and I'll tell you frankly, I don't like it."

"It's the disappearance, Jerry. I just can't shake it. I never considered myself a bad person. I did what I had to do…you know, for the country. Now…I'm not so sure. I mean, I heard all about this stuff from my grandfather when I was a kid, but I never believed it. I mean, who would?"

Jerry lowered his voice still more and almost whispered, "You're talking about 'The Rapture,' aren't you?"

Sam's eyes went wide, "You know about the Rapture?"

"I had a friend who used to talk about it," Jerry remembered, "but I'm a reporter, and I've trained myself to rely on facts, Sam – facts, and not stories and fables about people being taken up to heaven. There has to be a logical explanation for all this. Don't take me wrong, but I think your best move would be to get rid of that book and back to reality, advice I should take as well as you."

"Reality or not," Sam sighed, "I have a very bad feeling about this, and in my business, you learn to trust your feelings." He puffed out a deep breath and began to rise from the bench.

"Anyhow," he continued as he stood, "the next couple days will be critical. I'll be in DC for about a week, if you need me."

"Wait a minute, Sam," Jerry called, taking a deep breath of the chill December air. "I've got a lot more questions. Is the President going to stand with Israel?"

"Politically, there will be nothing but words -- a protest. Militarily? Well, Jerry, the basic sorrow of it all is that Israel now stands alone, and totally alone. There is nothing to be done. You of all people know that when we lost our foothold in Iraq and then Saudi Arabia that our military options diminished considerably, to say the least. We only have a token presence within the borders of Israel now, like I said, there is nothing that can be done."

Then the CIA agent spun around, calling over his shoulder, "I have to go."

And Sam Baskin walked away.

"Take care, Sam!" Jerry called after him. "It will be all right!"

But Jerry had his doubts.

Serious doubts.

CHAPTER FOUR

Journey's Start

5 DECEMBER: JERUSALEM: F45DQ17: IN THE FACE OF overwhelming evidence of large-scale military preparations, Israel today rejected the thought of a joint Russian/Arab invasion. A high ranking government official stated, "There will be no invasion; there is simply too much to be gained by all through peace."

6 DECEMBER: MOSCOW: G78RE44: US Secretary of State, Philip Dresson, met today with Russian leaders here in Moscow. The Russians unilaterally denied any hostile intentions. In an official statement, they declared, "These are nothing more than military exercises designed to unify the region."

7 DECEMBER: NEW YORK: N62PC91: The President of the United States addressed a full session of the UN Security Council this afternoon. In his speech, he urged all concerned to make peace their first priority.

9 DECEMBER: TEL AVIV: F57WK37: It is three days before the Jewish celebration of Hanukkah, and, amid speculation from all quarters, all is quiet.

* * *

At just slightly after 9:00 in the evening the plane carrying Jerry Westfield set down at Newark International Airport in the middle of a light December snow.

"Mr. Westfield," the attendant urged, "we're landing, sir. You'll have to fasten your seat belt."

Jerry's eyes opened slowly, and he shook his head, throwing off the remnant of the quick doze he had managed on the flight from Washington. He hadn't gotten much sleep, and he still felt worn out from the past week.

He'd had five days of seemingly endless interviews, and he had produced five articles for *The Chronicle*, mainly what he considered to be "color" stories. He had written about Washington during a crisis; about the contrasting opinions of two "highly placed" government officials without mentioning names; about what an invasion of Israel might mean to the "man in the street;" about contrasting views of America's own military strength in light of the current crisis; about alarming statistics the TV never told you. For that latter article he had used some of the figures Sam Baskin had supplied, without naming Sam, of course. What he had also never mentioned was Baskin's references to the Bible and the crawling that refused to leave his own stomach. It had been a successful week, and Bob Lewis had been pleased.

Even so, to Jerry's mind, to the reporter who had won the Pulitzer, there was no real story yet. At least there was not the one he was looking for. Something…something was missing. Perhaps it was something he had to find.

When the plane had rolled to a stop and the cabin door opened, he walked slowly into the busy terminal and stepped on to the moving walkway. In the distance, he could just make out Bill Foley standing there, sipping at a huge cup of coffee.

"Rough week?" Bill asked as Jerry stepped off the moving belt.

"You could say that," Jerry answered with a tired smile.

"Come on, we'll get your bag and clear out of here."

After they had fought the battle of the baggage area, the two men walked silently to the parking lot. One mark of a good friend, Jerry thought, was that he knew when not to say anything.

It was only after they were in the car that they turned and looked at each other.

Jerry said, "Bill, this is going to sound crazy, but I have to get Bob Lewis to send me to Israel."

"It doesn't sound that crazy," Bill replied, "but how can you go there now? No one has any idea what's going to happen next!"

"That's where the story is, Bill, and you know it. I have to talk to the people; find out what they're thinking. I can't do this story sitting at my desk or lunching at Sardi's – you understand that!"

"Oh, yeah! I know how it goes," Bill said, rolling his eyes. "You mean like during the riots in LA, when you almost got us both killed running in and out of burning buildings and talking to guys with guns in their hands! What is it with you, Jerry? Are you not happy unless you can sit on a keg of blasting powder with a lit fuse somewhere near your rear end?"

Jerry ignored the sarcasm except for a small smile that creased his face and continued, "Listen, Bill, I have an old friend who lives in Tel Aviv. He was in the Israeli Special Forces; retired now, I think. He actually fought in the Yom Kippur War of '73. He's always after me to come and visit. I can stay with him."

Bill sighed, and there was the briefest of pauses as their eyes met.

"Well, I don't think you'll have any trouble," Bill said at last. "Lewis is going to love this one. He'll have you on a plane tomorrow."

"Great," Jerry smiled, "but first I have to get some sleep. Can you drive me home?"

"That also," Bill Foley smiled, "will be no problem."

* * *

10 DECEMBER: JERUSALEM: F78DU23: The silence that currently pervades the Middle East is paradoxical To many, it brings a feeling of relief, while to others, the sense is that of overwhelming fear. Even so, life goes on in this tiny country which has now become the center of attention of the entire world.

* * *

Jerry reached down and flicked off the alarm when it rang at 6:00 AM. He had been up and packing since five, packing more carefully and thoroughly than he usually did, because he had a sense that this might be a long trip...a very long trip. His briefcase lay open on the bed, with the red cover of Jeremy Palmer's Bible clearly visible in it. Jerry looked at the case for a moment, his lips pursing slowly, then he closed it with the Bible inside. After all, it would be a long flight; he might need something to read.

Jerry slipped his small, black, well-worn personal phone book from a pocket and began to turn pages deliberately until he came to the name and number he desired. With just a small bit of anxiety, he began to dial the number of Jacob Klausman in Tel Aviv.

While he waited for the connection, Jerry wondered. It had been a while since they had last talked, a little over a year. Did the invitation still hold? Were Jacob and his wife still well? He would prefer staying with

Jacob than languishing in a hotel room, but either way, Jerry Westfield was going to Israel.

"*Shalom,*" said the deep voice on the other end of the line.

"Jacob? Jacob, it's Jerry Westfield!"

"Jerry," Jacob brightened, immediately switching to lightly accented English. "It's so nice to hear from you! How are you doing?"

"Fine. I'm doing fine. How are you and your family? Is everybody all right? Sarah? The kids?"

"Physically, everyone's fine. We are more than a little concerned about our present situation, however, as you might expect."

"That's why I'm calling, Jacob," Jerry said. "You said once that the next time I was coming to Israel I should give you a call and maybe stay with you. Well, is that offer still good? I'll understand if it isn't."

A joyous laughter filled the earphone, and Jerry knew that it was genuine and that he had his answer.

"Of course it is! Of course!" Jacob roared. "So, when are you coming?"

Jerry frowned a bit and said, "That's the catch. I hope to leave today."

"Come, my friend, come! It will be good to see you!"

"Thank you, Jacob. Believe me, it will be good to see you, too. I'll call you later with my arrival time."

"Very good!" Jacob said. "We will be ready. God be with you!"

"God…be with you my friend, and thank you again."

Jerry put down the receiver and took a deep breath. Staying with Jacob Klausman and his family would be just what he needed. The two of them had developed a special relationship. Even though they hadn't spent much time together lately, one phone call and it seemed to Jerry that they felt close as ever.

Jerry resumed his packing with a will. He could hardly wait to get to Israel and get started.

He was ready.

* * *

By seven-thirty that morning, Jerry Westfield was at his desk at *The Chronicle*. He was busy making certain he had all he needed for his journey, when he heard the booming voice of Bob Lewis.

"Well, Mr. Westfield," Lewis intoned, "it is the age of miracles, I see. Not only have you gotten in early, but it actually seems as if you are working. Are we writing something; going some place?"

"Good morning, Mr. Lewis," Jerry smiled his sweetest comic smile, "and how is our blood pressure this fine morning?"

Bob Lewis smiled genuinely and said, "Forget the amenities, Jerry. I talked to Bill late last night, and I got the authorization for the trip. I just want to go over a few things with you before you leave. Let's go into my office."

When the two men were seated, Bob Lewis reached down and pulled a small device from his briefcase.

Handing it to Jerry, Bob said, "Do you know what this is?"

"I think so. It's some type of modem, isn't it?"

"Yes, it is. It's similar to a P.C.M.C.I.A. Module."

Confidently, Jerry said, "I've used those before."

"This one is a little different," Bob remarked. "It has its own transmitter. It doesn't require a cellular phone. It transmits directly to satellite.

"Listen, Jerry," Bob Lewis continued, leaning closer, "you know what we're facing over there. Anything could happen at any minute. If you get in a situation where you get cut off, this device will allow you to transmit from anywhere in the world. All you have to do is plug it into the side of the p. c. and type. We'll pick up the signal on satellite. I also want you to take this."

Reaching behind his desk, Bob Lewis brought out a leather carrying case that Jerry knew was designed for a laptop. He handed it to Jerry. There was a silver-colored machine inside.

"It has a newly-developed lithium-ion battery," Bob explained. "It can last up to thirty-six hours between charges."

"Thanks Bob. I'll be all right. Say, some of this junk is really new. Where did you get all this stuff?"

Lewis smiled, "Don't ask. Just say that I have connections. Mary should be in by now. She's making your arrangements, and remember, you are to check in on a daily basis. Be careful. If things get bad, get somewhere safe and lay low."

Bob Lewis and Jerry Westfield sat facing each other for a moment filled with silence and a great deal more, all of it unspoken. Finally, Bob Lewis put out a huge hand which Jerry eagerly took in his own.

"We need you here," Bob Lewis said.

* * *

Mary Cortman was able to get Jerry on a flight leaving Kennedy Airport at 12:15 PM and arriving at Tel Aviv at 7:20 the next morning.

Jerry smiled.

That was more than enough time to catch up on some...some important reading.

* * *

11 DECEMBER: JERUSALEM: F65RQ84: Troop movements to the South, including Ethiopia, Sudan, and Libya are bringing new concerns to Israeli citizens and some government officials. Egypt and Jordan have issued a joint statement: "Peace is the only option." The Knesset, in closed session today, rejected Chief of Staff Daniel Aaron's plea for a total national mobilization.

CHAPTER FIVE

Invasion

AT 7:15 AM ON 11 DECEMBER AT TEL AVIV AIRPORT, the sun was shining brightly and the temperature was an even seventy-one degrees Fahrenheit. Jacob Klausman and his wife, Sarah, stood expectantly at the gate, waiting for the passengers to step off the plane that had landed just moments before. Jacob was in his mid-fifties and had lived in Israel all his life. A semi-retired Special Forces Officer, he boasted a firm if heavily-bearded chin, sparkling blue eyes and a body that he had worked at keeping in shape. Nowadays, he supplemented his pension by giving tours of outlying wilderness areas to adventuresome tourists. Indeed, few men knew the intricacies of the mountains and deserts of Israel better than Jacob Klausman.

When Jerry Westfield came into view, Jacob began to wave enthusiastically, and kept waving until the two of them were locked in a massive, bear-like embrace.

"It's so good to see you, Jacob!" Jerry beamed, when he could finally breath again.

"And you, my friend! You remember my wife, Sarah?"

"Of course I do," Jerry smiled genuinely as he kissed her cheek. "You two look great! Hey, thanks for letting me stay with you; especially on such short notice."

Sarah smiled back and said, "Living over here, you learn to do everything on short notice."

Sarah had been all of 18 years old when her family had moved to Israel in 1974, just in time for the Yom Kippur War. She had been born and raised in Brooklyn, and her new life in Israel had required many adjustments, all of which she had met and made with an unbounded enthusiasm. She had

31

been in Israel five months when she met the young and handsome soldier, Jacob Klausman. One year later, they were married.

"Come," Jacob said, "you must be tired. You'll have something to eat, meet the family and then get some rest."

Sarah laughed.

"You'd better watch your 'friend,' Jerry," Sarah said with twinkling eyes. "He will plan your whole life for you, if you're not careful."

They laughed together. The way Jerry felt at that moment, that would not have been such a bad idea.

* * *

As they drove, Jerry and Jacob talked about how they had met when Jerry had been sent to Israel on special assignment and Jacob had been delegated to keep the "prize-winning American reporter" out of harm's way. They had discovered that they had much in common, including a voracious curiosity and a streak of the stubborn, and they laughed loud and frequently at the memories that hung about them like a gang of raucous schoolboys. With each turn of the wheels, Jerry began to feel better than he had in days – in weeks, he decided! There was something exhilarating, almost intoxicating about being here. He regretted that he had not come sooner.

Jacob and Sarah Klausman lived in Jaffa, generally considered one of the oldest seaports in Israel. It was a picturesque town on the shores of the Mediterranean Sea, a short drive from the airport. Jacob and Sarah had restored one of the old blue-gray stone houses near the harbor. Narrow at the front, it rose in a type of timeless grandeur to a three-story height. Jerry had never seen the place, although Jacob had described it to him. When they pulled up to the house, Jerry stood there, trying to take it all in.

"Jacob!" he stated, his eyes still fixed on the stone structure, "this is beautiful! You may never get rid of me!"

Jacob laughed and said, "The beauty was always there, my friend, but it was shy and hiding itself. We merely helped to bring it out. Really, this has become Sarah's project. She is quite talented, as you will see."

"You've done well for yourself, Jacob."

"Have I? Wait now and I'll show you my real treasures."

As if by signal, a door opened and three beautiful, very healthy, crisp-eyed children entered the room and took places beside Jacob and Sarah.

"Joseph, Deborah, and Daniel," Jacob intoned with obvious pride, "say hello to Mr. Westfield…to your – yes – to your Uncle Jerry."

Introductions were made, and for a few minutes, Jerry Westfield basked in the joy of the Klausman family. When, at last, the children had left to follow other pursuits, Jerry turned to Jacob.

"You must be very proud," he stated.

"The Lord Almighty has been good to us," Jacob said. "We had our children later than most, but I like to say that this way they can still be the joy of my youth, the pride of my maturity, and the comfort of my senility! Now, come, let us go upstairs, where we can talk."

Jacob loved to spend time on the roof of his home. It was his favorite place to talk with friends, and with his God. It was flat, like most roofs of the older houses and all stone. A short wall surrounded it, with a three-foot iron railing on top of that. The iron railing had been Sarah's idea to keep the children safe. There were several chairs and a table, surrounded by a view that made everything possible and breathing difficult. When Jerry and Jacob were seated, Sarah excused herself and left.

She knew they needed time to talk.

* * *

When they were finally alone under a deep blue, cloudless sky, Jacob drew his chair closer to his friend.

"Jerry," he began, and the tone of his voice had changed considerably, "earlier this morning, I received some disturbing news from one of my sources. No, don't ask me – just one of my sources, OK? The Russians are moving a large number of war ships from the Black Sea south towards the Bosporus. By this time tomorrow, they could be in our swimming pool."

Jerry stirred in his chair. The Bosporus was a strategic, somewhat narrow waterway separating Europe from Asia and linking the Black Sea and the Mediterranean. Jerry, however, could not get himself that concerned about the movement.

"Look, Jacob, the Russians have done this sort of thing many times before. What makes this time any different?"

"Now! Now you sound like a newspaper reporter!"

Jerry smiled and spread both hands, palms up, to the clear sky.

"Up until now," Jacob continued, "everything has been done gradually – a few ships here; a few ships there. This time...they're getting ready for something."

"Then why is your government dragging their feet? What do they think is going on?"

"I don't know," Jacob answered honestly, and with some heat. "No one wants to believe what's going on. They close their eyes! The people want peace, they don't want to hear about war, and the government definitely does not want to disturb the peace process or the *status quo*. I tell you, Jerry, I am not alone in this. There are military officials who feel even stronger about this than I do. They say we may be forced to fight for our very existence."

"What about the new peace agreement with Syria? That's supposed to be fairly secure. Do you think it will hold?"

"Jerry," Jacob said, lowering his voice and looking around as if to signify that what he was about to say was not for everyone's ears, "I've seen intelligence reports showing that Syria has increased purchases of tanks and mobile artillery in recent months. According to an Air Force Commander in whom I place much trust, Syria is rapidly arming itself with even more modern weapons – from Russia!"

There was the sound of a door opening, and conversation stopped. Sarah walked out on the roof and came to where they were, placing a gentle hand on Jacob's shoulder.

"You are going to let Jerry get some rest, aren't you?" she asked with a smile. "I'm preparing a huge supper for Hanukkah, and I would like our guest to enjoy t!"

"Yes, of course," said Jacob, rising to his feet. "I promise you rest, and I give you rhetoric instead."

Then he looked directly at Jerry Westfield.

"We *will* talk later."

*　　*　　*

11 DECEMBER: 1500 HOURS: JERUSALEM: F12FY55: All reports indicate that tanks and artillery are beginning to advance quickly along all Israeli borders. Satellite reconnaissance continues to show a steady stream of troops and supplies flowing from Russia through Iran and Iraq.

11 DECEMBER: 1900 HOURS: JERUSALEM: F17FZ63: According to Israeli Intelligence, satellite photos confirm that the Russian fleet has reached the Bosporus and has begun to navigate through those waters. In the meantime, troop movements continue unabated on all fronts.

11 DECEMBER: 2015 HOURS: JERUSALEM: F 21FA03: It has been confirmed by Israeli Intelligence that Iraqi and Iranian forces have crossed into Jordan. Syrian forces are moving south along Highway Five from

Damascus. Accompanying them are Russian and German soldiers along with combined forces from Eastern Europe, the former Soviet Union. The tanks and artillery continue to race along the Highway. So far, they have met no opposition.

12 DECEMBER: 0320 HOURS: JERUSALEM: F31FA35: There have been unconfirmed but continuing reports that there is a noticeable and growing unrest between the Russian, German, and Arab troops currently massed at Israel's borders..

Dawn is less than two hours away.

* * *

It was 4:17 AM when Jacob Klausman woke from a fitful sleep, swung his legs over the side of the mattress, and looked at the digital clock beside his bed. He had not slept well, and as silently as he could, he slipped into jeans and a light shirt and headed for the roof. He had just started up the stairs when he heard the noise, a small noise, but he heard it, nonetheless, and he sensed rather than actually knew that there was someone on the roof.

He paused in mid-step and retraced his steps silently down the stairs. Quietly, he took his old US Army-Issue Colt .45 Automatic from its hiding place. It was a weapon he had used before, and he was extremely familiar with its operation. He drove home the clip, pulling back the casing and stripping a live round into the firing chamber. Then, as silently as he had come, he was on the stairs again, heading for the roof.

As he suspected, there was a man up there, and he was standing on one of the walls. Jacob brought the sights to a point midway between the shoulders of the shadowy figure silhouetted against the starry night sky.

"Stand where you are, or you're a dead man!" he said in Hebrew and in a strong voice filled with power and the crackle of command.

"Jacob!" came the terrified voice from the dark figure, "I don't know what you said! Don't do anything! It's me! It's Jerry!"

Jacob dropped the sights of the automatic and guided the hammer safely home, automatically flipping the safety.

"Jerry!" Jacob said, switching effortlessly to English. "What are you doing up here? Are you crazy? I almost…"

He didn't have to finish the sentence. They both knew.

Jerry stood there with his heart pounding loudly in his ears, shaking his entire body.

"I guess I'm a little…jumpy," Jacob said, coming beside Jerry and putting a strong arm around his trembling friend's shoulders. "So, you can't sleep either, huh?"

"Maybe," Jerry mused as his breathing began to come easier and in greater volume, "maybe it's, you know, jet lag – or all this talk about invasion."

"Come," Jacob said, leading the way to the stairs, "I will make some coffee for us. Strong coffee."

* * *

12 DECEMBER: 0503 HOURS: JERUSALEM: F74FC55: In the last few moments before dawn this morning, tanks and troops began moving through the mountains surrounding Israel. The front from the South includes troops from Ethiopia, Sudan, and Libya and appears headed towards the Aqaba. The central thrust seems headed straight for Jerusalem, advancing west from above the Dead Sea. Northern forces are moving directly towards the Golan Heights.

According to one eyewitness, the troops are so extensive they appear to be "a great cloud covering the land as far as anyone can see; like locusts heading for green fields. All you can hear is the rumbling of the machines. All you can feel is the desert moving under your feet."

When informed of the movements, Israeli Chief of Staff, Daniel Aaron, remarked, "For years the enemies of Israel have waited for this moment, and now it is here. Hate has brought them to this place, and now hate has them in its trance. They have achieved complete tactical surprise, and I believe that they feel certain of complete victory."

* * *

The first light melted away the darkness in great streaks of orange and yellow. At 0531 hours exactly, Israeli Air Force Captain Itzak Levy, F-16 Fighter Pilot, encountered the invasion force. At first, and for the first time in years, he doubted the accuracy of his senses. He pulled back on the controls of the F-16 and climbed higher to get a better look.

When he reported, his voice was noticeably shaken.

"Sir, we have a massive…a massive troop movement to the North and West. I repeat – massive troop movements to the North and West. There are tanks, anti-aircraft missiles, troops in the thousands. Invasion immanent. Request orders! Request orders!"

"Do not engage!" came the reply over the radio. "I repeat, do not engage. Help is on the way."

Fighter Pilot Itzak Levy looked down and wondered if he had been detected and a SAM missile streaking toward him even now. There was no indication that he had. The thought struck him that it was as if they looked upon him as a very small flea on a very large dog.

* * *

Almost immediately, the word came to scramble the fighters and activate defense systems, and throughout Israel, air raid sirens roared and barked and wailed and shattered the early morning air.

Jacob and Jerry heard the sirens in the kitchen where they lingered over their third cup of Herculean coffee.

"What's that?" Jerry asked, instinctively looking up.

"My dear God!" Jacob exclaimed. "They're attacking!"

Sarah, wrapping a blue robe about her, came running into the kitchen.

"Jacob! What's going on? Who's attacking?"

"The Russians…others. Quick now, get the children downstairs!"

"Where are you going?"

"I'll be there in a moment. Please, hurry!"

But Jacob was already on his way to the phone with Jerry Westfield close beside him. First, Jacob tried to get through to his contacts at a base in the Golan Heights. The phone rang and rang, but there was no answer. Finally, as he cradled his own receiver back on the hook, it rang in Jacob's hand, causing both he and Jerry to jump.

"Jacob!" said the voice at the other end of the line, "it's Tadeus!"

"Tadeus, tell me what is happening?"

"All Hell has come to earth, Jacob. They're coming at us from all sides – thousands of tanks and heavy artillery; millions of troops. I can't even give you an estimate, unofficial or otherwise. This is the fight of our lives, Jacob. Pray that God Almighty will defend us. Listen, take your family to the safest…"

A spurt of static filled the earpiece.

"Tadeus! Tadeus! Do you hear me?"

The line was dead. Jacob's eyes glistened as he raised his face to the sky and all but shouted.

"Oh, God of our fathers, are you not the God who dwells in the heavens? Do you not rule over all the kingdoms of the nations? Such power and might are in Your hands that no one can resist you. Look upon us today and save us from this great army!"

Jerry's eyes were fastened on Jacob. Rarely had he heard anyone but Jeremy Palmer pray aloud, and Jeremy's prayers were never like this. For a second, he felt like an intruder.

Jacob breathed deeply and said, "Our God will deliver us this day, my friend; I feel His Spirit."

Jerry looked at his friend and nodded. After a second, their eye contact dissolved and Jerry snatched at his computer and briefcase that contained the modem and transmitting device Bob Lewis had given him. Hefting it under one arm, he headed for the stairs to the roof.

"Where are you going?" Jacob asked in amazement.

"I have a story to write – remember?"

"Has the jet lag eaten away your mind? You could get killed up there!"

"I came here to get a story, Jacob, and I can't get it second hand. I can't describe what I can't see. You go to your family; they need you. If it gets too crazy, I'll hitch a ride with a Russian paratrooper and come down to join you, believe me."

And, not waiting for any reply, Jerry Westfield headed for the stairs.

Jacob understood that there would be no talking to this man. He also realized that his own wife and children needed him alive. Therefore, he stood for a further moment and watched as his American friend ran up the stairs and on to the roof.

Then, praying with upraised eyes that he would see Jerry alive once again, Jacob Klausman went to be with his family.

*　　*　　*

In New York, the news had hit like a sledgehammer against a feeble wooden door. Israel was under attack! At *The Chronicle*, the newsroom was exploding with activity.

Bill Foley, who almost always knocked first, burst into Bob Lewis' office. Normally, if Jerry were in danger, Bill would be right at his side. Now, Jerry was there, Bill was here, and he was becoming nervous.

"Have you heard from Jerry?" Bill asked.

"He called last night to check in with me, but that's it," Lewis answered, moving a few papers on his desk. "I'm certain we'll hear something soon. You'll know when I do, Bill."

Outside, in the main Newsroom, Mary Cortman sat at her desk going over travel vouchers. Suddenly, she was aware that the computer monitor on Jerry Westfield's desk had gone blank. She turned toward it and watched as Jerry's security code came on line. She jumped up and ran to Bob Lewis' office.

"Mr. Lewis!" she exploded, "Jerry is coming on line!"

Lewis got up so quickly, his chair tumbled noisily backward. He raced to Jerry's desk and sat, with Bill Foley arriving seconds behind, to peer over his massive shoulder.

The information began to fill the screen.

12 December, 0540 Hours (Jaffa/Tel Aviv): At 5:30 this morning, Israel's population awoke to the overwhelming sounds of air raid sirens and the screaming roar of F-16 fighter jets on their way to confront the enemy. From my viewpoint, I hear the sound of heavy artillery off in the distance as men, women, and children rush out on to the streets to defend their homes once again from an onslaught of hate and prejudice. Early reports attest that Russia and United Arab forces have combined to form what appears to be an overwhelming invading army.

Indeed, all of Israel's enemies have come against this tiny country today, against this country whose strong desire for peace may prove to be its only fatal weakness. Now I can hear explosions to the North and to the East. Fire and smoke are now visible just above the northern horizon.

Another explosion, and more flames and bellowing smoke to the east. From my vantage point, I can see tanks moving east into the sunrise, towards Jerusalem, while more Israeli Fighter Jets scream off into the clear morning sky.

I have witnessed the horrors of war before, and I pray Israel will be spared total destruction.

This small country where all roads seem to lead to God now looks to Him as their only hope of victory.

This is Jerry Westfield reporting from Tel Aviv, Israel.

– 30 –

PS (personal) – Bill, I'm still walking and talking. If there is a God, I wonder what He is thinking now? Bob, as usual, feel free to mangle my prize-winning writing any way you'd like. I know this is short, but I have to get moving. More later. JW

By the end of the message, a small crowd had formed, trying to read the screen over Bob Lewis' substantial back.

Lewis turned and faced them.

"Well?" he stated flatly, "We have work to do. Let's get to it!"

*   *   *

From the North, "Free Rocket Over Ground" or "FROG" Missiles were launched against Israeli airfields as well as selected civilian areas. The Israeli Air Force launched a counter attack to the North in defense of the Golan Heights. They were met with an overwhelming curtain of anti-aircraft fire, and the skies filled with SAM missiles.

West of Jerusalem, the battle was fierce and bloody. Israeli tank divisions encountered Russian and German forces and were outnumbered twenty to one. Against the mounting pressure of those odds, the Israelis could not hold ground. Battle lines began to slip, in the enemy's favor.

Southern forces pushed through the barren Negev towards the city of Dimona. Their numbers were vast and crushing. Defending forces melted like snow before the consuming fire.

The invasion advanced on all fronts. Crossing the plain above and below the Dead Sea, invading troops now began to move with some ease through the mountains around Jerusalem. From the air, Israeli fighter pilots reported with solemn voices, all bravado long replaced with leaden heaviness, on the vastness of the armies below and the desperate situation of their small country.

Two hours after the invasion began, the Israeli Command gave orders to pull back and form a new line of defense, as more and more tank divisions pressed in. joining in the fight for Jerusalem. Fighter Jets streaked in to land just long enough to refuel before they roared skyward once more, returning for another assault.

As Israeli forces consolidated their positions for a final defense, the combined invading forces launched what they saw as the decisive blow in an already overmatched conflict. Laden with a cargo of death, aircraft from Carriers in the Northern Mediterranean as well as land bases in Syria and Libya began to converge on Israeli positions.

Closer…

Closer…

Closer.

*   *   *

A Russian pilot, overlooking the battle from his fighter jet, noticed something on the ground and almost automatically noted the time. It was 1406 Hours, and the ground...the ground was moving. A rock slide of immense proportions, covering a huge area, was tumbling due east of Jerusalem and effectively cutting off the armies advancing there. This was something he had to call in. He tried. He tried a second and a third time as well. There was no answer, only the steady crackle of static.

The pilot had no way of knowing that Hell, itself was rapidly surrounding the troops on the ground. An earthquake of incredible size and vehemence was rumbling through the mountains of Israel, splitting and then splintering solid rock surfaces, ripping away all standing structures, leaving roads and highways in shambles and impassible, pushing Seismographs well beyond their prescribed limits throughout the Middle East. As far away as India, Eastern Europe, and Russia to the North, the tremors were boldly and fearfully acknowledged and experienced.

Nor was that the end of it. In the East and West, angry, black and boiling clouds had begun to appear and grow and spread, even as Chaos became the commander of the combined ground troops who were now being tossed and thrown like toys on a petulant child's bed.

The dark, heavy clouds met, and almost immediately it was as if a thick curtain had been drawn across the sun. In the dark and with the quake still trembling about them, an equally dark and unseen enemy gripped the invading forces – an enemy named Fear. A wind was rising, and it didn't take long before it grew to horrible, screaming intensity that drove the sand of the desert before it and brought zero visibility, burying both man and machine in hot, stinging sand and a hopeless, bottomless, terror-filled night. It was as if you were blindfolded, your hands tied at your sides, and you were thrown into a pitch black room where, every so often, you were slapped, prodded, or punched by someone or something beyond the ability of your mind to understand!

When the lightning began, ground strike after ground strike and over and over, there were men, tested and proven and brave men, who curled into corners and gave up their minds.

It was over an interminable hour before the wind -- the horrible, roaring, piercing wind -- began to subside, and that was when the rain began. Sheet after sheet of relentless, driving rain fell and fell and fell and fell. The troops, who could hardly see each other and certainly not their allies beside them, began, in their confusion and fear and frustration, to fire on each other.

More than one of the commanding officers, unaware that Israeli troops had retreated to regroup closer to Jerusalem, radioed that Israeli forces must have broken through to the South and East. Artillery and gunfire burned and sizzled through the falling rain, as ally fired upon ally never stopping to verify a target.

Huge, boiling rolls of deep brown water rushed down mountainsides and into the valley, formulating a thick mud that bogged down tanks and troops alike. The wind that had subsided for a moment began to pick up once more and hail, large hail, some of it as big as a hen's egg, added to the rain, bouncing from tanks and helmets, creating a drumming, deep roar that all could feel in their stomachs as well as hear, even through ears covered by clenched and trembling fists.

In the clouds, the wind shear and the hail combined and converged on the invading aircraft and, as Jerry Westfield would later phrase it, "swept them out of the sky like a giant hand!"

As this continued, Arab troops, advancing from the South, observed the carnage and cried betrayal, turning with vicious resolve on Russian and German forces in the valley just above the Dead Sea.

* * *

Military intelligence, in bunkers on the outskirts of Jerusalem, sat speechless with awe and shock at the incredible display of raw power that raged before them. It was as if some sort of horrific and terrifying beast were tied to a great chain that pulled taut just east of Jerusalem, allowing it to go no further. The earthquake subsided, but the clouds continued their assault. Aftershocks scraped and rent and tore and shook the desert floor for miles.

They continued throughout the long, devastating night.

* * *

It did not end until dawn. As the sun topped the eastern horizon, the terrible and almost deafening sound of it simply ceased as quickly as it had begun. A strange, almost reverential silence filled the void of its going everywhere.

From a small strip of undamaged runway, two F-16's rose to climb over the mountains and into the still, blue sky beyond.

"Recon One to base. Do you copy? Over."

"Recon One, this is base. We copy – repeat, we copy. Go ahead. Over."

"Sir," came Captain Itzak Levy's voice followed by a deep pause, "Sir, there's…there's no one left here. Over."

"Roger that. Have they moved to new positions? Over."

The two planes continued to scan the area, flying low over the terrain. Tanks and artillery lay motionless, half buried in the sand and mud, unbendable barrels now like twisted soda straws. Bodies, thousands and thousands of bodies in every tortured position ever associated with fear and panic, lay so close and near and over and on each other that in places, one could not see the ground.

"No, sir," Captain Levy replied. "When I said, there was nobody left, I meant...Well, sir...it appears they are all dead, sir. Over."

"Recon One, please repeat. Over."

"They are all dead, sir...dead! Over."

"Recon One, do I understand you correctly. You are saying that everyone over there is dead? Over."

"Sir, this is Recon Two," came the voice of the other pilot. "I confirm, sir. No one is moving down there. There are bodies everywhere. I see no survivors, sir...no survivors. Over."

There followed a silence on the cockpit radios of both fliers. It lasted about the length of time it took for Base to take in what had been just reported.

"Recon One," the radio finally crackled, "fly over the region and give me a location where we can cross. We have to get our people in there. Over."

"Roger that, base," Captain Levy confirmed as he began to turn north. "We'll check it. Over and out."

* * *

The confirmed report of the Recon flight was followed by orders to move in heavy equipment to begin removing the rocks and earth that had fallen on the highways east of Jerusalem. It would take weeks, even months before those roads were passable once more. Meanwhile, in Jerusalem itself, Israeli tanks and armored personnel carriers moved up and down the streets, while helicopters searched the damaged areas of the city for the injured.

News of the demise of the invading armies had flowed over the people like the oil of an anointing, and citizens poured out everywhere, helping each other, embracing each other, encouraging each other while comparing notes on the most incredible night of their lives.

* * *

Jacob Klausman had been out looking for Jerry Westfield for almost two hours, since the news had reached him of the unprecedented victory over Israel's foes. Finally, Jacob spotted him talking to one of the tank commanders.

"Jerry! Where did you go?"

"Jacob!" Jerry waved, jumping down from the Israeli tank. "Sarah? The kids? Is everyone all right?"

"Yes," Jacob said, embracing his friend. "We made it through the night. The house suffered some damage, but its nothing that can't be fixed and fixed quickly. Where have you been; I've been looking all over for you!"

"I stood on the roof as long as I could, Jacob, but it started to get hairy, so I left to see if I could hitch a ride to the front."

"To the front? You wanted to go *to* the front? You are crazier than I remembered! Don't tell me; I know. You can't write what you can't see!"

They began to walk, threading their way through the huge amount of jubilant people who filled the streets.

Jerry said, "I ran into this guy from the news network who had a jeep. I showed him my ID, and he actually recognized my name and let me ride with him. We got as far as we could before they stopped us. When the earthquake hit, it was so loud we couldn't talk to each other. Then, sometime after two o'clock, it got so black you couldn't see. Jacob, did you see that storm? I mean, the earthquake was so strong it shook your teeth, but the storm! I've never seen anything like that in my life! Jacob, I thought of you. I thought of your prayer – you know, what you said about God delivering Israel!"

As what he had just said hit home, Jerry stopped talking and walking at the same time, so suddenly that Jacob took two or more steps before he realized that Jerry was not keeping up. In his mind, Jerry was once more with Sam Baskin, his CIA contact, re-running the scene in the that damp park in Washington, and Sam was saying, *"Jerry, I'll tell you what else. If Israel wins this war, the worst is yet to come."*

Jerry stood, the blood draining from his face.

"Jerry! Are you all right?"

Jacob was holding him, shaking his shoulders. Quickly, Jerry shook his head and stood up to his full height.

"Yes. Yes, I'm fine. I have enough for now; I'd better send this story back to the paper."

* * *

Jerry's stories sped back to New York via satellite. With the world's interest riveted on Israel, Jerry's first-hand accounts caught the hearts of people and soon became *The Chronicle's* most read column. Many Jews, inspired by Jerry Westfield's stories of Israel's renewed faith and national pride, decided that it was time to make Israel their home. With Anti-Semitism growing throughout the world at a rate that was nothing less than frightening, many Jews chose to emigrate to the verified safety of Israel's borders.

* * *

ISRAEL CONTINUES IN CLEAN UP AND CHANGE
By Jerry Westfield
Special to *The Chronicle*

It is now one week since the invasion of Israel. The world is still reeling from the impact of this unprecedented and incredible event. With no overstatement, the defeat of the combined forces from Russia, Germany, Iraq, Iran, Libya, Ethiopia, Sudan, and other Eastern nations has shaken the world like no other event in history. The reaction of world leaders has varied from astonishment to incredible accusations that Israel actually lured those hapless, unsuspecting troops into a trap and launched some secret weapon that destroyed them all.

But, for those of us who experienced it; for those who lived through that night and watched from Jerusalem on the Cable News Network or from the ranks of the Israeli defenders, it was the supernatural power of their God that delivered them. Jews from all over the world continue to pour into this country, and there is excited talk on the street. Talk of a renewed expectation of the eminent coming of the Messiah.

Political ramifications are felt daily. The decision made yesterday by the new Cabinet Committee, led by the Prime Minister, to go back to all pre-negotiation borders has met with wide-spread approval among Israeli citizens. In a statement released this morning, the Israeli government stated, "In light of the attack on the State of Israel and its people with the intent to completely destroy the Jewish Nation, we consider all previous agreements that were based on peace and mutual respect to be null and void."

Today, Israeli soldiers continued to expel Palestinians and set up roadblocks and check points on all roads leading in and out of Israel.

Repair crews are working long hours on airports and highways, but the largest task still lies ahead – burying the dead bodies of the enemy.

The immensity of the job is staggering, as experts estimate that it will take between five and nine months until all the dead are interred. At present, wild animals and birds are already feeding on the carcasses of the fallen enemy, and the government has designated all able-bodied men to help cleanse the land.

Israel has designated the valley of Jordan above the Dead Sea as the official burying ground. So great is the number of dead, that traffic can no longer pass through that area until cleanup is complete. It is a monumental effort, and the Israelis are going at it monumentally. The valley has been re-named by the people, and is now generally referred to as 'The Valley of Hamon-Gog,' translated as 'Multitude of Gog' or 'Prince of the Northern Countries.' The irony is not lacking.

It is the greatest of understatements to say that things will never be the same here, or for that matter anywhere in the world again. Israel has seemed to have found their God.

The world stands in awe.

CHAPTER SIX

The Bait

JERRY WESTFIELD SAT IN THE SUN and thought about it. Now, inevitably, there was a power struggle underway for control of Eastern Europe and the Mid-East region. Following the unprecedented recent events, the economies and governments of the areas were in disarray, which was, Jerry knew, a euphemism for all encompassing, total, devastating chaos. There existed a vacuum in the power structure, and mankind, in its own parody of nature, made a mad rush to fill it and reap the substantial rewards. With a sad smile, Jerry stretched his body and mused that what they really needed was a king.

In reality, Jerry Westfield knew well that there was a man who would do for something akin to that very position, and that not-so-dark horse was causing a stir in world politics even now. A Greek by birth, but with a reportedly strong Jewish heritage, Demetrius Strapollos, the compelling force in the new Global Economy and Realignment Commission, was fast becoming the leading candidate. His European background along with his ties to the Mid-East seemed to tailor him into a perfect fit. Jerry recalled that this was the same man Ken Mailer was so enamored of; the one Ken had told him about just three weeks before in Washington.

Since then, Jerry had had the time to do some deeper research than looking in *Who's Who*. There were leaders who opposed Strapollos, but not one of them did so openly. Apparently, they also feared him.

Perhaps…just perhaps, with cause.

*   *   *

Approximately 1500 miles away, Ken Mailer reached into his burgundy-colored briefcase and pulled out a folder brimming with signed

47

documents. He smiled slightly, almost secretly, for this was a moment he had been waiting for – waiting for a long time. He looked down the long dark-oak conference table, and his heart began to beat and swell. He was all but intoxicated by the knowledge that he was there, seated with representatives from all over the world, and he, Ken Mailer, was one of their chief advisors. Finally, after years of careful courting and tedious prodding, the pieces were coming together. Soon, there would be one European Monetary System, and that would be a cashless one of which he was the chief engineer, with the rest of the world waiting and watching -- eagerly, very eagerly wanting to join.

The voices of the assembled representatives had risen to a low, sustained rumble when the huge, dark wooden doors at the side of the room opened slowly and Demetrius Strapollos, pausing but a moment to be framed in the doorway, entered the room and immediately dominated it. Immediately, the atmosphere changed and the mumbling ceased as Strapollos walked to the over-sized, black-leather chair that defined the head of the table. He stood there for a moment and brushed back his thick, black hair with one hand as his dark, onyx eyes surveyed the group. At six feet four inches in height, he physically dominated any other person in the room, and in the returned gazes of the people in that chamber, he might well have taken on the semblance of any Apollo on any Grecian urn. As always, he was impeccably dressed and every inch the businessman who thrived on confrontation.

"Gentlemen," he said as he lowered his tall and muscular frame into the yielding leather, "let's get started, shall we? Mr. Mailer, do you have those papers I requested?"

"Right here, sir," Ken Mailer answered with some pride. "They are all signed, notarized, and sealed, sir."

"Very good, Mr. Mailer," Strapollos said as he received the documents. He lifted his dark eyes to include everyone seated at the table.

"As you all know, to implement this transitional stage, we need all parties involved to be in a state of readiness. With the invasion of Israel and the incredible course of events that has followed in the Middle East, we will have to postpone our announcement. I propose a two-month delay. At that time, we will reconvene and move forward. In the meantime, gentlemen, I wish you to consider a proposal."

As he spoke, two men, as obviously pre-arranged, began to pass out large manila envelopes to each delegate. On the front of each package was a light-blue label with white edges which read,

CONTRACT WITH ISRAEL
Proposal for Peace.

There was a low grumble from several of the representatives as they read the title, but Strapollos continued without a pause, as though he had heard nothing but enthusiastically approving sighs.

"In this contract, we, as the European Community, would guarantee Israel's future safety and assist them in whatever rebuilding efforts may be needed," he told the gathering. "This will be in exchange for certain economic privileges in the area. Peace in this region, I remind you, will only benefit our cause and greatly enhance the future profits of everyone concerned.

"Anyhow, gentlemen, I'm certain that you will find it very interesting reading. I want each of you to call my office once you've had the chance to study it and give me your feedback and opinions. Then, I want to meet with each of you individually before we meet here again. We'll stay in touch.

"Mr. Mailer, I want to see you in my office, if you please."

With that, Demetrius Strapollos rose, smiled curtly to the assembly, and walked through the same door he had entered.

Everyone understood that the meeting was over.

*   *   *

"Ken," Strapollos began as soon as he was seated behind his gleaming mahogany desk, "how are we doing on our little project?"

"Well," Ken answered as his forehead wrinkled, "it's coming along, sir, but I'm...well, I'm afraid it's going to be at least another six months before we can implement."

Strapollos leaned a few inches closer to Ken, his dark eyes flashing.

"We don't have six months. I need that network up and running as soon as possible; I told you that when you signed on with us, didn't I? I want to know what they're eating; what they take in their coffee; who they're talking to; how many times they go to the bathroom. Am I speaking your language, Ken? Do I make myself clear?"

Strapollos had not raised his voice, but Ken Mailer began to feel a drop of sweat form just under his hairline, threatening to streak across his forehead.

"Yes, sir," he answered. "I understand, and that is precisely why we need time. In order for the surveillance network to be complete, we need to launch six more satellites. Six more, sir! The central control system is being installed in that special room in...or should I say under your home office even as we speak."

"Time," Strapollos said as he leaned back, "is a precious commodity, Ken, so let's not waste it. If you need something – anything -- let me know. Understand this: I'm giving you full authority in this matter. Europe is only the beginning, my friend. If we want to get the world united under one roof, we must act quickly and decisively. I know you understand, or you wouldn't be such a valuable part of the team. Isn't that so?"

Without waiting for an answer, Strapollos lowered his large head to the papers on his desk and said quietly, "Get back to me in three weeks with your progress, not the lack of it."

*   *   *

Ken Mailer left Strapollos' office swiftly, walking out the door and heading straight for the well-appointed lavatory. Although he loved the money and the power, he wasn't very good at confrontations; not very good at all.

Anyway, he thought to himself, *what was the big deal? Everybody knows that the "smart cards" are only the first step towards the microchip insertion. Its just science. Technology must go forward for the betterment of mankind* – Strapollos had taught him that.

He bent over the sink and splashed icy cold water into his face. He straightened, breathing through his mouth, and gazed into the mirror.

Besides, he thought, *if I don't do it, someone else will, and that person will be the one making all the money.* So what if those 'smart cards' and later those microchips also contained a virtually undetectable and almost microscopic additional chip, a chip that would allow Demetrius Strapollos to locate anyone, anywhere, anytime he wished. A similar system had been used for years in Europe for tracking livestock. Cattle or human being, Mr. Strapollos didn't see any difference, and neither did he.

As he walked out of the Men's Room, Ken noticed some of the delegates talking in the hallway. When they saw Ken, they silenced immediately and just stared at him, albeit with politeness and set smiles, but silently…silently.

Ken hesitated for a moment and then walked on. He knew there would be opposition to Strapollos' proposed treaty with Israel, but he would put his money on Strapollos anytime.

Ken Mailer dreamed of becoming Demetrius Strapollos' invaluable, irreplaceable, 'right hand man,' and he was not about to allow anything to get in his way.

Anything – or anyone.

* * *

In Israel, the massive clean-up effort continued tirelessly. The Israeli Army joined forces with huge groups of volunteers and work continued twelve to fourteen hours a day, six days each week, burying the dead soldiers if not their weapons. Hundreds of trucks and trailers were loaded each day with all types of firearms. These were brought to utility plants where they would be used as fuel. Many of the Russian weapons were made of *lignostone*, a synthetic product developed in Holland that burned at very high temperatures. So successful were the Israelis becoming in converting the weapons to fuel, Israeli officials proposed a considerable cut back on her coal imports from China.

Most importantly to Jerry and Jacob and Sarah and the others to whom they spoke, throughout the land, there existed a new sense of being bonded together, and the product of the bonding was a new, spiritual awakening. The religious community began to cry out with renewed fervor for the rebuilding of the Temple, so that sacrifices and offerings of Thanksgiving according to the laws of Moses could once more resume, and the people could give thanks unto their God for the miraculous victory over the invading armies. There was talk everywhere about a lasting peace and a renewed commitment to their faith.

With the dread 'cleansing' going on all about them, the atmosphere was somber, but there was something else as well.

Something…electric.

CHAPTER SEVEN

Inside the Trap

WHEN NEWS OF THE PEACE PROPOSAL reached the general population, the citizenry of Israel, there literally was rejoicing and dancing in the streets. *Finally,* people said openly, *finally someone with enough power to guarantee total peace!* Although not everyone was pleased, one had to look far and hard to find a dissenter.

Jerry had decided to stay on with Jacob Klausman and his wife, Sarah, at least for now. He had so many stories yet to write, and *The Chronicle* was feasting on Jerry's daily column. In fact, his reports on the invasion and its aftermath had placed Jerry high on the list for future awards, at least according to Bob Lewis and others at the paper..

The sun rose in scarlet grandeur, its early morning rays twinkling and dancing across the Mediterranean. Jerry and Jacob sat at the kitchen table, sipping coffee and taking in the beauty of it all through an open window. In that moment, that frozen moment, the events of the last two months seemed hazy…dim and distant.

It was Jerry Westfield who finally broke the silence.

"So, Jacob, what do you think about this whole thing…this Strapollos? Is he for real, or what?"

Jacob shrugged, and his lips curled downward, "I don't see why we need him or his New World Order. God is our refuge and our shield, or hadn't you noticed, even now?"

"Jacob, I've been here two months now, and I know you are a very religious man, and I respect that, but don't you think you might try to be a bit more objective? You know, I mean…realistic? Do you really expect God to do everything for you? I mean, the Bible says God helps those who help themselves, right?"

Jacob stared intently at Jerry and slowly shook his massive head.

"Jerry, you find that anywhere in Scripture, and I'll sign over the deed to this house!

"Haven't you learned anything from what has happened here, my friend?" Jacob asked, fixing Jerry's eyes with his own. "God does NOT help those who help themselves. God helps those who TRUST in Him. Where were Strapollos and his armies when the attack came? No one helped us then…only God. We don't need Strapollos, and he will only bring us trouble. Mark me well!"

Just then, Sarah invaded the kitchen in a vivid yellow and orange sundress. The room seemed to brighten even more as she said, "Still solving the problems of the world, I see. The United Nations should hear about you two."

"Someone has to," Jerry laughed. "It's a dirty job, but Jacob and I love it!"

"I'm glad you're happy," Sarah smiled back, "because I invited one of my friends over for dinner tonight. Her name is Ruth. You met her at the bank last week, Jerry, you remember? You'll like her; she's very interesting, and she's working on that crazy currency thing you always talk about!"

"Wait a minute," Jerry's smile dropped to half power. "You wouldn't be trying to…as they say… 'fix me up' with somebody, would you? You know how I hate that."

"Oh, come on now, Jerry; you'll like her. Besides, I need a fourth to make a good table. It's not another invasion, just a friendly dinner!"

"Help me out, here, Jacob," pleaded Jerry.

"You need to meet somebody," said Jacob, smiling and leaning forward in his chair. "You work too hard. You need to relax a little; have some fun; go somewhere!"

"So! You're in on this, too," moaned Jerry, throwing up his hands in mock surrender. "Well, I'll be nice, and I'll be polite, but that's it! I'm not ready for any kind of relationship right now. Besides, I hardly remember meeting this woman."

But, Jerry did remember her. He remembered her too well, and that was what made him hesitate now.

Jacob placed a hand on Jerry's shoulder and said, "Relax! It will be fine. Nobody's calling the Rabbi and hiring the hall. It's not the end of the world, you know – just dinner."

The phone interrupted, and Sarah moved to get it.

After a pause, she said, "Yes, he's here. Hold on please." She turned to Jerry, her eyes wide, holding the receiver out to him.

"It's for you," she said. "It's a Mr. Robert Lewis, and he's calling from New York City!"

Jerry snapped up the phone.

"Hello, Bob! What's up?"

"I need you to be in Paris tomorrow," Bob Lewis said without preliminaries. "I want you to cover the signing of the peace treaty."

Jerry could not resist a touch of sarcasm.

"Why, thank you," he said, " I am fine, and oh, yes, everything's going extremely well."

"Come on, Jerry," Bob Lewis' voice moaned, "you know I hate small talk. OK, so how are you? Doing fine? Stumbled over any dead leads lately?"

"Oh, Bob," Jerry sighed with a smile, "the force of your personality is overwhelming me!"

Lewis growled and answered, "I swear, if I weren't such a wonderful, warm, and benevolent person, beloved of children and old ladies, I'd fire your you-know-what! You have reservations on the 7:00 AM flight. Call me at the office when you get there. And, now listen closely, Jerry. My sources tell me there is a real power struggle going on – major differences of opinion between some of the countries involved. I know this sounds improbable, but some have even suggested possible assassination plots on some prominent world leaders are in the works, it's that bad. I want you to look under every rock. I mean it! I want everything!"

"I'm on my way," Jerry stated simply, all business once more. "It sounds interesting."

"And Jerry…"

"I know," Jerry interrupted, "be careful. I'll call you."

"What was that?" Jacob asked as Jerry returned to the table.

"I have to leave for Paris in the morning. They want me to cover the signing of the peace treaty."

"Peace treaty!" Jacob exclaimed, throwing back his head. "I'm sick from hearing about it! I mean it; my stomach hurts every time it gets mentioned! I hope it all falls apart!"

"Well," said Jerry, smiling at his friend, "whatever happens – I'll be there for it!"

* * *

In Paris, limousines slinked into the drop off area of the opulent *Hotel Louis XVI* in a steady stream disgorging leaders from all over the world. Demetrius Strapollos had insisted on Paris for the meeting, hoping to avoid any show of protest from right-wing Israeli extremists, 'fanatics' he had called them privately, who very vocally felt that Israel needed no other protector than their God. Nor, in truth, were these the only ones who objected, as a number of nations from the European Community saw no reason to sign anything with Israel. That, added to the underlying fear of Demetrius Strapollos that they all felt, and the festive occasion was underlined with tension.

Paris was coiling into a very tight spring.

* * *

Demetrius Strapollos was planning much more than a mere signing ceremony. Ken Mailer had been working for endless hours on the encryption method for the New World Currency, and Strapollos planned to seize this opportunity to announce its readiness. This was the right time, and he knew it – felt it.

When Ken Mailer walked down the long hallway to Strapollos' office in the hotel, he could see the two huge bodyguards standing on either side of the door. Strapollos had many enemies, and the armed guards were semi-permanent fixtures.

As for Ken Mailer, he was very, very close to attaining his goal of becoming Strapollos' right-hand man. Now, Ken was more than the 'high tech wonder' so many knew him as. Now, he was up to his ears in something very special -- espionage, and what he was about to do would certainly change his life – change it forever.

When he reached the door, the security guards acknowledged him with the slightest of nods. He refused to look at them, willing his gaze to be steady and straight ahead. He knocked, and when the voice within bade him do so, he entered.

"Good evening, Ken," Demetrius Strapollos said quietly. "I asked you to come, because I have some business for you to take care of."

"Certainly, sir. What kind of business, may I ask?"

Strapollos leaned back in his large leather chair and regarded Ken Mailer steadily. His handsome face carried the slightest suggestion of a smile, and it never changed throughout their conversation.

"I have a small problem for you to handle," Strapollos began. "It seems that one of our associates has a difficulty with my leadership. He questions my goals and feels I am gaining too much power. Ken, he is actually threatening to 'expose me' tomorrow before the entire world if I don't step down from, as he puts it, the 'self-appointed chairmanship of the

European Community.' What he intends to 'expose' is not your concern, nor should you concern yourself about it. Regardless of its content, the threat exists."

Strapollos rose now, uncoiling to his full six feet four inches of height and crossed to Ken. He reached out an arm and placed it gently, almost tenderly, around Ken's shoulders.

"Now, Ken, you realize how embarrassing that would be, and how it could jeopardize our announcement, don't you?"

Strapollos drew a white business envelope from his pocket and held it before Ken.

"Let me make myself very clear," he said, "so there will be no misunderstanding. I want this man out of the way. I don't need him to be here for the ceremony; the papers were signed weeks ago. He is an annoyance I can't afford and can definitely do without.."

He handed Ken the envelope and continued, "I want you to contact the man whose telephone number is in this envelope. When he answers, you will give him a second telephone number and a three-word phrase, both of which are in here. The gentleman you have contacted will take care of the rest."

With a cold suddenness, Ken realized fully what Demetrius Strapollos was telling him to do, and his hands began to sweat as he pressed them tightly against his side so they would not visibly tremble. The thought passed his mind that his anxiety was understandable, since he had never been asked to have a man killed before, let alone the leader of a major country.

Strapollos noticed his agitation and said, "Is there a problem?"

"Sir, I…I was just thinking…"

"Thinking?" Strapollos interrupted, adding only a slight quantity of cold steel to his voice. "You only have to convey a message. I have people to attend to details. It's all in the envelope. However, if you do not want to be part of this – part of our combined effort…I can have Mr. Meyer take care of it – that is, if you feel you can't handle it."

Mr. Auguste Meyer was the only competition left between Ken and the position of second in command. Strapollos knew that, and it was a card he played with great skill and invariable success.

"Oh, no, sir!" Ken said with apparent confidence, "I'll take care of it – right away!"

"Good," said Strapollos, indicating the envelope now in Ken Mailer's hands. "As I said, those are your instructions for the call. They are to be followed exactly – no deviations. Any problems, and you call me immediately on the coded line.

"And, Ken," he said with his voice calm and quiet and soothing once more, "remember that this is what we have been waiting for. It's our time now, Ken, our time!"

Ken walked out the door with the envelope in his jacket pocket and a feeling he could not describe gripping his heart. Something was happening to him. He had been changing slowly for some time now, and he could feel something – was it power? – rushing through his veins, hot and heady and very, very real. Success was what mattered, success and pleasing Mr. Strapollos. If only he could pull this off, there would be nothing Mr. Strapollos would keep from him.

Nothing!

He would become the second in command, the right hand man, to the one who, he knew, would become the most powerful man in the world.

*　　*　　*

The clock on the mantle was chiming six o'clock in the evening, and Jerry Westfield sat nervously on the couch in his friend's living room. Sarah was busy putting finishing touches on "the dinner," and Jacob watched the evening news. Jerry looked up as the lights of a car pulling into the driveway flashed across the front windows.

"Jacob," Sarah called immediately, "Ruth is here; would you get that?"

Opening the door and his arms at the same time, Jacob smiled, "Hello, Ruth! How are you?"

Ruth Cowen walked into the room.

Jerry had courteously risen to his feet, and now he was staring at the woman who stood before him. He had honestly not remembered her looking so...well...so good. She was around 38, he estimated, standing five feet three or four, with the blackest, raven hair he had ever seen and a face dominated by large, jade-green eyes.

"It's good to see you, Jacob," she said. "Thanks for having me."

"Our pleasure! Say, you remember Jerry Westfield, don't you?"

"Certainly," she replied, holding out an ivory-fingered hand. "How are you, Jerry?"

There was a second's pause, and Jerry blurted, "Good. I'm good!"

Behind Ruth's back, Jacob rolled his eyes and made a face of feigned agony at Jerry.

"Ruth!" came the call from Sarah, "join me; I'm in the kitchen! So glad you could come!"

When Ruth had left the room, Jerry Westfield flopped on to the sofa and slapped the top of his head. Jacob was next to him in an instant, smiling widely.

" *'Good! I'm good!'* " Jacob taunted playfully. "The Pulitzer Prize winner is such a brilliant conversationalist!"

"Give me a break, will you!" Jerry replied, tossing a throw pillow at his friend.

Jacob sat back and let out a hardy roar. He was enjoying this; really enjoying it.

He had never before seen his friend so disarmed or so at a loss for words.

* * *

Dinner was a wonder. It had been no small task for Jerry to keep his weight down while living with Sarah's cooking, and tonight was no exception. Everything smelled irresistible; everything excited the appetite.

The conversation at the table was mainly between Sarah and Ruth, with he and Jacob as speechless bystanders, but Jerry determined that he would change that. Gathering himself mentally, he jumped into the conversation.

"So, Ruth," he started, "Sarah tells me that you're working with the bank on this new world-wide currency?"

"Yes, we're getting the computers ready for the on-line change-over to the World Wide Marketplace."

"Is that what they're calling it?"

"Yes, that's the new format. We received it yesterday. We're still waiting for the final installation instructions, but we hear through the 'grapevine' that an announcement is short-coming."

"What do you, personally, think about all this?" Jerry asked. "Is it going to work?"

Jacob laughed. "Always a reporter! Always asking questions!"

"Oh, I don't mind," Ruth smiled. "I believe that it will help everyone. It will make buying and selling on the World Wide Web so much easier. And, it should practically eliminate theft. Actually, there's only one thing that causes me a little...well...concern."

"And that is..." Jerry said softly.

"I'm a little worried about this man, Strapollos. He's becoming very powerful, and I...well, I don't like to see any one person with that much control."

"Now you're talking," Jacob interrupted, slapping one huge paw on the table. "That's what I've been saying all along!"

They would have continued, had not the shouting from outside the window become so loud that it could not be logically ignored.

"What is that, Jacob?" Jerry asked as he rose from the table. "What's going on out there?"

* * *

Jacob and Jerry got to the front door at almost the same time and took a step or two outside. The women stood in the doorway, framed in the warm light from within. All four watched as the figure of a man came walking, came reeling, came prancing down the street with a growing contingent before, beside, and behind him. Some were following silently, while others were shouting back, wildly gesticulating, telling him to be quiet; to get off the street; to get out of their neighborhood. The figure in the center of the whirlwind would have looked quite ordinary were it not for the way he reeled and shouted and intoned.

As the center of attention came nearer, Jacob and Jerry could hear that he was crying out in Hebrew. Jerry understood only a few words, but Jacob translated with remarkable ease.

"Woe to Israel!" the man cried, his voice loud and shrill and cutting. "Woe to Israel, for she has agreed to a covenant with death! Woe to Israel, for the Lord God says, *'I and I alone have delivered you from the hand of the enemy, yet you have made a covenant for peace. They cry peace, peace, but there shall be no peace. Your covenant with death shall be annulled, and your agreement with hell shall not stand. When the overflowing scourge shall pass through, then you shall be trodden down by it.'*

"This is the word of the Lord, the God of Abraham, Isaac, and Jacob.

"Woe to Israel! Woe to Israel..."

And the man continued down the street intoning, moaning, weeping, repeating the message again and again, with people being added one by one to the roiling, mumbling crowd that followed him.

* * *

When they were back inside with the door closed firmly behind them, Jerry turned to Jacob and saw the unsettling mask that had painted itself on his face.

"Jacob, are you all right?"

"I don't know," Jacob replied. "I've never felt quite like this before."

"Come on, Jacob," Jerry urged, "don't let this guy get to you. He's a fanatic. A looney! They're coming out from under every rock, lately. You should see what we have in New…"

Jacob's entire body swung around to face Jerry. "He is a prophet of God, Jerry! We have talked, and you know that I've been feeling this way all along! All that man did was take what I have felt and put it into words by the will of God!"

Slowly, Jacob turned and walked to the table. He placed both hands on it and hung his head, as if the weight of his thoughts had become incredibly heavy.

"Jacob, are you all right?" Sarah asked, looking intently at her husband.

"I'm sorry, everyone," Jacob stated, not answering Sarah directly. "I beg you to excuse me, but I must go upstairs for a while. I…I do need…to be alone."

Jacob headed for the stairs to the roof and began to mount them slowly. Sarah knew what he was going to do.

He needed to pray.

* * *

When Jacob was fully gone, there followed a long, awkward silence, as if no one knew what to say, which was, indeed, the fact. It was Jerry Westfield who finally found some words.

"Well," he said, "I'll admit it; that thing gave me the chills."

"Nothing like that has ever happened before," Sarah stated firmly. "You've been here long enough, Jerry. You know that."

Quickly, Ruth added, "It's a first for me, too. I've never seen anything like that!"

Again, they were silent. Then Sarah asked, "Anyone want a cup of coffee? I'll put some on."

"I know I could use one," Jerry snapped quickly.

Ruth shot a quick glance at Jerry and then at Sarah.

"Count me in," she said. "Just make sure it's strong!"

* * *

The three of them sat at the smaller table in the kitchen, rather than the larger one in the dining room and sipped coffee and spoke of movies and fashions and desserts they had sampled in various restaurants -- frivolous and unimportant matters. The incident outside the door was not mentioned. Finally, Ruth used an early appointment to excuse herself, and Jerry Westfield, with only a little silent prodding by Sarah, offered to walk her to her car.

"It was really nice meeting you," Jerry smiled.

"Even with the 'interruption,' I had a good time," Ruth commented as she slipped into her vehicle.

"Yeah…er…yes. Me, too." Jerry mumbled, one hand on the roof of her car, staring at Ruth through the rolled down driver's window.

Neither of them spoke for almost half a minute, until Ruth said simply, "I have to go now."

"Would…would you consider going to dinner sometime?" Jerry suddenly blurted.

There was another pause, a very slight one this time, and then Ruth smiled and said flatly, "Yes, I would. Sarah has my number. Why don't you call me when you get back from Paris."

Jerry realized that he was smiling, too.

"I'll do that," he said. "I'll do that! Good night!"

The car roared to life and sped away as Jerry stood there, not moving for quite some time. It had been an eternity, it seemed, since he had felt like a babbling teenager, and yet, at the same time, so…at ease…so comfortable with a woman. Was there something about her? Something different…

He shook his head and took a deep breath of the night air. Then he headed toward the house. He had better stop acting like a schoolboy and get some sleep.

After all, tomorrow would be a long day.

A long, long day.

*   *   *

When Ken Mailer was finally back in his suite, he opened the envelope and spilled its scant contents on the coffee table. On the single sheet of white paper were two phone numbers and a phrase along with one line headed "INSTRUCTIONS:" all very neatly typed. The first number he was to call at 12:30 AM, and the other he was to pass on to that contact along with the phrase. He checked his Rolex; it was 11:29. An hour… just one hour from now, and his part would be over. It wasn't so bad. Not so bad at all.

Ken Mailer lay back on the brocaded couch and stared at the ceiling, dreaming and waiting – waiting and dreaming -- for the golden power and glory that he knew would be his.

* * *

At 12:30 AM precisely, Ken Mailer took up the phone and dialed. At the other end, it was picked up by someone who spoke English with a plodding, heavy accent, precisely what accent, Ken could not determine.

There were no preliminaries, no greetings. The voice stated flatly, "You have something for me?"

"Er…yes, yes, I do," Ken answered with only the slightest tremble in his voice. "I have a phone number and a three-word phrase."

"Say."

"555-2398; One Step Down."

"Acknowledged," said the voice on the other end.

Then the line went dead.

That was easy, Ken thought to himself. That was very, very easy. His breathing eased and his grip on the phone loosened as he placed it back in its cradle.

Then, needing to be fresh in the morning, Ken completed his written instructions by burning the envelope and the typed sheet of paper in the working fireplace of his suite and flushing away the ashes in the lavatory before he went to bed.

* * *

His wake-up call came at 6:00 AM, and Ken Mailer sluggishly rolled over to lift the receiver and place it back on the hook. He'd had less than five hours sleep, and he rubbed his eyes sluggishly as he sat up in bed. As had been his habit since college, the next thing he did was to clutch at the remote and turn on the TV, which, like all the TV's he owned back home, had been tuned to the Cable News Network.

He was half way to the shower when he heard it.

"This just in --Explosion in Italy kills President Mario Pulzarrio!"

Ken Mailer froze where he stood, pajama top in his hands, his mouth wide.

"Pulzarrio?" he said aloud to no one. "That's the target… Pulzarrio?"

The TV commentator continued, "We now have reports that Police authorities say a group calling themselves 'Liberators of Enslaved Humanity' have taken responsibility for the bombing. We take you now live to Paris where Italian Vice-President Antonio Severelli is about to make a statement to the Press."

The cameras shifted to a small conference area which Ken recognized as being in the *Hotel Louis XVI*. Very obviously, the room had been quickly prepared for the announcement. A network reporter in Paris continued the narration. "This is Pierre Bonault for CNN, live in Paris. As you can see, Vice-President Severelli is noticeably shaken by these events as he approaches the podium. The President was not only his political ally, but also his very close, personal friend. It appears that Signore Severelli is ready to speak. I repeat, this is live from Paris..."

Cameras zoomed in to a tight close-up of the Vice-President's pale and obviously stressed face. It was the face of a man who had suffered a great loss but was facing it with courage and determination.

"Ladies and Gentlemen," he began, speaking in English. "I don't know what to say. I am filled with grief and anger at this horrible tragedy. I have lost a good friend, but Italy has lost a patriot. I regret that I cannot stay for today's ceremonies, but you will understand that I must leave immediately for Rome. I will say this, however. Those miserable cowards who are responsible for this murder will not go unpunished. I will do all that is within my power to find them and bring them to justice. Thank you..."

The reporter in Paris continued his commentary, but Ken Mailer didn't hear him. He stood there in his bare feet, gooseflesh covering his arms, totally stunned. The phone rang three times before he could gather the awareness and the willingness to pick it up.

"You have served me well, my friend," came the voice of Demetrius Strapollos. "Well done."

"Sir?"

"You have seen the news?" Strapollos asked, his calm voice nonetheless victoriously exultant.

"Yes, sir, I have."

"Very well, then. Meet me for breakfast in half an hour in my suite. There is much for us to discuss."

Ken's eyes brightened, and the chill across his bare shoulders vanished. He all but sang, "Yes, sir!"

He hung up the phone and skipped into the shower. As the hot water soaked his skin, he began to smile. He knew, now, just how powerful a man Strapollos was. Now, Ken Mailer looked deeply within his heart and he found…nothing. His hands were steady now, and his mind and heart had followed. He realized with intense clarity that he felt no remorse; no pain – only exhilaration. It was as if he had just crossed over a huge bridge…

And mercilessly burned it behind him.

* * *

In spite of the news, it was a beautiful, spring-like morning in Paris, even though there was a slight chill in the early March air. One by one, the sleek, black limousines began to arrive at *Elysee Palace*, where the signing would take place. Almost all the major players were in place, and some of them suggested that the signing be postponed in light of the tragic assassination of President Pulzarrio of Italy. Since it had taken two months of preparation to gather these heads of state in one place at one time, however, Demetrius Strapollos affirmed, with the deepest of personal regrets, that proceedings would continue.

* * *

Jerry Westfield literally threw his bags into his hotel room, one of them actually landing on the bed, spent less than five minutes freshening up in the bathroom, and was off to get an early jump on the herd of reporters even now flowing into the *Elysee Palace*.

Jerry had barely shown his pass and gained entrance when he spotted a familiar figure walking down the stairs, clad in what Jerry knew to be an extremely expensive, cream-colored suit with an opulent pure silk tie.

"Ken!" Jerry shouted, "Ken Mailer!"

Ken stopped at the bottom of the stairs and turned slowly.

"Jerry?"

"Well, Ken, I figured you'd be here somewhere. From what I hear and see, you're moving up in the world."

"Just what do you mean?" Ken snapped, his face suddenly cold and ominous. Then, as quickly as it had happened, the cloud passed and he was himself again. "Of course, you mean the article on the economic summit."

"That and this obscenely-priced suit. That necktie alone must have set you back a hundred. You've come a long way, my friend," said Jerry, indicating the surroundings with a sweep of his hand "Very impressive; very impressive, indeed."

"Thank you, Jerry, and the tie was two-fifty, marked down from three hundred," Ken said with the very slimmest of smiles. "Look, I'd like to talk, but I have so much to do. You can understand…"

"No problem. We'll catch up with each other later."

Ken Mailer nodded and vanished into the crowd.

Something's wrong, Jerry thought, although at that point, unaware of late night phone calls and the animal heat of power, he had no idea exactly what that might be.

* * *

Jerry found his seat, claimed it, and waited as the main room filled to capacity and beyond. At the appointed time, various heads of state took their places amid a barrage of flashing lights from the bank of photographers present. There was a somber silence about the proceedings otherwise, as the assassination took more than the edge off what was hoped to have been a joyous occasion. Nonetheless, it was impossible not to feel the electric hum of excitement with so many leaders – so much power -- in one room.

When the last dignitary was seated, Demetrius Strapollos walked in slowly, followed, two paces behind, by Ken Mailer. Every eye held firm as the tall, dark man seated himself next to the President of France. There wasn't a person in the huge room who did not know that this day belonged to Strapollos and no one or no thing was going to get in the way. The applause began slowly at first and built into a swelling grand crescendo that Jerry Westfield could feel through the soles of his feet.

Strapollos rose, holding out one hand palm down, and the applause quieted. He stepped up to the bank of microphones and, with one wide sweep of his eyes, he began.

"Ladies and gentlemen, honored heads of state, most distinguished guests, and members of the press… I shall be brief. This is a very special ceremony in which the European Community is pleased to announce that we have sponsored a peace agreement with Israel and her surrounding neighbors in which we pledge to protect the sovereignty of the nation Israel against any and all invaders.

"There are certain provisions of this agreement that will benefit everyone. There is, for instance, a commitment of 2.5 billion in rebuilding funds. The nation of Israel has the right to…and will have…our assistance in rebuilding, including the construction of the Temple in Jerusalem. In exchange, this agreement clears the way for an international peacekeeping force within Israel's borders.

"At this time, it gives me great pleasure to invite the Prime Minister of Israel to sign first, after which, I will sign for the European Community."

To tremendous applause, Israeli Prime Minister Daniel Ahira leaned forward and signed the document. He straightened and smiled for the cameras, after which he handed the pen to Demetrius Strapollos.

Strapollos took the instrument with a blank face and lowered it to the paper, signing his name in rapid jerks of his large hand.

When it happened, it happened quickly. At first, and for the most fleeting of seconds, Jerry thought that the vibrating floor was from the tremendous applause, but when the violent shaking began and continued, he realized that it was more than that. The windows in the room began to rattle in their foundations, and in that moment of hesitation as eyes jumped first here then there, there followed a second horrendous jolt. Recording equipment and personal decorum flew everywhere and were left behind as people began scattering, clawing, crawling for the exits.

Jerry was on his feet at once, and he made it through the door just as the third and what would be the final jolt hit. Behind finely papered walls, pipes cracked and water began to flow everywhere, cascading down the steps and into the expensive carpeting. Nostrils flared as the smell of gas filled the air, followed almost immediately buy a loud, explosive noise as a ball of fire shot out a second floor window. People began screaming then, passing hysteria one to another as children might toss a ball; pushing and shoving and stepping on and over each other in a desperate attempt to get to the doors – to leave the rooms of Hell behind.

* * *

Jerry Westfield was one of the first to make it out, and he had made it across the driveway, over a short stone wall and onto the lawn which fronted the *Elysee Palace*. Even as the sirens of emergency crews grew louder in the distance, he opened his briefcase, digging out his notebook computer. In seconds, he was sitting cross-legged on the cold grass, linked to satellite and typing live on to the Internet and *The Chronicle* office in New York.

* * *

DATELINE PARIS:
ISRAELI PEACE ACCORD:
This is Jerry Westfield reporting live from the Paris Peace Accord.

What started out as a beautiful day, filled with bright sunlight and the expectation of political harmony, has suddenly turned into a living nightmare framed in chaos. As dignitaries from all over Europe and the Middle East gathered at the opulent Elysee Palace *to celebrate a new union between the New World Order and the Nation of Israel, ceremonies were abruptly halted by what appears at first glance to have been a violent and destructive earthquake, its size and strength still unknown.*

Emergency vehicles are just now arriving on the scene, their screaming sirens competing with the shouts and screams of the wounded and traumatized who were applauding with such enthusiasm just moments ago. From my viewpoint it seems obvious that injuries are considerable. I can make out fires on the second and third floors of the building, and I see several firemen apparently shutting down the gas main that feeds this street. Black smoke is etched vividly against the clear blue of the March Parisian sky.

The timing of this earthquake, if that's what it was, was extraordinary. At the precise moment of the signing of the peace agreement. Just as Mr. Demetrius Strapollos inked his name on to the agreement and before he could put down the pen, the quake hit. Obviously, to many involved, this will be a dark cloud over what should otherwise have been bright and jubilant proceedings. We shall see if this turns out to be the real story in the end.

Signing off – more to follow -- this is Jerry Westfield for The Chronicle.

* * *

With his equipment packed away, Jerry Westfield picked up his briefcase, brushed off the dirt he had accumulated on his person, and walked among the tumult of screaming, running, gesticulating people to his rented car which waited for him at the foot of the long entranceway.

As he pulled out into the Parisian traffic and began to drive the several blocks to his hotel, it occurred to him with growing amazement that there was little or no damage outside of the Elysee Palace grounds. In fact, the further he got from the place, the less damage he could observe.

With his mind racing in high gear, he drove back to his hotel.

* * *

The door of his hotel room slammed shut behind him, and Jerry laid his briefcase on an armchair. Without sitting, Jerry took out his personal, black PDA and located the number of Ken Mailer's cell phone. The phone rang and rang before it was answered.

* * *

Ken Mailer activated his cell phone on the eighth ring.

"Mailer here!"

"Ken, this is Jerry Westfield. Are you all right?"

Ken took a sharp intake of breath as he glanced at the face of Demetrius Strapollos who sat beside him in the dark limousine that quietly made its way through the narrow Parisian streets.

"Yeah," Ken muttered. "Eh...yes., Jerry, I'm fine. How about you?"

"I'll live. That was quite a ceremony, wouldn't you say?"

Ken was becoming more and more nervous. He glanced again at Strapollos, and then turned his attention back to the cell phone.

"Yes," Ken stated, "That's very unfortunate. Very unfortunate. Er...listen, Jerry, I can't talk right now...I'm in the middle of a meeting."

"Sure thing," Jerry returned. "I'd like to meet with you tomorrow before I leave. Ten in the morning – that's good for you, isn't it?"

Jerry Westfield never was one to be put off.

Ken Mailer, realizing the persistence of this particular reporter once he was on to something, merely said, "Sure, that's possible."

"Great," said Jerry with a smile in his voice, "I'll meet you in the hotel coffee shop at ten, OK? My turn to buy, remember?"

"OK," Ken replied. "Agreed." He was happy to be off the phone.

"Mailer, who was that?" Demetrius Strapollos asked gently.

Ken shrugged nonchalantly and smiled weakly as he said, "Just an old friend."

"Of course," Strapollos answered flatly as he stared out the window.

* * *

Less than an hour later, Jerry Westfield sat on the foot of his bed, jotting notes for his meeting with Ken Mailer and trying to keep up with his racing mind, when the phone broke into his thoughts. Jerry picked it up on the second ring.

"Westfield," he answered.

"Jerry?" came the familiar voice, "Jerry, its Jacob! I saw about the earthquake! Are you all right?"

"Yes, Jacob," Jerry answered, his voice brightening, his lips curling into a smile, "I'm fine! It was quite an experience. I'll tell you and Sarah all about it. How are things with you?"

"Eh!" Jacob sighed, "the same type of craziness as always. Everybody is talking about this 'amazing' peace agreement. But, as long as you're all right, that's all that matters."

"Really, Jacob, I'm fine. I think I might be on to something. I have a meeting with that 'friend' of mine I told you about. I want to see if there's something else to this peace accord.

"Oh, yes, I'm also flying back tomorrow. I'm scheduled to arrive at 4:15 or 1615 Hours as I should say to an old soldier."

"Soldier, yes, but not that old," Jacob quipped. "I'll be there to meet you. And, Jerry..."

"Yes."

"Watch your back," and there was, suddenly, the hard steel tone of the Special Forces officer in his voice. "Watch your back."

* * *

In Jerusalem, as throughout Israel, news of the peace accord paradoxically caused renewed turmoil. Those opposed to the treaty demonstrated openly in the streets, boldly proclaiming that God was vehemently opposed to the contract Prime Minister Ahira had signed. The new 'prophets' walked the streets and narrow ally ways at all hours now, predicting doom for Israel and the entire world. While few people took them with any great seriousness, their very presence made most feel intently uncomfortable.

Rebuilding the Temple was each day's major topic. The only point of real contention relative to that project was when the Messiah would appear. To many, it was only the Messiah who could lead them back to the Temple Mount and start the work. Many speculated that he was already among us, perhaps one of the teachers of the Torah or among the Rabbis. Others claimed that he would appear only after the Temple was completed.

But, the majority opinion by far, the one that existed in whispers and hurried conversations at dinner tables and in elevators and at concession stands, was that it must be the man called Demetrius Strapollos. He was, after all, the one who had commissioned the Temple to be built and claimed, besides, that he would protect Israel from any future attacks. Some even adamantly claimed that Strapollos' father was a Rabbi in Greece and of the lineage of the Tribe of Dan.

The debate continued for weeks and weeks, and support for Strapollos grew ever stronger. Finally, banners with his name on them began to be hung from buildings and bridges and walls and billboards, clearly and blatantly proclaiming him as the one -- the coming Messiah.

Curiously, while these banners fluttered in the warm Israeli breeze, reports from all over the world were coming in featuring a new phenomenon -- nature turned ugly. Fierce, damaging storms were commonplace, and reports of small-scale volcanic activity and minor earthquakes became more and more frequent, not that many in Israel took particular note of these reports.

None of it, indeed, was enough to deter or change Israel's or the world's growing fixation and delight with their new hero.

Demetrius Strapollos.

CHAPTER EIGHT

Tightening the Grip

KEN MAILER WALKED CAUTIOUSLY into the hotel coffee shop at 9:59 AM for his ten o'clock meeting with Jerry Westfield. Jerry spotted Ken first, and with a wave motioned him to the table. As Ken approached, Jerry's mind registered that Mailer looked…tired, almost worn out.

There is, Jerry phrased silently in his mind, *no happiness in him.*

"Good morning, Ken!" Jerry said aloud. "Some coffee?"

Ken nodded, and Jerry poured a cup from the carafe on the table.

"Thanks for taking the time to meet with me," Jerry smiled. "Hey, old pal, did you get any sleep last night? You look beat."

"I'm a trifle overworked right now," Ken answered curtly as he adjusted his knife and fork and spoon and unfolded his napkin and folded it again. "How are things going for you?"

"Not bad. I'm living with old friends in Jaffa while I cover this beat for *The Chronicle.* They're good people, and I like being with them.

"But, let's not talk about me! How do you like working so closely with somebody like Demetrius Strapollos?"

Ken's brow furrowed, and one eyelid twitched. "What do you mean?"

"I think you know what I mean, Ken. Excitement – hoopla – New World Order – new currency – new leader – and all this mystery surrounding your boss. You know, of course, that some people are hailing him as the new Messiah. I think you'll agree that doesn't happen every day, my friend."

Ken Mailer tried very hard to control his hands and to make certain his face was calm, even placid, but it was becoming more and more difficult.

"It has its benefits," Mailer said smoothly. "He is a demanding man, but that, as they say, comes with the territory. If you do your job well, produce for him, you are well taken care of...taken care of very well, indeed."

"And, if you don't produce?"

"You get replaced," Ken answered matter-of-factly and without emotion.

A moment passed as they both sipped at the dark liquid in their cups, studying the brew intently and avoiding eye contact. Finally, Jerry looked up and leaned closer.

"We've known each other a long time, so let's be straight, all right?" he stated. "There are those who think Strapollos is very dangerous. People seem to disappear when they get too close to this man, especially when they disagree with his agenda."

Ken lowered his cup with enough force for the silverware to move.

"That...that is a bunch of political garbage!" Ken exclaimed. "Mr. Strapollos is just what this world needs. It is his heart's desire to bring everyone together under one roof; one united global community, where there will be protection and prosperity for all!"

Jerry had heard canned answers before, but usually they came from politicians.

"Sounds like I should stand," he said, "for the singing of the New World Anthem. I've been around, Ken, and this guy can't be that good – you know it, and I know it!

"In fact," and Jerry leaned back, held Ken's eyes with his own, and decided to try something that had been bouncing off his brain since yesterday, "some sources tell me that he may have had something to do with the death of President Pulzarrio of Italy."

Ken's heart began to pound, and he gripped the sides of the table, pushing back his chair as if to rise.

"That's ridiculous!" he almost shrieked, thrusting one manicured finger at Jerry's face. "You could get yourself in deep trouble, Jerry, making accusations like that! Lose that kind of thinking -- lose it! And while you're at it, lose some of those 'sources' as well!"

I've got something, Jerry thought, but the only thing he didn't want to lose just yet was Ken Mailer. There was too much more he wanted to know, and Ken was proving almost too easy.

"Calm down, Ken. I didn't say I believed that stuff, did I? I just wanted to get your opinion, that's all. Would you like something to eat? Anything?"

"No. No, thanks. Coffee's fine."

Ken Mailer settled himself into his chair, lifted his cup and took a deep swallow. He knew he had gone too far, and now he had to get things back together; back where he was in control.

"Let's forget about what other people say," Jerry smiled. "What's your take on what transpired yesterday?"

"You mean the earthquake?" Ken replied, his voice normal and even once more even if his mind still raced furiously. "I'll admit that it was pretty strange."

"Oh, yes, considering that as soon as he signed the agreement, all Hell broke loose!"

"Well," Ken said with an indelible smile now stamped across his face, "I suppose Mr. Strapollos is more powerful than we thought."

Jerry forced a small laugh. This was another dead end. He shifted gears.

"Ken, I met this woman..."

"Wait a minute!" Ken interrupted, and the smile seemed to grow human for the shortest of moments, "you said *'woman?'* Jerry Westfield is dating again?"

"Take it easy," Jerry laughed with a wave of his hand, "there's really nothing to it. She's a friend of a friend. We were introduced; we had some conversation – that's all.

"What I was going to say is that she works for a bank in Jaffa, and she was telling me a few small things about this new currency system. I told her I knew the guy who designed it, and she was very, *very* impressed."

"Now you're using *me* to impress the ladies?" Ken laughed, inwardly rejoicing for the change of subject. "Well, that's a switch!"

"You know," Jerry said as if an idea had just been born in his brain, "I can use all the help I can get. Maybe you can tell me something about this new system that will impress her? Like...like when is it scheduled for implementation?"

"Phase One will go into effect June first of next year," Ken said proudly as he leaned back in his seat, now on solid and comfortable ground, and prepared to speak lovingly of his child. "The new system will be operational in the European Community and the New Middle East region, including North Africa. Phase Two is slated to begin throughout the rest of the Eastern European block countries and Russia by the end of next year. That should bring stability to the entire region."

Jerry looked up from his black coffee, "And the West?"

Ken's eyes became worried and cleared in a single second. He said, "We're ironing out those details right now. I really believe that once

73

the West sees the new system in operation, it's going to be a very short time before they and the entire world are connected. Believe me, the benefits are tremendous, and they're already extremely interested."

"Ken" Jerry asked honestly, remembering the Ken Mailer he had known in college. "Why? Why do this? What do you want to accomplish?"

Ken did not even have to think about his reply.

"To unite all the world into one global family," he answered, his voice becoming what one would use with a very precocious child. "No tariffs; no trade laws; no currency barriers – one world and one people. First, we implement the currency system, and the rest will take care of itself."

Ken pushed his chair back, looking at his watch.

"Got to go!" he smiled, feeling that he had come out ahead. "I have a top level meeting to attend in Brussels. Tell you what, Jerry, I'll have my secretary mail you all the details. Call my office, ask for Carol, and tell her where you want it sent."

Ken was on his feet, pumping Jerry's hand.

"Till next time," Ken smiled, hoping that would be far, far in the future.

Jerry smiled wanly.

"Thanks for your time, Ken," he said, but Ken was already walking away, displaying to Jerry a ramrod straight back.

Almost to himself, Jerry half sighed, "…take care of yourself."

And he meant it.

* * *

Back up in his room, his bags already packed and the meeting with Ken Mailer still buzzing in his skull, Jerry snapped on the Cable News Network on TV. He was not pleased with what had just taken place with Ken Mailer. You didn't have to be a psychiatrist to know that something was definitely wrong.

Jerry Westfield reached inside his briefcase and brought out Jeremy Palmer's Bible. Once more, Jerry felt an emptiness that it was hard to describe, let alone live with. How he wished he could talk to his old friend, and somehow, he felt close to him when he looked at the Bible Jeremy had loved so well.

Perhaps, just perhaps, there were answers left in that book -- answers scrawled by Jeremy's hand in the notes his friend had scrawled across the pages of this red leather bound volume.

Jerry glanced at his watch. 10:36 AM. There was plenty of time. He opened the book.

It was in the Gospel of Matthew, stuck in the binding, that he immediately found a slip containing the words, *'Signs of the Times'* and the notation *'Mat. 24:4-8.'* He remembered joking with Jeremy about the very phrase, asking if he could advertise *The Chronicle* on one of those signs. Jeremy had smiled, but he hadn't laughed. Immediately, Jerry regretted his own inane attempt at humor.

The verses were easy to find, since Jeremy had highlighted them in vivid yellow. He was about to read them when a flurry of color and noise on the TV caught his eye.

The screen announced a special report in large bold letters.

"…We will take a look at the phenomenon of escalating natural disasters taking place around the world," the television reporter was saying. "This is live feed from Central America, where an estimated million people are homeless and thousands have been killed by the effects of Hurricane Arleen, an absolutely unprecedented storm which has ripped through this region causing widespread devastation. Emergency officials say they are using gasoline to burn unburied bodies to prevent the spread of disease.

"Today, rescue teams across the region resumed searching for survivors of the cataclysmic floods and landslides.

"The greatest losses were reported in Honduras, where an estimated 10,000 people died and 800,000 – that's 15 percent of the population – were forced to flee their homes. Countless more are presently in the midst of a great famine, lacking fresh water, food, and medicine.

"In neighboring Nicaragua, over 3,000 people are known dead while 4,000 others remain missing, and more than 600,000 remain homeless nationwide. This is just the latest in a series of natural disasters to hit the area in the last several months."

Jerry snapped off the TV with a shake of his head. He had personally covered stories just like that, and he was well-acquainted with the incredible hardship brought on by this type of 'natural' tragedy.

But, this was not what he intended to think about in the time he had left before he had to leave for his plane. He pulled Jeremy Palmer's Bible closer and began to read the highlighted verses.

Jesus answered: "Watch out that no one deceives you, for many will come in my name, claiming, 'I am the Christ,' and will deceive many. You will hear of wars and rumors of wars, but see to it that you are not alarmed. Such things must happen, but the end is still to come. Nation will rise against nation, and kingdom against kingdom. There will be famines and earthquakes in various places. These are the beginning of sorrows.

I don't understand, Jerry thought. *I wish you were here, Jeremy. I wish I could ask you some questions right now. I still can't bring myself to believe that this book can…what… predict the future of mankind? That's just not rational; not sane!*

Jerry lay back and allowed the Bible to close on his lap. His thoughts were coming too fast, and he needed distraction before total confusion set in. He grabbed for the remote and the TV flared to life once more.

"…flooding evacuations on Sunday," the same reporter continued, "in the aftermath of the recent heavy rains in portions of southern Kansas and northern Oklahoma in the United States. At least 100 deaths are reported

"A pair of rain-swollen rivers took aim at Arkansas City, Kansas, a town of about 12,000 people surrounded by the Arkansas and Walnut Rivers. Both rivers crested Sunday, with the Arkansas hitting a record 15 feet above flood stage.

"About 5,000 people were forced to evacuate, as water six to seven feet deep poured into homes on the south side of town.

"Flooding elsewhere throughout the region has caused thousands to abandon their homes and has caused untold millions of dollars in damages."

There will be famines and earthquakes in various places, Jerry recalled.

On the TV screen, reports of destruction continued.

* * *

It was raining hard in Nivelles, the fashionable suburb of Brussels, when Ken Mailer arrived at the opulent front gate of the Strapollos mansion. The driver held open the door of the limousine, and Ken ran up the steps to the stone porch just under an overhang. He slid his ID card through the scanner, waited for a confirming beep, then pushed in the private entry code that only he and Strapollos knew.

There was a click, and the huge, thick, ornate door opened to admit him.

Ken stepped inside, shaking off what little rain had fallen on his shoulders. The foyer was huge and impressive. Even now, after many visits, Ken still took time to drink it all in. The floors were of marble and polished to mirror perfection. The mahogany staircase rose imperiously through the ceiling. Louis XV and Louis XVI period furniture hugged the walls, which were covered with original oils and gold-framed mirrors. Ken never grew tired of just...looking.

A side door opened noiselessly, and a man he knew only as Walter, Mr. Strapollos' personal servant, entered quietly. Ken knew that he was far from a mere butler, however, since hidden behind the politeness and mannerly ways most people witnessed was a man who was fluent in four languages, an expert in handguns, a fifth degree black belt, and fanatically loyal to Demetrius Strapollos. No, hardly your normal butler.

"May I take your coat, Mr. Mailer?" the man asked. "Mr. Strapollos is waiting in the study."

"Thank you, Walter," Ken said. He checked his appearance in one of the gold-ringed mirrors and crossed to the study, where he knocked firmly and then entered.

"Do come in," said Strapollos as Ken walked through the dark wood door, "we've been waiting for you."

"Sorry to be late, sir," Ken explained, "but the weather held everyone up. I believe everybody is late this evening..."

Ken was going to say more, but the words lumped within him; would not come. Sitting next to Demetrius and looking quite comfortable was Auguste Meyer, Ken's main and perhaps only adversary within the Strapollos organization.

"Why, hello, Auguste; what brings you here tonight?" Ken could hardly get the words out of his throat, let alone force them to sound normal.

It was Strapollos who answered, "Auguste tells me that you had breakfast this morning with Jerry Westfield."

"Yes, yes I did," Ken said, keeping his voice level. "He's an old friend of mine from college. Is that a problem, sir?"

"What did you talk about?" continued Strapollos flatly, ignoring Ken's question..

"Old times and small things. You know, sir, like...he has a girlfriend...where he's staying. That sort of thing."

Strapollos' eyes were unblinking as he repeated, "Old times and small things..."

Ken tried to take it all in. There was Strapollos staring at him; his rival, Auguste Meyer, sitting with a cold, sardonic smile on his face.

That was when Ken Mailer felt something stir deep inside. After what seemed to be a forever of fear and worry, Ken found all that anxiety replaced by something that stirred hot and acid, rumbling and building, and directed at one source and one source only...Auguste Meyer.

Meyer was younger and bigger than Ken, but right now, that didn't seem to matter. Ken took an unflinching step toward his rival, and his voice was strong and hard.

"If you have something to say, Meyer, why don't you just say it?"

The grin was gone from Meyer's face, and he jumped to his feet.

"I heard you!" he almost screamed. "I heard you spilling your guts to him! Don't deny it!"

The thing that had boiled inside Ken a moment ago, took form into a deep and abiding hatred for Auguste Meyer. Without conscious thought, Ken's arm rose and a finger jabbed out in Meyer's direction.

"Liar!" Ken's voice blazed. "You heard nothing! I did not say a thing that would damage our project or Mr. Strapollos. I'm tired of you sneaking around looking for any way to take my position. You haven't produced one thing to advance the project since its inception! If there's a fly in the ointment, you're it!"

Auguste Meyer said nothing, although his face had taken on a crimson hue, and veins in his forehead worked overtime. In what seemed a single motion, Meyer unbuttoned his navy-blue blazer and drew a pistol from his waistband. In less than a second, the gun was pointed directly at Ken Mailer's head.

"You're the fly, Mailer," he breathed. "Do you know what you do with a fly? You smash it!"

Ken closed his eyes. The pistol was a Luger, he knew, although the exact make and model he could not identify. *Funny,* he thought, *the things you think about when you're going to die.*

He wondered if he would have time to pray.

Or, for that matter, if he could pray at all.

The shot, in the confines of the study, was like a bolt of hot thunder rolling inside his head.

I'm...I'm...not...dead, Ken thought. He opened his eyes.

Auguste Meyer had sunk back into the armchair in which he had been sitting. His expression was blank and almost benign, except for the small, purple-red hole in his forehead and the thin, deep scarlet line of blood that flowed from it, down his face, over the bridge of his nose.

He was, of course, quite dead.

"Well done, Walter," Strapollos complimented.

Ken turned slowly to see Strapollos' butler, Walter, standing in the doorframe with something still smoking in his hand.

Strapollos rose and spoke to his servant while motioning at the body in the chair.

"Take this out, Walter, and see that no one finds it."

"Very good, sir," the butler said evenly. "Everything shall be taken care of."

Strapollos turned to Ken who was standing with his eyes fixed on the red drops that now stained the floor next to Auguste Meyer's chair.

"Don't concern yourself about this, Ken. It will all be cleaned up, and nothing will show. That's one of the advantages of highly polished marble floors, don't you think?

"Ken," Strapollos continued, "would you care to sit down? You're not looking too well."

"I…I," Ken stammered, taking in the room with a wide sweep of one slightly trembling hand, "I don't understand?"

Strapollos smiled. It was a small smile, but for a moment, his eyes almost twinkled.

"There is little to understand," Strapollos assured Ken. "I knew he was up to something, and I've been watching him for weeks. He had become unstable, and he was selling technology on the side. Of course, we monitored his every move. I was waiting for the right moment, and what you did and said just made it easier to solve the problem.

"After all," Strapollos went on, "I can't have anyone killing my right-hand man, can I?"

"Excuse me, sir," Walter interrupted as he removed the pistol from the corpse's hand. "Dinner is ready to be served."

Strapollos rose and motioned to Ken Mailer who began to walk towards the dining room on legs that felt almost numb. At that moment he was thinking not of dinner or a dead man in an expensive chair or crimson beads on a marble floor. His thought carried one message…a single theme.

Right-hand man? Right-hand man? He had heard those words, hadn't he, and directly from Strapollos. Besides, except for working breakfasts and lunches, Strapollos almost always ate alone, particularly at evenings, and here he was about to dine with the most powerful man on earth.

He had made it!

He felt the marble floor beneath his feet again, and his appetite at once grew ravenous. He, Ken Mailer, had made it to the place for which he had yearned and longed and fought. He was Demetrius Strapollos' right-hand man!

The fact that it had taken the death of another to achieve that goal didn't seem to bother Ken as much as he might have thought it would.

Well...at least not considering the outcome.

CHAPTER NINE

Messiah and the Prophet

WHEN THE GOURMET DINER WAS FINISHED and the last crystal goblet cleared away, Demetrius Strapollos rose and ushered Ken Mailer into the den, where Strapollos sank his tall body into an easy chair and laced his fingers across his chest. That was a certain sign, Ken knew, that he wanted to talk.

"Ken," Strapollos sighed, getting directly to the point, "I believe we have touched on this before, and you are aware that the people of Israel strongly believe that only the Messiah can lead them back to the Temple Mount and initiate the rebuilding of the Temple. Let me be frank with you and go the final step. I believe I am that man."

Ken's eyelids fluttered. He was not a religious man, personally, by any means, preferring agnosticism to adherence to what he conceived to be an outmoded moral code that would certainly not have gotten him to the position he now occupied. Even so...the Messiah? That was taking things up a notch – big time! The Messiah!

"In order for this to become a reality," Strapollos continued, "I have carefully chosen a man to help us attain our goals. He sincerely believes that I am that leader, and he is committed to making it an actuality in the very near future. I have asked him to join us this evening, and I believe he should be here now. I tell you this, because he will be working very closely with you on the project from here on out."

Strapollos reached over and pushed a button on a device resting on a mahogany side table.

In less than ten seconds, Walter appeared in the doorway.

"Is the gentleman here?" Strapollos asked.

"Yes, sir. He arrived a few minutes ago."

"Very good, Walter. Show him in, please."

Ken's mind was reeling as both he and Strapollos stood to greet the evening's new guest. Ken could hear the footsteps of the men as they approached, and presently Walter entered, followed by their new associate.

He stood just inside the doorway and his deep black eyes surveyed the room. He was wearing a long, jet-black robe and a wide-brimmed, black hat. The man's features were long and distinct, his beard was darker than black, and his raven hair hung in two large braids.

"Ken," said Strapollos, "I'd like you to meet Rabbi Michael Eissen."

Ken could not help staring. *A Rabbi? Well, of course!!! What a move of pure brilliance on Strapollos' part.* He reached out his hand.

"Rabbi. It's a pleasure."

Rabbi Eissen did not take Ken's hand, but he did acknowledge him with a small but polite nod in Mailer's direction. Quickly, Ken allowed his hand to drop to his side.

The three men sank into chairs as Walter closed the door quietly as he left.

"It is good to see you, sir," the Rabbi stated when all three were seated. "It is an honor to be here with the both of you."

Ken felt slightly uneasy, but he had no knowledge of this man and no way of knowing that Rabbi Michael Eissen was the very powerful leader of a very right wing party in Israel. Many, including many religious leaders, considered him to be extremely dangerous, and many more were outraged that he was ever allowed to use the title *'Rabbi.'* His faction believed that now, today, was the critical time to take control of their country. Among other things, they wanted their nation to return to the Law and Temple Sacrifice. Many, however, were suspicious of Eissen's motives. Now that Israel was on the mend from the Russian/Arab invasion, many – perhaps even the majority – were anticipating their Messiah to come and take control.

For men like Demetrius Strapollos and Rabbi Michael Eissen, this was the singular, most cherished opportunity of a lifetime.

"Thank you for coming, Michael," Strapollos began. Then his glance turned to Ken.

"Ken, Michael will be taking over the duties of public relations. He has his own constituency that will work with him to help us, shall we say, 'prepare the way.' I want you to work closely with him to make certain that all goes well. Whatever he needs, you are to make sure he gets it."

Strapollos leaned forward and gazed intently at Ken.

"The Temple must be built," he emphasized. "I promised peace, and there will be peace. Nothing must get in the way of that objective – no thing and no one. Do you understand?"

Ken nodded enthusiastically, and Strapollos continued.

"On Saturday, you will fly to Tel Aviv and begin preparations."

Ken hesitated and said anxiously, "Sir? I have so much to do already. The satellites are almost in place, and we're scheduled to test the system next week. I...I'm really going to be needed here."

"You will be back in plenty of time," Strapollos answered. "I want you there to get this started. Make sure the right people are in place, then come back. As time progresses, Michael will take over that aspect completely, and you will be free to concentrate on the new monetary system, your outstanding area of expertise..

"You'll get your tickets and reservations at the office as usual, and Michael will meet you at the airport. He'll fill you in and set up meetings with the people we have chosen. Remember, Ken, you are to be there to represent our technical and financial commitment to these people. Whatever the need, you supply it. Whatever they need...

"And, now, Ken, Michael and I have some items to discuss that I am certain are of no interest to you. I'm so glad you could make it for dinner."

Rising with Strapollos, Ken instinctively realized that he was being dismissed. He shook hands with Strapollos and nodded to Eissen.

Then, the 'Right-Hand Man' left the room.

*   *   *

When Ken Mailer had gone, Rabbi Eissen and Demetrius Strapollos sat for a while without words, simply regarding each other.

It was Strapollos who spoke first.

"It has been a long time, Michael," he said. "I believe the last time of any import that we spent together was in England, where you were immersing yourself in -- what was it? -- the occult practices of Babylon and the great dictators of World History."

"Ah, yes," Eissen sighed, "but that was several years ago, and even then, I knew that we would meet again. It is the unseen hand of destiny that brings us back together, I believe that."

Rabbi Eissen moved slightly closer and continued, "When I heard of the peace accord, the realization flowed over me like warm water. I knew I had to contact you. Your time has come, Demitri, your time has come.

"There are many of us who believe that the world is ready for a new leader, especially, of course, one who will bring prosperity and order with Israel at the center. Believe me, for I've been there and seen it, the people in Israel are ready for the Messiah, longing for him -- and you are that man.

"We must move immediately but carefully, for there are still those who would oppose you. Right now, there are too many to dispose of individually and adequately, but," Eissen concluded confidently, "you will win them over. I promise you."

"What are your plans?" Strapollos asked, his eyes meeting Eissen's in a moment of total understanding.

Eissen's face never changed as he answered. This had been gone over many, many times with his compatriots and in his own mind. He spoke with the confidence of familiarity.

"First, we will stage rallies; then we will purchase commercial time on Israeli television. We will represent you as the promised Messiah of old. Once we have the support of the people, the Israeli government will have no choice but to follow.

"Then, we will plan a well-heralded visit by you. The visit will coincide with the celebration of the placement of the cornerstone of the Temple on the Temple Mount. It will be a major celebration throughout Israel, but what is most important, it will seal your position with the people. You will be...Messiah!"

"Excellent," Strapollos nodded, and for the first time since they were alone, a slim smile parted his lips. "Keep in contact with me on a daily basis. Daily, you understand. I want to know about each aspect of the operation."

"Certainly," Rabbi Eissen said as he leaned back deeply into the soft chair.

It occurred to Strapollos that never before, at any time, was any man as close to ruling the entire world as he was at this moment. It was a strange, exhilarating taste in his mouth, something he could not place which was, nevertheless, quite good...quite enjoyable...quite stimulating.

There was a soft knock at the door, and without looking up Strapollos said, "Yes, Walter. What is it?"

The door opened, and the butler entered.

"I was wondering if either of you gentlemen would care for something to drink?"

He paused and looked around the room. Demetrius Strapollos sat quite alone in the richly paneled den.

"Sir? The Rabbi...he left?"

"Yes, Walter. We were finished for the evening. Actually, I believe I would care for a brandy."

"But," the confusion in the servant's voice was palpable, "I...I don't understand. I've been waiting just outside the door. I don't know how he could have gotten by without my seeing him."

"Quite all right, Walter," Strapollos said calmly. "I know you are very good at what you do, and that's why you're here and paid so well. As to what happened, there are things that are neither your fault, nor your privilege to know."

Strapollos managed a smile.

"Now," he said, "about that brandy..."

CHAPTER TEN

The Calm Time

THE MOON OVER THE CITY OF JAFFA was huge as it hung low in the sky and danced and sparkled and shimmered on the waters of the Mediterranean. The night sky and the roof of Jacob Klausman's house were a perfect match, and Jerry Westfield loved being there. He sat blissfully alone with the stars for nearly an hour before Jacob came up to join him.

"I can see you really like it here, and that gives me pleasure," Jacob began. "But, then, why not? It's beautiful."

"Yes, it is," Jerry remarked and then swept arm and hand across the expanse of sky. "It's all beautiful. If the human race could just manage to stop killing itself, the world would be a really great place to live."

Jacob took a deep breath and sat down next to his friend.

"It is the creation of God, Jerry. No one else could make such a beautiful and perfect thing. I love to come up here and pray; I feel so close to Him."

Jerry rose slowly and leaned against the outside wall. It was a moment before he spoke.

"You know, Jacob, I think I need a few days off."

Jacob looked at Jerry with a huge smile on his face and said, "Finally, he gets the message! It's what I've been saying all along, Jerry – you can't work all the time; you need a break! Take a few days, Jerry; enjoy the land that is your heritage – meet the people; take a moment to smell the geraniums."

"That's 'roses,' Jacob. The phrase is 'take time to smell the roses.'"

"You smell your roses," Jacob smiled, "and I'll smell geraniums, and we will both get pollen up our noses!"

They laughed, friends together under the speechless beauty of the night sky.

A twinkle came into Jacob's eye, and he asked, "Tell me, have you called Ruth since you got back?"

Jerry plopped himself into one of three chairs surrounding a small wooden table and gazed off into the dark.

"No," he said firmly, "I haven't!"

Jacob took another great breath. "So what are you waiting for – the phone rates to come down? You told her you would call her as soon as you got back. I thought you said you enjoyed her company?"

"I did. I just...needed some time to...think...that's all. I mean, I only got in this afternoon!"

Jacob laughed out loud.

"I understand," he said. "My friend needs time to – what? – Find himself? Well, maybe you will feel better in the morning, eh? Right now, my friend, let's just enjoy the evening."

The two men sat together in silence, enjoying each other's company without words. Each man relaxing in the cool night breeze and wondering and dreaming scenarios of what the future would hold.

Neither one of them even came close.

* * *

The following morning, Jerry walked into the sun-filled kitchen and found Jacob and Sarah sitting at the table, talking over mugs of steaming coffee.

"Well, look who's up!" Jacob smiled. "It's almost 10:30!"

"Did you sleep well?" Sarah asked.

"Yes, I did!" Jerry affirmed, turning to Sarah and playfully ignoring his friend. "It was the best sleep I've had since...well, since I was two years old at least. You know, I was lying there this morning, and I was thinking. *The Chronicle* and I would like to take you two out somewhere, somewhere really nice...perhaps dinner and maybe some dancing. We could go to that little club we passed last night, coming from the airport. What was it called? Yes, the '*L'Chaim*,' that's it. It looks like a nice place, right? Sarah...er...do you think Ruth would want to join us?"

Sarah's eyes brightened as she replied, "She called me this morning from work and wanted to know if you were back yet. I told her some of the things that happened to you, and she was very concerned, so, yes, I think she would be glad to hear from you. You know, her work number is on the pad next to the phone. I wrote 'Ruth at Work' on the pad and drew an arrow to the number, just in case any of us should want to contact her, you understand. You could give her a call right now; see what she says?"

Then, in her best don't-you-dare-say-a-word-to-the-contrary tone, Sarah added, "Jacob and I would love to get out. Wouldn't we, dear?"

"Sure, why not?" Jacob laughed, throwing his hands in the air in an I-give-up gesture. "I don't dance too much, but I hear the food is great, and you know I love great food."

But Jerry had already ripped the page with Ruth's number from the pad and was heading upstairs to the roof with the cordless phone, dialing as he went. After several rings, a voice came on the other end, just as he emerged on the roof.

"Good morning, Mizrahi Bank, Ruth Cowen speaking. May I help you?"

"Hi! Er...this is Jerry...Jerry Westfield. How are you?"

At the other end of the line, Ruth's voice changed, became so much softer.

"Jerry, how are you? I heard you were in that building in Paris when the earthquake hit. Sarah told me what happened. I'm happy to hear you're all right. You are all right, aren't you?"

"Yes, I'm fine," Jerry answered, "It was...let's say it was quite unusual. Right now, I'm just overjoyed to have a few days off, some time when I don't have a deadline. In fact, that's the reason I'm calling."

Jerry swallowed and tried to collect himself. This was the first time in so many years that he was going to ask a woman out to dinner when it wasn't for an interview or an arranged affair such as a press awards dinner.

"I was wondering if...you know...maybe...well, if you'd like to go for that dinner we spoke about? I mean, if you're free this evening. I know tonight is short notice, but I never know when I'm going to be off."

"I understand," Ruth replied. "I think that would be wonderful."

"I...I thought it would be nice for the four of us to go. Sarah and Jacob are free – I mean. If that's OK with you?"

Ruth answered immediately, "I would like that very much. Where did you have in mind?"

"I...I thought we could go to that new club just outside the airport. It's called the '*L'Chiam*,' I think. How about I pick you up at seven? Sarah has your address. Would that be all right?"

"That would be fine," Ruth said, and her smile came over the phone. "I'll see you then."

Jerry felt lighter, as if he might rise from the roof of his own volition.

"Seven o'clock it is! Bye!"

Jerry clicked off the phone and walked down the stairs feeling pretty satisfied with himself.

"So, what happened?" Ruth exploded. "What did she say, as if I don't already know?"

"I pick her up at seven," Jerry answered proudly. "I think I'll call the place and make sure they reserve a table for us."

Jacob and Sarah looked at each other and smiled.

It was going to be a special night.

* * *

At the Mizrahi Bank, after she had hung up the receiver, Ruth Cowen sat at her desk, staring at the wall before her. There was something… something about Jerry Westfield that she really liked. Perhaps it was his honesty…or the almost innocence of his boyishness. She was so used to men coming on to her filled with slick confidence and slick words, that it was refreshing to talk with someone like Jerry who was obviously nervous but not afraid to be himself in front of her.

It might stand a chance, she thought. *It just might stand a chance.*

She picked up her pen and went back to work.

* * *

Jerry pulled his car up the u-shaped driveway of Ruth Cowen's apartment building. He parked the car and began walking up the steps to the front door, which was covered by a dark green canopy and attended by a doorman. As he approached the entrance, he could see into the lobby, and he watched as Ruth Cowen walked out of an elevator and straight toward him. Her black hair glistened in the lobby's light, and the pale blue dress she wore accentuated her dark features.

Jerry's hands had begun to sweat, and he wondered why he had suddenly regressed to a teenager on a first date. With a firmness and determination, he wiped his palms on his trousers and extended a hand to greet her.

"It's good to see you again, Ruth. You look beautiful!"

"Thank you, Jerry. It's good to see you…and in one piece."

They laughed and walked out to the car. Jerry opened the door for Ruth, and after she was seated, he walked around to the driver's side, thinking, *Jeremy, old pal. Maybe you were right. There is a God!*

"Where are Sarah and Jacob?" Ruth asked as Jerry got behind the wheel.

"We have to go back and pick them up. The baby sitter hadn't arrived, so I told them not to worry, because I'd pick you up first, and then we would come back for them."

"Fine," said Ruth, "It will give us a chance to talk."

*   *   *

"So...er...have you lived in Israel all your life?" Jerry asked when they had pulled on to the main road and were settled in traffic.

"Actually, I haven't," Ruth answered. "I came over here about ten years ago from Long Island."

"Really? What made you decide to come to Israel?"

Ruth answered in a matter-of-fact voice, saying, "I came over here after my divorce. I needed a new start, and this seemed to be the best place where I could really start over."

Great job, Westfield, Jerry thought to himself. *What a great way to start off!*

The light turned red, and Jerry brought the car to a stop at the intersection.

He turned to look directly at Ruth and said, "I am so sorry, Ruth. I should never have asked."

"Please don't be sorry," she replied, her eyes straight and honest. "It lasted all of two years, there were no children, and, believe me, I am as glad of that as I am to be here. I made a bad mistake, Jerry. I married a charming and sophisticated guy who simply couldn't keep his hands off other women. I made a very common mistake -- I was naive enough to believe that I could change him. Like most who try that, I was dead wrong. I'm here now, and I love it."

The light changed and Jerry drove on while Ruth continued.

"Thanks to Jacob, I have a good job with a great future. Both he and Sarah have been great friends to me. I met Sarah at a community welcoming party when I had been here one week. She is actively involved in that, helping people get settled when they arrive. She told me her husband could help me find a job. I had been involved in banking in New York, so Jacob introduced me to some people he knew at the Mizrahi Bank in Tel Aviv, and...well...here I am.

"But, enough of me!" she giggled. "I understand you are a Pulitzer Prize winner?"

Jerry wanted to tell her not to stop talking about herself; that he could listen to her for a long, long time. Instead, he said, "Yes, that's true. I got it for covering the race riots in Los Angeles in 1992."

"You must be very proud of that. I never met anyone who is so famous."

"Famous?" Jerry smiled. "Oh, I'm not famous – infamous maybe, but not famous!"

They pulled up to the Klausman home, and Jacob and Sarah were waiting for them.

"Here we are," Jerry stated the obvious.

And he said it with a touch of real regret.

*   *   *

Once inside the velvet interior of the club, they were seated and began the ritual of ordering drinks, talking, and browsing the menu.

Ruth reached over and touched Jerry's hand.

"I told you some of my story," she smiled. "How about you?"

"I don't think there's much to tell," he answered, taking a deep breath. "About six years ago, my wife filed for divorce on the grounds of incompatibility. That translated to the fact that I was never around for her. I didn't blame her then, and I don't now, either. She was absolutely right. We were never able to have children, and with me on the road so often, months at a time, it must have made for a pretty lonely and empty life for her.

"I tried to get home as often as I could, really, but it wasn't enough. She ended up with some guy, and they got married a month after the divorce became final. She got most of everything in the settlement. I guess, deep down, I felt I owed her that much. I didn't fight very hard at all."

Ruth had not let go of his hand all the time he had talked.

"That's very sad." she said. "It must be hard for you, being on the road so much and alone all the time?"

"Well, it's not always that lonely. I meet a lot of interesting and powerful people in my travels, which makes my life very interesting, and once in a while I luck out and get to stay with very special people like Sarah and Jacob Klausman.

"However," he paused, "it's not often I get to meet someone like you."

Ruth and Sarah smiled, and Jacob rolled his eyes to the vaulted ceiling.

Sarah leaned across the table to Jerry and whispered, "Jerry, would you like to dance?"

"Why, of course," Jerry replied, rising and holding out his hand to his friend's wife.

91

"Not me, you moron!" she breathed in frustration, the index finger of her right hand jabbing furiously across the table at Ruth. "Her!!!"

There was a pause, and then the four of them roared in laughter.

"Come on, Jerry!" Jacob urged. "I think that tonight, even I will give this dancing a try!"

Jerry took Ruth's hand and guided her onto to small dance floor. She came to him smoothly, as if they had been accustomed to this for a long time.

The band took up the theme, as a man and woman carrying microphones were highlighted on the stage by a blue spotlight.

Jerry was not familiar with the music, but it was soft, and the dancers felt the passion in the performer's voices as they sang:

> How many nights I've searched
> Within my waking dreams,
> For something that would last
> Beyond the sunset's beams…
> And reached out in the dark,
> Not knowing what I'd find,
> But hoping there would be
> Someone…to last,
> Beyond the Edge of Time…

The song continued, and Jacob and Sarah could not keep their eyes off their two friends. Although they had said nothing to each other, it was obvious to both of them that something was happening between Jerry and Ruth.

Something special.

End of Part One

PART TWO:
Pale Riders

I looked, and there before me was a pale horse!
Its rider was named Death, and Hades
was following close behind him...

Revelation 6:8

CHAPTER ELEVEN

Of Dreams and Disaster

HIS GRANDMOTHER SAT IN HER OLD CHAIR, the large, overstuffed one in the living room; the one that smelled of her ancient perfume, even when she was wasn't sitting in it. She had that old, crackly, black-leather Bible in her lap, and she was reading to him. He curled at her feet as she read aloud, one finger gently tracing the lines because of her failing eyesight, the other hand stroking his head softly, lovingly.

He was so happy. His grandma liked to tell him stories, especially from that book, and he loved to hear them. There were so many of them – Jesus and Moses and Daniel and big old Peter, the fisherman – so many. Now, she was reading to him again.

His happiness grew and swelled and filled him so completely that it pushed out tears from the corners of his eyes. They were tears just like the last time he had seen grandma, in the place with the candles and the low, hushed voices.

That's when he remembered.

"Grandma," he said.

The old woman stopped her reading and looked down with a warm smile.

"Yes, son, what is it?"

"Grandma…you're dead…aren't you?"

"Why, yes, boy, I am," his grandmother continued, her smile never fading, her voice loving and reassuring, "but that doesn't matter. I've come to tell you a story."

"You have?"

"Yes, boy, I have, but it's one you already know. It's one I told you when I was alive; before the funeral."

"Which one, grandma?" he asked. "You told so many?"

"Think, son, and you'll recall," his grandmother smiled. "Trust in God, you hear? Trust in God, and never believe…that one…"

Her thin, aged finger pointed to the left, and his gaze followed it to the door of the room. It took him only a second to realize that the door was moving, moving in and out like a living, breathing thing. With the certainty of instinct, he knew there was someone, or something, behind that door, waiting desperately to get in, something he did not want to meet.

The sound began, like that of a great, indescribably wild thing that thirsted and longed for something red and hot.

And, he was afraid.

"Grandma!" he screamed. "Grandma, help me! Don't let him get me!"

But his grandmother was already growing transparent, fading away, leaving him with the breathing door and the ripping sound and the ravenous beast.

"Trust in God," her fading voice said. "Trust in God, and never believe that one…never!"

He reached for his grandmother, but she had gone. The unearthly growling became louder…louder. The door began to splinter!

No!!!

Robert Lewis sat bolt upright in his bed. His breath was coming in short, wild bursts, and he was aware that his chest was heaving. The perspiration flowed from his dark brow on to the white sheets, and in the deepness of night and his own bedroom, he felt chilled and clammy and vulnerable.

His eyes swept the place. Everything was quiet, undisturbed in the dim light that filtered through drawn curtains. The door of the room was…just a door. The only sound was the occasional rush of traffic on the streets outside.

It was a dream; just a dream, and his grandmother, God rest her, was asleep in her grave.

At least, so he hoped and prayed.

*   *   *

It was late Saturday night in Jaffa, and Jerry Westfield sat in his room, his attention riveted to the small TV set he had bought for his own use and intended to leave for the Klausmans when he finally went back to America. He was fascinated and incredulous of the reports coming in from all over the world, and he watched the Cable News Network with Jeremy's Bible in his lap, trying to forget the words he had read in that book.

"In what the U. S. Weather Bureau has called 'the most unusual and devastating weather pattern in recorded history,'" the TV reporter intoned, "unprecedented late March and early April Hurricanes continue to form and wreak havoc in the South Atlantic. Today, the Weather Service announced that even more devastation may be on the way following directly in the wake of Hurricane Arleen.

"In the United States, government and private relief agencies are mobilizing supplies for the ravaged areas of central Florida with as much haste as possible. After punishing Central America last week with torrential rains, leading to an estimated 27,000 deaths, Arlene turned northeast and battered Cuba and Florida on Wednesday night and early Thursday with heavy rain and high winds. The storm itself rolled across Florida on Friday morning, cutting a path of destruction one hundred and fifty miles wide from Tampa to Boca Raton. The high winds destroyed hundreds, perhaps thousands of homes, tore up crops, downed power lines, and demolished a number of business structures.

"Florida Governor Harold Jordan told a CNN reporter," and the screen changed to a picture of an elderly man, his gray hair whipping in the wind, fatigue painted across his face like a bold danger signal. "'The death toll is over 2,000. Fifty percent of our major infrastructure is either destroyed, damaged, or just torn apart. Our agriculture is in shambles! All our major crops, our export products are...gone! This is something that happens maybe once in every...I don't know...two hundred years? Now, we hear there may be more storms coming our way? If they hit, I don't know...God help us...I don't know what we'll do...'"

Again, the commentator appeared, saying, "As if in confirmation of the Governor's fears, the National Hurricane Center in Miami has reported that a string of storms is beginning to line up in the Southern Atlantic like a huge convoy of impending destruction. The Hurricane Center is warning that coastal evacuation may be necessary as far north as Virginia. Meanwhile the death toll in Honduras from Hurricane Arlene has risen to almost 12,000 people, with another 21,000 reported as missing. In addition, over one million people are homeless, drinking water is in extremely short supply, and both food and fuel are being rationed. One official coined the phrase 'virtual famine' to describe the current lack of vital supplies.

"As the death toll rose steadily toward the figure of 27,000 across devastated parts of Honduras, Nicaragua, El Salvador, and Guatemala, Hurricane Arlene achieved her niche in history, becoming the most powerful storm ever recorded, eclipsing the Great Hurricane of 1780, blamed for 22,000 deaths in the Eastern Caribbean.

Russ Scalzo and Steve Mamchak

"Nicaraguan officials claim that Arlene has left thirty percent of the population homeless, and that it would cost an estimated three billion dollars – well more than half the nation's annual economic output – simply to rebuild what was destroyed.

"In an interview with Cable News Network, Nicaraguan President Allionzo Perez reminded everyone that there remains a personal horror far beyond the economic situation."

President Perez appeared, seated at a desk, as he reported, "'We are told by fishermen that the stench of death near the coast is sickening.'"

"By yesterday, the official death count was 12,000 in Honduras," the commentator continued, "7,800 in Nicaragua, 2,239 in El Salvador, 2,228 in Guatemala, 1,100 in Mexico, 858 in Costa Rica, and 255 in Panama and Jamaica combined.

"Nor is the situation of out-of-control natural phenomena any less trying in other parts of the world. In China, an earthquake measuring a hefty 7.3 on the Richter scale hit an area 30 miles southeast of Beijing in Langfang. An official in that region has contacted Richard Taylor, our Far East Correspondent. Taylor has quoted the official as saying, 'We are in need of medicines, because we have so many respiratory problems and fungal infections. We are very worried about epidemics breaking out. We need tents, temporary tents to get these people out of our shelters. We have sometimes 1500 to 1600 people in each shelter. This can cause the spread of diseases – even epidemics.'

"The impact of these and other natural disasters is being felt everywhere, as the situation continues to worsen in financial districts around the world. This is true particularly in the insurance industry, where extremely high claims are being filed.

"Today in a news conference held in Los Angeles, Robert Vanson, Spokesperson for Homeowner's Equity Securities, told reporters, 'The Insurance Industry has taken some pretty hard blows. Considering that we are facing the potential for more severe losses in the next few weeks, at this time we are very concerned about our ability to compensate those in need. Despite this, I assure you that it is our intention to do all we can to meet those claims from the distressed areas of our country.'

"However, Homeowner's Equity Securities is not the only company facing this problem.. The list includes all major Insurance and Security Companies, including National Corp Insurance, Home Insurance Group, Farmer's Insurance Group, and dozens of others. When asked what happens to the average family when the money runs out, Robert Vanson replied, 'We are working with Congress on this situation right now, and we are confident that we will be able to come up with some satisfactory answer.'

98

"Even with that reassurance, homeowners across the country are growing concerned and restive. In South Carolina, a homeowner, when asked about his insurance company, responded in this manner: 'Why should I continue to pay for insurance coverage that I'll never be able to use? I paid those premiums to protect my home, so that my family would always have a place to live! If they can't make good on our claims, I might as well save my money!'

"Nor is that gentleman the only person holding such an opinion. A recent CNN poll indicated that public confidence in the Insurance Industry is reaching an all-time low. If this ground swell of public sentiment continues, it will not only amplify the crises they are currently facing, but it may cripple the Insurance Industry as well and have a major impact on the economy, not only in America, but throughout the world.

"Will the American Congress be able to bail out these crippled companies? What about the cost of rebuilding in other devastated countries? When will these natural disasters stop?

"These are questions everyone is asking, and questions that will only be answered by time.

"For Cable News Network's Week in Review, this is Roberto Mandez signing off. Peace!"

Jerry Westfield snapped off the remote and the picture died. Never, could he recall, either in the history he had read or within the scope of his own experience, had there been anything like this.

It wasn't...he searched for the word.....

It wasn't...natural.

* * *

Jerry rolled on his side and shut off the small light beside his bed. He lay in the dark for a while, his mind still filled with the tragedy and turmoil he had heard and seen on the TV just moments before. He wanted...he needed a good night's sleep, but he knew it would not come easily.

When his cell phone rang, it startled him, and when he answered, he was a little too loud.

"Hello!"

"Jerry? Jerry, it's Bob Lewis."

Jerry paused for a moment, and when full comprehension came, he said, "Good Grief, Bob, what's going on? Did you forget your time zones? It's just past midnight over here, you know?"

"Sorry," came the reply. "I need to talk to you, Jerry. Right now.

"Look," Lewis continued, and there was something strange about his voice, "We've known each other for quite a while, now, and most of the time, I think we've been on the same page. I need to get your opinion on something, and I need it without your usual side trips into absurd humor, all right?"

That did it. Jerry was upright at once, shaking off whatever sleep had settled on him, sitting on the side of the bed, taking a breath to prepare himself for whatever Bob Lewis would say next.

"Of course, Bob," he said, "you have my full attention, and it can stay between us if you'd like. What's on your mind?"

Jerry could hear Bob Lewis pause, and he knew that Bob was collecting his thoughts.

"Jerry," Lewis said finally, "what's your personal take on Strapollos? I have some really bad feelings about him."

"Well," Jerry began slowly, "there's not much that's known about him. I mean, he came to prominence so fast, that no one seems to have had the time or inclination to write about his personal life. I can tell you this, however, he's becoming increasingly powerful and dangerous. But, I'm certain you're aware of that."

"That's the part I don't like," Robert Lewis sighed. "It really bothers me that so little is known about him. Here's a man who, as you wrote in your last article, is surfacing as the major political and economic leader in he world as well as being hailed in Israel as the new Messiah, and nobody seems to know where he even comes from? I find that upsetting."

There was a pause, and when Robert Lewis spoke again, all vehemence had left his voice to be replaced by a weariness you could feel across the wireless miles.

"When I was a boy, and my grandmother was alive," Robert Lewis continued, "she would tell me stories from the Bible, and some of them were stories about what was going to happen in the 'near future,' as she put it. One of those stories was about a man the Bible called 'The Antichrist,' who would take control of this world

"You know, I grew up, and I never placed any real credence in those tales, but lately…lately…"

Jerry could here Lewis breathing deeply. Jerry gave him time.

"This is going to sound crazy, I know that," the man continued, "but lately, I've been dreaming, and I'm a kid again, with my grandmother. She's sitting in her old chair, and…and I think she's trying to tell me something about…about some horrible danger that's right outside the door, ready to break in."

Lewis paused a second before saying, "I think I know who it is. It's…the Antichrist!

"I'm sure this is insane to you, Jerry, but have you ever heard any of this stuff before?"

Jerry didn't answer at once. He couldn't, for his own mind was racing too far out of control. Heard about this? His friend Jeremy Palmer, who vanished from the face of the earth with his wife, Kathy, had told him, warned him really, about the Antichrist, not once but many, many times. A shaken Sam Baskin of the CIA had done likewise on a wet park bench in Washington, DC. Now, his boss, Robert Lewis, tough and skeptical Managing Editor of *The Chronicle*, had told him the same thing. What is this?

Am I paranoid? Jerry thought about it very briefly and could come to no decision. He was always so certain these tales were just fantasies… but now. These people weren't red-eyed fanatics screaming in your face or trying to run some scam for their profit. These were sensible, logical, even skeptical people from diverse places who had come to the same point, the same question, and the same fear. It couldn't be…could it?

"Jerry? Jerry, are you there?"

Suddenly, Jerry realized that the phone was in his hand, and he had been staring at it, unable to answer.

"Ah…yeah…yes, I'm here," he said to his managing editor in New York. "I was just thinking about what you told me, and I think I want you to know that you are by no means alone. Several other people have told me the same thing over the past six or seven months."

Jerry continued, "Bob, you know I'm not one for hocus pocus and Twilight Zone stuff, but I will tell you, I would be a fool not to recognize some of the parallels between what the Bible says and what's happening in the world.

"I'll tell you what, Bob, if you give me the go ahead, I'll start checking around, and I'll see what I can find out, OK?"

"That's exactly what I want you to do," Lewis answered quickly, "but please be careful; certain people may not like you snooping around!"

Jerry smiled.

"Don't worry, I'll take care," he told Lewis. "By the way, Bob, how's the response to my column on *The Chronicle's* Web site?

Bob was genuine in his response, "Great! People just love it! I mean it! In fact, you're starting to get more hits than the sport's page!

"And, by the way, you'll be getting some new equipment in about a week."

"What kind of equipment?" Jerry asked. "You know I don't like carrying around a bunch of junk that only gets in my way."

When Lewis replied, his voice had taken on enthusiasm.

"Jerry, it's a new, notebook computer with a built in camera and loaded with the latest satellite broadcast technology. The best part is that it's even smaller than the one you have now. You're gonna love it!

"Look, Jerry…I gotta go! I want to hear from you on this, OK? I'm serious. Take care."

Slowly, Jerry hung up the phone. He had better just go to bed. His brain was aching from information overload, and he would have time to think about it in the morning.

Jerry laid down and rolled over.

In only two hours and sixteen minutes, he was asleep.

* * *

Along with the rising of the morning sun and the cries of the white sea birds soaring along the Mediterranean coast came the morning newspaper – and the headlines that could not be missed:

COMING TO THE TEMPLE MOUNT:
DEMETRIUSUS STRAPOLLOS AND THE CORNERSTONE

* * *

Jacob Klausman was up and dressed early, getting ready to take a group of adventurous tourists on a tour of the Wilderness of Israel. He was reading the paper and finishing his last swallow of coffee when Jerry came into the kitchen.

"Did you see these headlines?" Jacob announced in a bellowing voice as he slammed the newspaper down on the table with enough force to cause the sugar bowl to jump.

With a smirk and a raised eyebrow, Jerry stated, "Do I take it then that you don't approve?"

Jacob rose from the table, pushing his chair back with more than sufficient force to have it tumble backward had Jerry not intervened.

"This man!" Jacob fumed. "This Strapollos! I tell you, Jerry, he is nothing but trouble! There is no good thing going to come of this, and you know it, and I know it! Strapollos has his own agenda – his own benefit – in mind, not that of the people of Israel!"

Jacob stood gazing out a kitchen window, and he breathed deeply, regaining control.

"People are so gullible, Jerry. A year ago this man was just another 'politician,' and now? Now, everybody loves him. I don't know who he really is, but he's NO Messiah I can tell you that!"

Jerry had finished pouring his coffee, and now he took his mug and joined his friend at the window. After a moment of shared silence, Jerry spoke.

"Jacob, my friend, I think it's time I begin what is called in my profession a little 'investigative reporting'. Since everybody wants to know who this guy really is, I'm going to find out. He has to have a beginning somewhere, and I'm certain I can work up a history on him. Who knows, maybe I can arrange an interview when he visits Israel next month?"

Jacob turned from the window and stared directly into Jerry's eyes. The lightheartedness that generally characterized Jacob Klausman to the world was gone for the moment, and in its place was a deep concern and a determination and steeliness Jerry had seen before only on very rare occasions.

"Don't do anything foolish, Jerry. This Strapollos is dangerous – very dangerous. I understand that you realize this, but as your friend, I feel I must remind you."

Jacob reached out and embraced Jerry in one of his famous bear hugs.

"Thank you, my friend," Jerry said.

Jacob nodded.

"Well!" exclaimed Jerry, breaking the mood and changing it, "you have a good day for exploring, old friend. Try not to get lost out there, all right?"

Jacob laughed.

They both knew that there was no one who understood every nuance of the land better than Jacob Klausman.

CHAPTER TWELVE

The Cashless Society

SEVERAL HOURS AFTER JACOB KLAUSMAN had headed off into the wilderness with his small band of tourists leaving a trail of pale dust behind, a messenger arrived at the house in Jaffa bearing a large, heavily taped envelope for Jerry Westfield. He had to sign his name in three places in order to take possession.

The return address showed the package to be from the office of Ken Mailer, and Jerry used his pocketknife to cut through the outside wrappings.

Inside was a second envelope, and taped to it was a note on light blue paper, hand-written by Mailer himself.

The note read:

Jerry,

> *As I promised you in Paris, here it is. You have three days, starting now, to do your story. After that, the rest of the media gets it. Your paper may publish the entire document on the Web any time after 12:00 noon, Wednesday, New York time.*
> *Good luck!*
> *Ken M.*

Inside the inner envelope was all the information Ken had promised on the 'Cashless Society,' and Jerry knew that it would be in exacting detail.

It was over seventy pages long.

*   *   *

Jerry Westfield spent the next two days reading until his eyes and head ached, trying to digest what he had read, and becoming familiar with

104

the new computer Bob Lewis had sent him Special Delivery from New York. He was also looking for any insights into the mind and possible motives of Demetrius Strapollos, so it was slow going, at best. Finally, he began to write his column for the next day.

He had just finished his article and was reading it over while sipping coffee and listening to the news channel on his small TV. He was about to send the document thousands of miles to Bob Lewis, when the Cable News Network that Jerry had on for background noise, interrupted with an announcement that the United Nations had called an emergency meeting to discuss a far-ranging economic proposal from Demetrius Strapollos.

Jerry's eyes widened. The timing was impeccable. His story would hit the paper and the Internet the same day as the coverage of that UN meeting would hit the dailies around the world. While other papers were reporting about reporting it, *The Chronicle* would have the entire story on the front page. This would make *The Chronicle* and Robert Lewis very, very happy.

Jerry had the exclusive story he had asked for.

And it had been handed to him.

*   *   *

COPY TO FOLLOW – COPY TO FOLLOW – COPY TO FOLLOW

For The Chronicle, *this is Jerry Westfield reporting from Israel.*

The continual upheaval caused by unprecedented natural disasters is steadily wearing down an already fragile world economy. In an effort to put an end to the looting that continues throughout the world in the wake of these natural disasters as well as the "Great Disappearance" in November of last year which swept away millions of people from every nation on earth, the United Nations is meeting in emergency session at their New York headquarters to discuss a proposal by Demetrius Strapollos, President of the European Community, to bring the world together under one economic umbrella.

According to this proposal, a radical and new world-wide economy would be established everywhere, leaving behind the now tattered ruins of old national currencies and leaping ahead into a new world order, uniting the nations for the first time since the fabled Tower of Babel. When implemented, it would truly make the world one people under one economic structure.

The proposal itself is lengthy and sometimes complex. In this report, let's take a look at some of the highlights.

First, the proposal would wipe out all previous debt by third world nations who have experienced great loss of life and destruction of crops and businesses due to the recent outbreak of storms and earthquakes. This would be extremely welcomed by these suffering nations, since the United Nations Committee on Disaster Control has estimated that it may be twenty years or more before these devastated countries recover fully, making it virtually impossible for them to ever pay back the large loans now outstanding.

Next, the proposal would unite the resources of the world in one, strong, global economy and marketplace, erasing tariffs and trade laws and creating a true Global Community which would have the ability and power under the committee leadership of selected world leaders to help those in need anywhere around the world without discrimination.

The new currency would be digital in nature. This would allow easy control and equitable distribution for each individual in the new value system. Individuals would return all paper monies to an assigned location (their local bank office, for example) for proper crediting. All assets would be evaluated by local authorities and given value based on the new "Standard Unit" measure, or "SU," as it is being called, which will be set and approved by the leadership committee.

At that time, an identifying number will be given to each person, similar to the Personal Identification Number, the "PIN" of present "smart card" technology currently in use in virtually all banking institutions. Individuals will be able to access their accounts in the same manner they presently do via ATM's and other Cash Machines.

All employers will be required to electronically deposit payroll checks and other income their employees earn directly into their respective accounts.

Repayment of personal loans or payments to individuals by individuals will be transferred via their personal "Smart Cards" by the people themselves in the same way cash or checks today are used for payment, requiring only their personal ID numbers to make the exchange. This will enable all transactions to remain strictly digital in nature. No actual monies will be involved.

Banks and other financial institutions will continue to give interest on units (monies) as they did before. They will also continue to make loans as they may see fit to do so.

These are the highlights of the proposal being considered by the United Nations at the present time. The entire text will be available on The Chronicle Web Site *after 12:00 Noon, New York time, Wednesday.*

This proposal is revolutionary to say the least. In its raw form, it seems to make perfect sense, but what will future generations have to say about the decision that faces us today?

Is it fair and reasonable to say that we are entering a new age? Is it an age that began when mankind sat down in front of the first computer and was fascinated by what he had created? Technology has taken us to many new worlds, and for all we know, this may be the next one.

The question remains, however, what kind of world will it be? Will this proposal of Demetrius Strapollos truly bring people together? Will this mean one world leader and one world government? Only time will bring the answers.

Personally, for today and tomorrow there are other questions that need more immediate attention. The proposal from Demetrius Strapollos is something formidable to ponder, but the next question that comes to my mind is even more personal and equally as ponderable.

Who is Demetrius Strapollos?

Where did he come from, and what are his plans?

How did he get to his current position so fast?

Stay with us. We will try to provide answers for these and other questions of note in a new series of articles beginning next week and entitled:

DEMETRIUS STRAPOLLOS: WHAT'S INSIDE, DEVIL OR ANGEL?

From Israel, this is Jerry Westfield.

-- 30 --

END TRANSMITION – END TRANSMITION – END TRANSMITION

*   *   *

Jerry's story hit, and the public reacted. In some quarters, there was celebration, unbounded and joyous, while others received the news with equally enthusiastic and very public outrage. In one Far-East city, an *ad hoc* committee was formed to propose the President of the European Community for the Nobel Prize, while in a town square in a small village in Sussex, England, Demetrius Strapollos was burned in effigy.

The proposal itself was hardly a surprise. Most National leaders had had it in hand for more than a week. Moreover, Ken Mailer had been working hard, logging thousands of air miles weekly, heading to meetings all over the world, answering endless questions and clarifying endless issues against this day.

Even though he had predicted and expected the diverse reactions, Ken Mailer had no idea that everything was going to happen as quickly, as smoothly, and with as much predictability as it had.

Above it all, Ken was happy, deliriously happy. Now, it was time for the next step in the giddy dance.

It was 7:00 AM, New York time, which made it 2:00 PM in Israel. Ken lifted the phone and placed the call to Jerry Westfield.

There was a little groundwork to be done.

*   *   *

Jerry Westfield walked the warm streets of Jerusalem, basking in the afternoon sun and looking for people to interview. He was on the search for reactions to the plans for the coming Temple Mount celebration, which would be attended by Demetrius Strapollos. What better way to get that reaction than to talk to the people who lived and worked and walked on these Jerusalem streets?

He had spotted one colorful prospect and was about to approach when his cell phone rang.

"Jerry!" came the voice, "It's Ken! Ken Mailer!"

"Ken!" Jerry replied, genuinely surprised to hear from him and to perceive the enthusiasm and liveliness in his voice. "How's it going? You must be incredibly busy. You're the last person I would ever expect to hear from today."

Ken was more than merely excited, and Jerry could feel the man's passion bursting through the phone.

"I just wanted to touch base with you on something, Jerry. You know, I mean you KNOW that we're going to need some favorable press over the next few weeks, what with the new economic proposal and our visit to Jerusalem next month. Well, I was hoping you might be able to…you know…help us out a little."

Jerry Westfield had an excellent idea of exactly what Ken wanted, but Jerry also wanted Ken to spell it out plainly before he commented on it.

"I don't see that you need my help," he said into the phone, trying to sound as humble as possible. "You appear to be doing just fine as it is. Did you have anything specific in mind?"

Thousands of miles away, Ken Mailer smiled. *Now I'm making progress*, he thought. *He's interested. Time to sweeten the pot!*

"Well…ah…Jerry," Ken said, pretending to be thinking of this on the spot, "well…how about you covering the visit from the inside?

You know, you could meet us at the airport, travel with us during the celebration, interview members of the team. Then, after the ceremonies, I could...let me see – yes, I could arrange a meeting – a personal interview between you and Strapollos, and it would be live on the Cable News Network!"

Ken's voice dropped a bit, as if he were trying to regain control. When he spoke again, his tones had the practiced ring of great sincerity.

"Jerry, your influence is greater than you imagine. Let me say, old buddy, that you're being over in Israel has not hurt your career. Honestly, your presence and professionalism would add a measure of credibility to these proceedings for many people throughout the world. You know what they say – a few kind words can go a long way."

Jerry could hardly move. If he had not expected something very much like this, the shock would have been even more intense. Basically, Ken Mailer was asking him to do something that went against everything he personally held sacred in journalism. Still, he wanted to keep playing Ken at the end of the line, because he really did want an interview with Strapollos. He took a deep, silent breath, and tried to keep his voice calm.

"Ken," Jerry replied, amazed at how evenly he was speaking, "I have to tell you that I don't think I'm your man. You know that I write about what I experience – the facts. I'm neither a PR man nor a Spin Doctor; I don't do Public Relations for anyone. If, as you say, people know me and read my stuff, it's because I do write only the truth, and the truth as I see it.

"Look, I would be very happy to cover Mr. Strapollos during his visit to Jerusalem. But, I would need the freedom to ask my own questions and report exactly what I find. Do you understand what I'm saying?"

Ken understood, all right, but this was not the answer he had in mind. Demetrius Strapollos had given him direct orders to recruit Jerry Westfield and get his endorsement. Strapollos was not the type of man who liked to be disappointed. His employer wanted everything to go smoothly, and Ken realized how critical a conversation he was engaged in at this particular moment. He knew he had to navigate carefully.

"Jerry," Mailer said firmly and politely, "I appreciate your concern for the facts. Certainly, I understand your position, but I'd really like you to realize that I simply cannot – that's CAN NOT -- have you asking anything you want anytime you want. Frankly, Jerry, this 'Inside Strapollos – Devil or Angel' approach, or whatever you're calling it, is a little disturbing. The questions for your interview will have to be submitted in writing at least two days prior.

"I'm sorry, Jerry, but that's just how it is. I know we can work this out if you're willing to go by our guide lines – and that's all they are, just guide lines -- which I don't think are unreasonable, given the situation. What do you say?"

Jerry smiled. This was precisely what he had hoped for. *It was ironic, wasn't it? There you are, walking the streets of Jerusalem, looking for a way to get answers about Demetrius Strapollos, and the opportunity rolls in from a thousand miles away over your cell phone.* Jerry had expected the "offer" to deify Strapollos, but he had only barely hoped that an actual interview would come from it. Now, if he could watch Strapollos for a long enough period, maybe, just maybe, he would find a spark to shed light on this mystery man.

Jerry breathed a deep sigh into the receiver, as if he were giving in to a greater good only at great personal cost, and said, "OK, Ken. I'll come up with some questions and fax them to you over the weekend for your approval. I appreciate the opportunity, but please understand that this is going to be a news story. I will report on the events as they happen. This cannot become a promotional stunt or a personal endorsement. I won't be part of anything like that."

"Of course not, Jerry!" Ken exclaimed, seeming stunned that Jerry would even suggest such a horror. "Absolutely nothing of the sort! I promise, we'll work out details over the next couple weeks. Right now, I have a breakfast meeting with Mr. Strapollos, and I have to get ready for that emergency UN meeting.

"Jerry," Ken added as sincerely as his training would allow, "thanks for your help. We'll be talking soon."

"OK. Ken. Good luck."

Jerry flipped the phone closed and eased it back into his pocket. He found a stone bench and sat on it, still lost in his own thoughts.

Even though he expected some sort of contact and offer from Ken, who could believe that everything would turn out the way it had.

It was as if someone – or something – was orchestrating every step.

*   *   *

When Jerry returned to the Klausman home later that evening, he found Ruth Cowen standing in the kitchen, deep in conversation with Sarah. A quick glance at the dining room table assured him that Sarah had prepared a beautiful setting where an equally beautiful dinner was likely soon to be served.

Sarah all but squealed with delight, "Look who's home! We hadn't heard from you, so we figured you were coming back. We were hoping you would show up sometime! I planned a little dinner party to celebrate your big story."

"You really took them by surprise, my friend," Jacob added, clapping a large hand on Jerry's back, "with that special report on the new economy. Do you know that you've been getting credit all day long on the different news networks? We even got a couple phone calls asking for you!"

"Hey, I'm sorry about that," Jerry said. He felt badly about those calls. He never intended nor wanted his work to disturb the family he had learned to love so much.

"I haven't given this number to anyone," he continued. "I've always used my cell phone. Maybe they got the number from somebody at *The Chronicle.*"

Sarah smiled, "I'm asking, do we look upset? We are happy for you!"

Ruth had moved to Jerry's side. Softly, she took his hand and kissed him on the cheek.

"We're all happy for you," she whispered.

Jerry looked into Ruth's eyes; eyes that, at the moment, held something deep and warm that Jerry would like to have gotten to know.

With his usual hearty laugh, Jacob Klausman broke the moment.

"Let the man go upstairs and get cleaned up! Can't you see I'm starving!"

Without comment, Jerry smiled, returned Ruth's kiss and headed upstairs. When he had disappeared completely, Sarah turned to her friend.

"So," Sarah said, "you two look like you're getting along well."

"You could say that," Ruth replied.

Then, they both broke out laughing.

In truth, their relationship had progressed nicely since their first date some ten days ago. They had spoken on the phone every day since, and with the exception of one day when Jerry was entangled in deadlines, he had met her every noon in a small café just around the corner from the bank.

Ruth smiled. Jerry was more than pleased that Robert Lewis had consented to leave him right where he was. As for herself – well, with attention shifting to Jerusalem again, Jerry might be there for quite some time to come.

Yes, she decided with a smile, quite some time.

* * *

To begin, everyone gathered around the dinner table. When the children had finally been settled, Jacob spread his hands and lifted his face.

"Blessed are you, O Lord, our God, who brings forth bread from the earth!" he prayed. "Lord God Almighty, we thank you once again for all Your blessings that You have so richly bestowed upon us. Guide us, O Lord, and keep us in Your mercy and power. God grant peace to Jerusalem."

Sarah fed the children first, while everyone else sipped at glasses of Jacob's favorite wine.

"So what did you find out today, Mr. Star Reporter?" Ruth asked with twinkling eyes.

Jerry smiled.

"Actually, I had a fairly interesting day," he said, leaning back in his chair. He wanted to phrase his next statement in as matter-of-fact a tone as possible, knowing the opposite reaction it would have.

Therefore, he yawned and continued, "Oh, yes, I got a little call from Ken Mailer, asking me if I wanted to join the Strapollos entourage next month – as their guest reporter, of course."

Jacob nearly choked on his wine, sending a fine mist of it across his shirt; Sarah froze in mid-step, her mouth open; Ruth just laughed, her eyes flashing.

"You are joking," she asked, "aren't you?"

Jerry began to study the color of the wine in the clear glass, his face contorted in an enigmatic grin.

There was a pause which Sarah broke.

"He's just kidding around…"

"Not at all," Jerry continued. He was enjoying this. "I am truly serious. Nor is that all. At the end of the ceremony, I will be doing an interview with Strapollos which will be broadcast throughout the world via satellite on the Cable News Network. Not a bad day, I'd say. Not a bad day at all."

Ruth Cowen threw up her hands and intoned, "You're incredible! How does this stuff happen to you?"

Jacob Klausman was the only one not smiling.

"Jerry. you are going to sit right there next to that devil and ask him questions?" he half-stated, half asked. "Suppose he doesn't like what you ask him. What then? Did you think about that?"

Jerry turned his attention to Sarah and said, "The dinner smells great! I love the way you cook, Sarah."

Jacob rolled his eyes and raised his hands to the ceiling.

"Jacob," Jerry said, turning to his friend, "What do you think he's going to do, give me a live hand grenade to hold while he sticks a knife in my heart on world-wide TV? He wants to enhance his image, not destroy it. "

Jerry leaned closer and placed a hand on Jacob's shoulder.

"Look, they require that I submit the questions in advance so they can approve them, so it will be fine. Besides, my friend and my boss, Bob Lewis, wanted me to find out about this man; you are just as curious as Bob, Jacob; I want to know all I can about him – what better way to start than the so-called 'up close and personal?'"

"And you, Jacob Klausman," Sarah added with a pointed finger, "be careful who you call a devil. We don't know one thing about this man."

"That's just it!" Jacob exclaimed. "We don't know anything about this man, and everyone is ready to crown him king! You know something, I hear that renegade, Michael Eissen, is heading up a committee to anoint Strapollos as Messiah. Eissen's talk is inciting the people to near riot! What's more, nobody is doing anything about it!"

Ruth, who had been smiling, was suddenly serious.

" I read in *The Post* today that there was a survey taken of 5,000 Jews in Israel, and eighty percent of them believe that Strapollos could be the Messiah. Fifty percent said he *was* the Messiah. Just last night, I saw one of those 'infomercials' listing all the reasons we should embrace Strapollos as Messiah.

"I don't think this is going to go away. Who knows what the consensus will be by next month when the 'message' has had thirty days more to work and then he actually does arrive?"

"Maybe I should go see this Rabbi?" Jerry mused, his tone contemplative. "Maybe I could get him to grant an interview before I deal with Strapollos?"

Jacob held his glass with both hands and said, "Let me tell you something. This man, this Michael Eissen, has…forgive the cliché…a dark side that not many know about."

"What do you mean, 'a dark side?'" Jerry asked. "He watches too many 'Star Wars' movies?"

"You forget," Jacob answered, ignoring Jerry's attempted humor, "that I was Special Forces, and I still have some contacts there. I have known Rabbi Michael Eissen from a distance for a long time. Do you know that before he became a Rabbi, he studied under a renowned practitioner of the occult for five years? Yes, and there were those in the rabbinical community who vehemently opposed his becoming a rabbi here in Israel, an opposition so strong, he traveled to the United States where – please forgive me, Jerry – they accept everything as equal without discernment. Then, he spent three years in England doing extensive research on the religious practices of ancient Babylon, among other things. Finally, he resurfaced in Israel and quickly found a following that has been growing ever since.

"Jerry, believe me when I tell you -- he is a very dangerous man."

Everyone's eyes were fixed on Jacob. For a moment, there was nothing but silence, then Jacob spoke again.

"My father, a man of strong political opinions, always tells me, 'Jacob, love the Lord our God, and it is also wise to know your enemy.'"

There was another silence, and then Ruth broke in, forcing a smile.

"Hey!" she said, "I thought this was a celebration?"

Glad for any excuse to release the tension, they all laughed. Jerry held his glass high.

"Yes, it is!" he stated. "I would like to propose a toast! To the greatest family on the face of the earth! For their hospitality, their friendship, and their love – God bless the Klausman family!"

To that statement, at least, there was no dissention.

*　　*　　*

Begging exhaustion and an early start in the morning, Jacob and Sarah went up to bed almost directly after dinner, leaving Jerry and Ruth together on the living room couch. Ruth leaned her head back on Jerry's shoulder, and he slowly ran his hand through her raven hair.

The moon rose over the Mediterranean and fractured the sea into a thousand, a million fragments of blue-white light that sparkled in the gentle velvet darkness of the evening. The couple on the couch watched through the living room window and spoke no words for a long time.

No words were needed.

Finally, Jerry spoke softly to her ear.

"I forgot what it was to feel this way."

She lifted her face and kissed him gently.

"And I," she whispered. "And I..."

The moon rose higher. The night embraced them.

"I'm sorry," Ruth said at last. "I really am, but I...I have to get to work in the morning."

"I know," Jerry breathed reluctantly. "I'll walk you to your car."

When he looked at his watch, Jerry was amazed at how much time had passed. Even so, they stood by the car speaking of everything and nothing for another half hour before Ruth pulled away.

Back in the Klausman home, Jerry contemplated turning on the news for a few moments. He rejected the idea quickly. This night had been so wonderful, that he wanted to relish it; to savor it; and dream about it. He would not let the news of the world spoil that.

With his step soft and with a smile recalling the evening that nourished his heart as much as Sarah's cooking did his body, he shut off the light and went upstairs to bed.

CHAPTER THIRTEEN

The Speech

KEN MAILER, THE BLACK LEATHER PORTFOLIO containing his speech firmly held under one arm of his sharply tailored, dark-blue suit, walked down the long hallway leading to the platform of the General Assembly. Neither he nor the people who walked with him said a word, and, in truth, that silence suited him well. Here he stood, second in command to the most powerful man on earth, about to address an emergency session of the General Assembly of the United Nations. Ken welcomed the silence so he might bask in that moment's glory.

As he mounted the platform there was scattered applause from throughout the great hall. Ken took in the place swiftly and in a single glance, from the impressive high ceiling to the rows of tables, each representing a nation of the world, to the ambassadors and dignitaries that he...he, Ken Mailer...would soon address.

Then he was shaking hands enthusiastically with others on the platform, fastidiously arranging his speech on the great lectern, having his photograph taken again and again and again and again.

Easy now, easy now, easy now! Ken thought as he stepped up to the bank of microphones. *Remember it's one step at a time; let's do this perfectly -- just the way it was rehearsed.*

There was renewed and polite applause throughout the assembly, followed by the scrape of chairs and the rush of people "settling in" for what was about to come. Various officials donned earphones; translators in booths leaned forward instinctively; everyone waited.

Ken Mailer looked out over the waiting General Assembly and smiled warmly. *Just the way it was rehearsed...*

"Madam Secretary, Distinguished Representatives of the Nations of the World, Honored Guests of the United Nations, Ladies and Gentlemen," he began.

Just the way it was rehearsed...

"First of all, may I personally thank you for clearing what I know to be very busy and exacting schedules in order to attend this extremely important emergency meeting of the Assembly.

"This meeting was called to introduce you to what I believe with all of my heart to be a new and glorious age of global economic security. If that sounds presumptuous on my part, then I beg you – I beg you -- to hear me out. You see, I believe that once you are aware of what I am about to tell you, you will share my enthusiasm, share my vision, and share *our* goal – our one and common goal.

"There are none here today who are not aware of the incredible challenges, monetary and otherwise, that lie before us – before us all. I will not, for I need not, belabor that point. Yet, as difficult as those tasks may be, I cannot...*cannot*...help but feel that we have been brought to this point by nothing less than – do I dare to say it? – by destiny itself!

"Today, I lay before you a blueprint that will enable us to build together a true global community and help secure the future prosperity of one world – *our* world! Today, I take a step, not for myself, but for everyone on the face of this globe! Today, we begin working together as one family, for one people, for one tomorrow! Today, we truly become a family of Nations United. Today, we truly become brothers and sisters working hand in hand for a common good. Today, we truly begin a journey out of the mire and out of the mud and upward toward the solidity of that rock on which we shall build a future that will be secure, productive, and filled with golden promise – not for any one nation or person or interest, but for everyone!"

The applause filled the hall. Some delegates were on their feet while others nodded enthusiastically while clapping with equal vigor.

Just the way it was rehearsed...

When the noise had quieted, Ken Mailer continued.

"Of course, with every new beginning there are always sacrifices and changes that will have to be made somewhere along the way. I trust you have all read and studied the proposal you received. A copy has also been sent to every leader of every nation on the face of the Earth.

"Now, we realize that at this point, we are only advisors to our national leaders and officials, and we also know that ratification of such an agreement is, at best, months away.

"Having said that, let me add that I am confident that what is accomplished here, now and over the next few historic days, will be the beginning of nothing less than a new and vibrant era in world history, starting here; starting today!"

The applause was a great deal more controlled, but it rumbled across the walls deep and sincere, and Ken, although his face never changed; never showed anything but sincerity and concern, was amazed.

"I would like to begin," Ken continued, "by addressing the International Monetary Fund. I feel a brief look at its history is in order, and may I say, also in our best interest. The IMF was originally chartered after World War II, and it was designed only to make temporary bridge loans to troubled Western currencies pegged to the dollar, which at that time was linked to the Gold Standard.

"However, when the Bretton Woods arrangement was ended by President Richard Nixon in 1971, the IMF desperately began to search for a new mission. First, it made loans to prevent sovereign debt from defaulting, especially in Latin America. Then, it broadened its scope to prop up entirely failed economies in an effort to create a global financial safety net.

"However, A recent study by the Heritage Foundation found that more than half of them, more than half of the 89 lesser developed countries that received IMF loans are no better off economically than they were before, and, amazing as it sounds, 32 nations are actually worse off today.

"In light of this history; in light of Asian and South American markets in virtual disarray; in light of the global natural disasters we have suffered over the last six months which have rendered the economies of many countries either helpless or practically non-existent, we find ourselves at the edge of something no one wants -- a *de facto* economic meltdown!

"This could not be allowed to continue. We had to prevent any further economic erosion. Therefore, along with Mr. Demetrius Strapollos and other members of the European Community as well as many of your national leaders with whom I have met personally over the past year, we have designed a plan to replace all current currencies with a digital system we call, 'The Cashless Society.'"

There was a scattering of applause from the delegates, many of whom were, Ken knew, already convinced and just 'going through the motions.' Ken took a deep breath, remembering the look of almost saint-like sincerity they had rehearsed.

"Truly, this is a new beginning. Soon, we will be able to secure the economic future of our world while still preserving the economy of those who have been able to retain their personal assets and corporate holdings through these most difficult and trying of times."

Ken Mailer was suddenly aware that there was a stirring of some sort on the platform, but he could hardly stop to find out what it was. He cleared his throat and continued.

"It is essential to all future progress in this area that the first 'building block' action be the introduction of a stable and reliable digital currency…"

All at once, the Secretary General was on her feet and Ken was aware of her approaching him at the lectern. In her hand she carried a sheet of green paper. There was a flash of anger in Ken that his speech was being interrupted, but that passed too quickly for anyone to notice. *This doesn't matter,* he told himself, for they had even rehearsed what Ken might do in just such an event, and here it was happening. Now, all he had to do was remember.

Just the way it was rehearsed…

Ken paused and turned to the Secretary General.

In a hushed, solicitous, and almost reverential tone, he asked her, "Is there something wrong?"

With a solemn face, the Secretary General extended the paper to Ken, who took it and slowly began to read.

With cameras flashing and TV camera personnel focusing in on the moment, Ken Mailer raised an unsteady hand to his suddenly pale brow and appeared to breathe very deeply. Slowly, ever so slowly, he lowered the green paper and turned back to the podium.

"Ladies and gentlemen," he said in a level, flat voice, that many would later swear brought actual chills to their spines and gooseflesh to their arms, "I…I have just been informed that a major earthquake of approximately…6.8 or higher on the Richter Scale has hit almost the dead center of Los Angeles, California. At present, there are no further details."

He paused for a moment and lowered his head. With his eyes closed, he could still sense and hear the sighs and gasps echoing around the room as the murmuring grew louder.

"Please," Ken said, his arms outstretched in a plaintiff plea for silence which came almost immediately. "Please! This is a tragedy that cuts to our hearts, and I do not have it in my own heart to continue in the light of the pain which so many of you have experienced in your own lands and which many of us are experiencing at this moment."

From the depths of his being and with brimming eyes permanently caught in the flash of a host of cameras, Ken Mailer raised himself up and addressed the ceiling of the room.

"What will those people need? Will there be any means left to help them? I can't...forgive me...I can't help but see this horror as underscoring the urgency, the vital urgency, of our situation. What will be necessary to compel us to take action as soon as possible?"

Ken hung his head once more to murmurs of affirmation all across the Assembly. When his head lifted seconds later, it was evident that he had regained an amazing control of himself, and the room hushed at once.

"I realize that there is much to discuss and many questions to be answered that are not appropriate to address at this time and in these circumstances. Yet, if we are to have a future – if those people who even now are suffering in Los Angeles and across our globe are to have a future -- we must tackle those questions, and we must do it soon. Therefore, I am asking that the Secretary General adjourn for this afternoon, and that emergency arrangements be made in order that we may meet tomorrow in smaller groups in order that your questions may be answered more specifically, and that we may begin open discussions.

"I further propose that by whatever means you can, there be another meeting of this General Assembly at the end of the week to vote on whether to initiate further studies or to accept the proposal as written and make recommendations on how we should proceed.

"I know this is quick – yes, I understand that -- but we all have eyes to see! Time is running out, as the tragedy that even now is being acted out by the people of Los Angeles will well witness!

"We have a responsibility to the citizens of this world to help restore economic order and normalcy as quickly as possible!

"Our people cry out from their misery; they beg us to help stop their pain; they look to us, their leaders, to stop talking – stop talking and start acting!

"We, as leaders; we, as countrymen; we, as part of the family of humanity need to come together as one people, one government for the common good of all.

Ladies and gentleman– we...can...do...no...less!

"Thank you...thank you very much..."

The applause was thunderous, but Ken Mailer did not smile, he dared not do that, for that was not a part of the script. In rehearsal, he had been told what to say and how to act if something about a natural or even man-made disaster interrupted his speech. He had had more than sufficient practice in how to adapt it to various situations, and it had worked! It had worked just the way he had been told it would.

But...how...how had they known there would be that sort of interruption? How did they know there would be any interruption? Confusion pounded on the gates of his mind, but Ken Mailer refused to let it in. After all, did it matter? He could always think about it -- later.

Now, as the Secretary General adjourned the session, Ken walked over to those sitting on the platform, shaking hands and beginning the long and tedious process of answering all the questions they had.

But, he would get through it. He would do it in the same flawless manner in which he had given the speech.

Just the way it was rehearsed...

* * *

Half a world away in his exquisite mansion in Nivelles, the fashionable suburb of Brussels, Demetrius Strapollos took a slow sip of amber liquid from the crystal balloon glass and snapped off the TV coverage that had been live from the United Nations.

He settled back in the black leather chair and allowed a small smile to play across his lips. He had enjoyed the entire performance – enjoyed it immensely.

"You rehearsed him well," he commented to the man sitting next to him. "A good start, wouldn't you say?"

From the edges of his vision, Demetrius Strapollos could just make out the wide-brimmed black hat moving up and down in complete approval.

CHAPTER FOURTEEN

The Two Meetings

IT OCCURRED TO JERRY WESTFIELD that he really, truly loved a challenge, and if there was an air of mystery about it -- well, that was all the better. As a child he had consumed puzzle books of every type and description, and as an adolescent and young teen, the books of S. S. Van Dine, Rex Stout, Agatha Christie, P. D. James, and particularly Conan Doyle were constant companions, sometimes read again and again. His sharp and cutting instinct for problem solving had been based on the steel of logic and honed by the masters of the art.

All this played in Jerry's mind as he left the Klausman home early on the morning following Ken Mailer's United Nations "triumph," as some of the news media had been calling it. Ken's speech had started Jerry thinking, but not about the cashless society.

Jerry had wondered about the man Ken so idolized, Demetrius Strapollos, and for some reason that brought him to Strapollos' not-so-silent partner, at least in Israel. Rabbi Michael Eissen was on his mind, not only because of Jacob's severe reaction to the man, but also due to the general mystery that surrounded Strapollos's chief advocate in Israel. With some pleasure, Jerry determined to get information on the Rabbi, and to do it this day.

He got into his rented car and headed for a store he knew where he could pick up a cup of early morning coffee and a copy of *The Chronicle*, since the place imported newspapers from all over the world.

He was standing in line at the cash register, sipping his black coffee and contemplating what approach *The Chronicle* would take in covering Ken Mailer's speech at the United Nations when he noticed a box on the counter. In it were a dozen or more round buttons, approximately two inches in diameter. They were white with twin bands of light blue at the top and bottom and between them, printed in red and dominating the surface, some in English but the majority in Hebrew, was the legend:

THE MESSIAH HAS COME!

When it came Jerry Westfield's time to pay for his purchase, he smiled and asked, "Do you speak English?"

"I'm from Jersey City, Pal," the counterman smiled. "Some people claim it's English, but I ain't so sure."

"I'm from across the river in New York," Jerry laughed, purposely pronouncing the city's name "*Nu Yawk*" He smiled as he offered his hand. "I know what you mean. Mind if I ask you a question?"

"Go ahead, Pal. Business is slow."

Jerry indicated the box of tri-colored buttons and asked, "Do you know where this stuff comes from?"

"Sure. You know anything about Tel Aviv?'

"A little. I can get around there."

"OK, over on Kiel Street in Tel Aviv, there's an office building with a banner on it about as big as the building itself. When you see it, you'll know. You can't miss it, Pal."

"Thanks for the directions, Joi-sey," Jerry smiled. "Thanks a lot!"

"You're welcome, N'Yawk," the counterman answered.

They smiled at each other, and Jerry took his change and began to leave.

"You really can't miss it!" the proprietor called after him.

"How's that?"

"It's also the headquarters of Rabbi Eissen!"

*   *   *

Joisey was right, Jerry thought, *that banner is just about as big as the building itself.*

He stood before the structure on Kiel Street in Tel Aviv and took it all in. The huge banner fell from the roof to just above the entrance. It had the same coloring as the buttons, and although it was in Hebrew, Jerry had no trouble translating . The banner read,

COME CELEBRATE
THE TEMPLE DEDICATION
WITH
DEMETRIUS STRAPOLLOS
15 MAY
AT THE TEMPLE MOUNT!

Obviously, Jerry had found the place he was looking for. He took a breath of the warm air and entered the lobby.

Inside, it was much like any other modern office building, and were there not signs in Hebrew, he might have been anywhere in the world. There were two elevators to the right and two to the left, and in between was a gleaming black directory display with white letters indicating the location of the various offices in the place.

Jerry's eyes quickly scanned the board and found the office suite of "Rabbi M. Eissen" on the third floor, Suite 302. He got on an elevator and pushed the button marked three.

When he stepped out, he found himself faced with a hallway covered in a myriad of posters proclaiming the celebration at the Temple Mount. There were also many photographs, the largest of which was one of Demetrius Strapollos signing the agreement with Israel, taken, Jerry knew, about one second before the earthquake hit.

Jerry turned the gold knob on the black door marked "Suite 302" and entered the office. Before him was a receptionist's desk where a well-dressed, attractive young woman was just finishing a phone conversation. She hung up the receiver and smiled at Jerry with highly professional, polished pleasantness.

"Good morning. May I help you, sir?"

Jerry paused only a second before he dug out his press card and held it up for her to see as he answered, "Yes. My name is Jerry Westfield, and I'm a reporter from *The Chronicle*, a newspaper in New York. I would like to see Rabbi Eissen."

The receptionist's eyes brightened, and the smile grew broader.

"You're the American reporter I keep hearing about!" she exclaimed with what seemed to be a genuine smile which turned into almost a pout. "Well, I'm really sorry, Mr. Westfield, but you *will* need to make an appointment if you wish to see Rabbi Eissen."

"I wouldn't take up much of his time," Jerry tried. "I only want to ask him a few small questions."

Her smile never changed, but now here eyes became steady and definitive.

"Well, I'm afraid he's not here right now, and even if he were, I really couldn't allow you to see him without an appointment. Certainly, you, Mr. Westfield, of all people, must understand."

Jerry was only half listening as he scanned the doors in the wall behind the receptionist's desk. The first one he came to that had a name on it belonged to a Mr. Joshua Zimmer according to the brass letters.

"I see," Jerry confirmed. "In that case, will you please see if Mr. Zimmer is in. I'd like to see him if possible."

Somewhat taken aback, her face still refused to change, and she motioned Jerry Westfield to a bank of chairs along one wall of the reception area.

"Please have a seat, sir, and I will see if Mr. Zimmer has time to see you now."

Jerry nodded his thanks and sat facing the young lady, about ten feet away. He hoped desperately that he had hit upon the name of someone significant in the organization and not the person who was in charge of ordering paper clips and toilet paper.

It was less than a minute later that, still smiling, she put down the phone and turned to Jerry.

"Mr. Zimmer would be pleased to see you now, Mr. Westfield. His office is directly behind me. Please go right in; he's expecting you."

Jerry smiled at the receptionist and crossed to the door of Joshua Zimmer's office. Out of habit, he knocked with three staccato raps of his knuckles and entered.

"Do come in, Mr. Westfield! What a pleasure!"

The man who greeted him was in his early fifties, with thinning hair and thick glasses above a full gray beard. He stood about five-eight or nine inches tall and easily weighed over 300 pounds. He lurched around his desk, extending a well-fleshed hand in Jerry's general direction.

As the two of them greeted each other, the man continued, "I am so pleased to meet you. I am Joshua Zimmer, Rabbi Eissen's personal secretary and administrator. Please, what may I do for you? How may we help you?"

Jerry Westfield's face never changed as he thought, *Good going, Jerry! You hit a home run!*

Outwardly, he said, "I deeply appreciate your taking the time to see me like this, Mr. Zimmer, and on such short notice, but I was wondering if I might ask you a few questions concerning the Temple Mount Celebration?"

The heavy man smiled and motioned to a chair which Jerry took as Zimmer settled his bulk in the oversized chair behind his desk.

"Before we begin," Zimmer offered, "would you care for some coffee? A soft drink, perhaps?"

"No, thank you," Jerry responded. "I just had some coffee. About the Temple Mount Celebration…I was wondering…"

"Well, Mr. Westfield," Zimmer interrupted, "Mr. Mailer, with whom you are well-acquainted, has informed us that you will be interviewing

Mr. Strapollos on Cable News Network the evening of the Celebration. I assure you, we are all looking forward to that day with great anticipation – great anticipation!

"As far as the Celebration itself is concerned, I don't know what more I can tell you. We have issued press releases which you should have gotten. I will happily make one available to you now if you wish."

"Thank you so much, Mr. Zimmer," Jerry replied, still smiling, "that would be very helpful, but, you know what would be even more useful would be some information on Rabbi Eissen. He is an interesting man, you'll agree, and somewhat controversial in his own right, is he not?"

Unlike Jerry's face which he had trained to remain placid in all situations, Zimmer's countenance underwent considerable alteration.. His eyebrows sank behind the rims of his glasses, his lips pursed, and he began to pull at his beard in short, brisk strokes.

He took a moment before he answered. When he spoke, it was obvious to Jerry that the man was choosing his words very, very carefully.

"I suppose," Zimmer said slowly, "you could say that. But, I am certain you realize that any man with strong convictions, such as Rabbi Eissen, would be considered 'controversial' in some quarters. I mean, don't you think?"

I'm not going to scale that wall, Jerry thought. He tried another approach

"Oh, of course. By the way, how long have you known the Rabbi?"

The eyebrows lifted above the glasses as Zimmer responded, "Oh, for quite some time now! We met in the United States about…let me see…eight years ago – at a convention."

"And what type of convention was that?"

Without a pause Zimmer replied, "It was a meeting on spiritual awareness, exploring the powers of transcendental meditation and other phenomena of a 'spiritual' nature."

"Don't you think that's just a bit unusual for a Rabbi?" Jerry asked.

"No!" said Zimmer who returned to his beard stroking with increased vigor, "I don't think it's unusual at all! After all, knowledge is essential at all levels. It gives one a greater understanding of…of life… and the hereafter."

Jerry leaned back in his chair and continued to press.

"From what I understand, the Rabbinical Community here in Israel doesn't exactly share that same, shall we say, 'liberal' view. In fact, many of them oppose Rabbi Eissen and have stated openly that they feel he is not fit to be called a Rabbi nor to lead the people in such an historic and monumental event as this.

"Of course, that's what others have said. What are your feelings about that, Mr. Zimmer?"

Joshua Zimmer leaned back in his chair and removed his glasses, rubbing the two indentations on the bridge of his nose with thumb and forefinger. He set his eyeglasses on the desk and continued stroking his beard as he regarded Jerry.

"I can answer that in one word, Mr. Westfield – jealousy. Everybody wants to be the one to introduce Messiah to Israel and the world. It is nothing less than history in the making, so you can hardly blame them for that. While, certainly, it is most unfortunate that some of the religious leaders have...declined...to attend the ceremony, and are so...outspoken as to their personal opinions, still it will be a grand and glorious day, as you will personally witness, Mr. Westfield."

Jerry nodded and grinned. All this propaganda and euphemisms were to be expected, certainly, but he wanted to concentrate on Eissen.

"Exactly what part does Rabbi Eissen play in all this?" he asked.

Joshua Zimmer leaned forward and his eyebrows flared as a slight grin lit his round face. He was on familiar ground now.

"We believe that Rabbi Eissen is the prophet, the one who was spoken of through the prophet Isaiah: 'A voice of one calling in the desert, *"Prepare the way; make straight paths for him."'"*

Inside, Jerry felt a familiar bolt of energy run through him. It was the same shock wave that came to him every time he sensed that something was wrong, that what he had just heard or seen was twisted; didn't make sense. Of course, it had been forever since he attended Hebrew School, but he remembered the verse Zimmer had just used. He also was familiar with it because Jeremy Palmer had read it to Jerry many times as well, and Jerry knew that Joshua Zimmer had misquoted. Jerry knew the verse actually concluded, *"...prepare the way of the LORD."* He could not tell if the error were by accident or design, but Zimmer was continuing, and Jerry listened closely.

"Rabbi Eissen will also have and exercise certain authority given to him by Mr. Strapollos that will enable him to organize various religious groups and religions into one, since Messiah is for all people, you see, not only the Jews. Mr. Strapollos wants to join everyone – Arabs, Jews, Christians – into one great body of people. That is the way it should be!"

Jerry was growing excited, not at the rhetoric, certainly, but at the fact that he was getting more than he ever imagined. He kept taking notes and thinking of ways he could dig deeper with each question without getting Zimmer too upset.

"So," Jerry continued, trying to keep his voice flat and level, "you are saying that you believe that Demetrius Strapollos is more than a world leader; he is also the world's connection to God?"

The beard-stroking stopped, and Zimmer's eyes bore into Jerry Westfield, and there was something hot behind them.

"You should remember that much from Hebrew School, Mr. Westfield. I assume you did attended Hebrew School?"

You smug, pompous puppet! Jerry thought, but he merely said, "Yes, I did, but it was a long time ago. Please, do continue."

Zimmer picked up his glasses from the desk and dangled them from his fingers.

"The prophets of old told of the coming of Messiah and the fact that, when he appeared, he would restore Israel to her former glory, making Jerusalem the capital city of the entire world."

Jerry looked up from his notes and asked, quite solicitously, "But, how do you think the rest of the world will react to this? Think about it for a moment, you're asking all the other countries of the world to do away with their sovereignty and accept this man as…as…King over all the world. Somehow, I just can't see that working too smoothly, do you?"

Jerry's voice had begun to rise toward the end, but apparently Mr. Zimmer didn't seem to notice.

As he replaced his eyeglasses and pulled open a desk drawer, he asked, "Have you read your own newspaper today?"

"I got it," Jerry sighed, "but I haven't had a chance to go through it yet."

Zimmer removed a newspaper from his desk and spread it on the surface before Jerry.

"This is today's edition of *The Chronicle*, Mr. Westfield. If you will read the lead article, you will find that Mr. Strapollos' economic plan is gathering both praise and momentum across the entire globe. With the exception of a few very minor demonstrations here and there, it appears that we may have a new, world-wide economic system in place before very much longer."

"And you're saying this will pave the way for everything we've discussed so far?"

Zimmer's eyes were locked to Jerry's as he leaned forward and said, "You give people prosperity, and they will accept almost anything…"

Then the bond broke, and with a massive shifting of his weight, Joshua Zimmer was on his feet, shaking Jerry's hand and leading him toward the door to the office.

"Well, I sincerely hope I have been of some service to you," Zimmer smiled. "But, as you can understand, I have duties that must be attended. I am sure we will meet soon again."

Half way through the door, Jerry turned to Zimmer.

"We will meet soon," he said before departing, this time his eyes catching a glint of fire. "Soon."

Of that, Jerry was certain.

*   *   *

When the door had closed behind him, and Jerry was once again at the desk of the well-dressed receptionist, he pulled himself up to his full height and intoned, "I would like to make that appointment now to see Rabbi Eissen, as soon as possible."

The receptionist looked up from her desk, seemed as if she were about to say something and then thought better of it, and began to hammer on the keyboard in front of her.

"There are several openings later next week, Sir, but I am afraid that I will have to check with Rabbi Eissen before I can make any such appointment for him. If you will give me a number where you can be reached, I will call you as soon as I can and let you know what the Rabbi says."

Jerry reached into his coat pocket and handed her his personal card with his name, affiliation with *The Chronicle*, and the number of his cell phone on it. He smoothed back his hair, smiled at the receptionist, and walked briskly out of the office and into the hallway.

While he waited for the elevator to make it's trip to his floor, his gaze was again drawn to the bigger-than-life photo on the wall of Demetrius Strapollos signing the seven year contract with Israel, the one that was taken just before all Hell broke loose.

Inside his mind, Jerry could hear the words of Joshua Zimmer, *"You give people prosperity, and they will accept almost anything..."*

Had it not been that same, bread and circuses philosophy that had bred fanatical allegiance to dictators and madmen throughout the world? When Hitler had come to power in a devastated Germany, the economy got better; times got better; individual incomes got better – at least for a while. Who cared what happened to a few unruly Jews and other dissidents, as long as there was whipped cream for the pudding and the trains ran on time!

You give the people prosperity, and they will accept almost anything.

Of all that Zimmer had said, that was the phrase that stuck in Jerry's mind.

Stuck...and held on!

* * *

Jerry started his car and headed toward the bank. The interview with Zimmer had worked out better than he had hoped, but it had also taken longer than expected. If the traffic cooperated, however, he might still be on time for his date with Ruth. After all, that was a priority he didn't want to postpone.

He didn't really want to hear the increasingly depressing news broadcasts, either, but as he wove his way through the Tel Aviv streets, he knew he had an obligation to keep abreast of all that was happening in the world, so he reached over and snapped on the radio. He figured he owed it to his profession.

"...top of the hour, and we are covering these stories:

"In Los Angeles, the cleanup continues for those hit by yesterday's earthquake which registered an extremely powerful 6.8 on the Richter scale. Many people were left injured and homeless and wandering the streets, but unlike previous quakes in this area, help was not readily available. With so much storm destruction across the United States and the world, help remains limited in that area and slow in coming. In the city itself, it is reported that looting is out of control, and some units of the National Guard, already spread thin throughout the state, have been ordered into the area in what Mayor Stanley James has called, 'a feeble attempt' to maintain order.

"Elsewhere in America, a record number of tornadoes in the Midwest and unprecedented hurricanes on the Atlantic and Gulf Coasts have produced near devastation in some areas. Usually reliable government sources have been quoted as saying that Congress is doing all it can, but financial resources are running dangerously low.

"Here in Israel, Jerusalem continues to prepare itself for what many are claiming will be the greatest celebration in this country's history or, for that matter, the history of the world. On May fifteenth, the anniversary of Israel's birth, European Community President Demetrius Strapollos will head the dedication ceremony that will place the cornerstone of the New

Temple on the Temple Mount. Religious leaders from all over the world will be attending. Some minor demonstrations are expected and security for the proceedings will be extremely tight, we are informed.

"In New York, the United Nations is continuing meetings to determine if and how to implement the new 'Cashless Society.' Meetings are expected to continue into next week with a possible high level meeting at week's end in the Security Council chamber involving most, if not all, world leaders…"

The news continued, but Jerry pulled the car into a parking space, twisted the key, and radio and motor died together.

The news was no better than it had been for days, but right now, Jerry Westfield chose to put that on a shelf in the back of his mind, for he had other things to think about, at this moment more important than anything else. He had made it in time for his standing lunch date with Ruth, and everything in him looked forward to that and that only.

Funny, Jerry thought, *for years, all I could think about was work.*

* * *

The clock on the steeple of the dark gothic church struck two deep-throated peals which floated into the black, starless night and soon died in the light mist that covered everything in its glistening damp. Within sight, there was no one on the deserted streets to hear the clock or feel the cold of the dark moisture.

Out of that night, a pair of headlights broke the sullen darkness and a black stretch limousine rolled silently down the street and made a quick turn into a warehouse entrance. The large garage doors that had opened as the car approached now closed automatically and soundlessly once the vehicle was inside.

In the warehouse, the car stopped and its motor faded as the front doors opened. The driver got out and held the rear door for his passengers, while on the other side a large man armed with an automatic rifle stood up and carefully scanned the deep, shadowy interior of the building.

Slowly, two men emerged from the interior of the limousine, each wearing a long, black overcoat over dark, well-tailored suits. They stood next to the car for a few seconds while three other men emerged from the shadows. They, too, were dressed well.

The five men met and shook hands in the dimly lit interior of the warehouse. One of them motioned to the side, and they made their way to a door while the driver and guard continued their vigil.

Inside the room was a table, five chairs, and a small light bulb, shaded by a tin cowl that hung from a cord in the ceiling. Had the light been brighter or had any of the men cared to look closer, it would have been noted that floor, ceiling and walls were lined with quarter-inch lead panels. It was a place designed for secrecy...deep secrecy.

Two of the men placed small briefcases on the table. Even in the limited light, the emblems of Spain and Portugal could be plainly seen.

"I am happy you could make it, gentlemen," one of the men began when the door had been closed and locked. "We have spoken on secured phones, but we have, to my knowledge, never met. As a measure of our sincerity in this night's endeavor, I shall take it upon myself to introduce us all.

"I am Pedro Arano, President of Spain, and you," he continued, staring directly at the man across the table, "are Manuel Cisco, President of Portugal. These other gentlemen are Luis Alvarro, David Reasor and Darren Willis, all trusted Special Forces personnel assigned to the United Nations from various special agencies."

Pedro Arano took a deep breath and sat bolt upright in his chair, and all eyes were on the President of Spain.

"I will not waste time. We all know why we are here. Our nations cannot and will not sit passively by as the power of one man continues to grow and grow. We have all come to realize that his very presence is a threat to our existence. Need I remind you of our deceased colleague, President Pulzarrio of Italy? Need I ask if anyone here actually believes that he was assassinated by a group of fanatic terrorists?

"Let us speak plainly. Demetrius Strapollos is responsible for that outrage. Demetrius Strapollos is responsible for the trouble our nations face. Demetrius Strapollos must be stopped!"

Agent Luis Alvarro leaned forward into the conversation and asked, "Shall we detail exactly what we have in mind?"

"On fifteen May," stated President Cisco of Portugal, speaking for the first time that evening, "Strapollos is planning a trip to Israel to celebrate the Temple Dedication. That is when we make our move.

"President Arano and I need you three to find several men, Arab or Jew, who despise him enough to kill him. There will be thousands in attendance and security will be excessive, but you gentlemen particularly understand that security has never stopped an assassination before and shouldn't now. Of course, the assassins will be shot and killed, but only after they have seen to the demise of Strapollos. That is to be understood as well as the fact that you will be greatly compensated once the job is done."

Agent Reasor, late of an elite CIA team, was the first to notice something. He was not certain what it was exactly, but it was as if a shadow, an unfamiliar, dark, floating shadow had flitted at the edge of his vision, and he felt a breath of cold and clammy air blow across his face.

At once he was on his feet with a blue-black automatic pistol in his hand. The other two acted instinctively, unceremoniously pushing Cisco and Arano to the floor and covering them with their own bodies as weapons appeared in their hands as well.

They froze that way for two seconds, perhaps three, and then muscles began to relax, the Presidents of two great European nations were gently picked up and carefully brushed off, and all five slowly sat once more in the chairs around the table in this dimly lit, lead-paneled room.

"I'm sorry," Agent Reasor said. "I thought for sure I saw something."

"That's OK," Agent Willis commented coldly. "Better a false alarm than two dead Presidents."

There was a short silence before Manuel Cisco said, "The gold we promised you as a down payment is in the trunk of my car. Take it out now, because I have to be getting back."

"We must all realize," President Arano cautioned, "that we cannot meet again, ever, even after this is done. The remainder of the gold will be where we agreed, and you gentlemen can pick it up any time after fifteen May."

They all nodded in agreement, and no further words were spoken. In silence, the door was unlocked, and they shuffled quickly from the room. In equal silence, the three agents moved the heavy gold into their car.

When all work was finished, both vehicles left the way they had come, leaving behind only the hushed emptiness of the place.

Even the streets were silent as death as they drove off into the cold, dark night.

📖   📖   📖

CHAPTER FIFTEEN

A Walk by Night

IT HAD BEEN A LONG DAY; of that, Jerry Westfield was very sure. The interview with Joshua Zimmer was still fresh in his mind. Indeed, it had dominated his lunch with Ruth, and he had spent the remainder of the afternoon and early evening in trying to fight off a growing and nameless uneasiness about this whole affair that was drawing so pressingly close – an uneasiness that would not leave even the most private rooms in his mind. Demetrius Strapollos and Rabbi Eissen and Ken Mailer and now this Zimmer character – his head ached, figuratively and literally.

He was, therefore, extremely glad to find himself, at long last, sitting on the edge of his comfortable bed in his well-lighted room in Jacob Klausman's warm and friendly home in Jaffa. With the day slowly attaining the status of memory, he idly ran his fingers along the leather top of his briefcase, and his mind turned to one of the items he knew was inside – Jeremy's Bible, the same one he had taken from the Palmer's empty house so many months ago.

He had been so busy lately with all that was happening and escalating at a pace so far beyond his control, that he had barely enough time to keep up his relationship with Ruth...yes, Ruth...than spend time reading anything but the latest morning briefings and periodic messages from Bob Lewis.

He opened his briefcase and removed the red-leather Bible. Moving to the desk in the room, Jerry began to thumb through the pages, not really certain of where to read or if he really wanted to read at all as much as look at the notes in the margins in his missing friend's handwriting and somehow come a bit closer to the memories he cherished of Jeremy and Kathy.

Jerry remembered how Jeremy Palmer had often talked to him about the book called *Revelation* (or was it "*Revelations*") so he opened to it. He satisfied himself that the title was singular and even stored away for future need that it was easy to find as the last book in the Bible.

He read. Starting at the very beginning, he read every word. He read about the seven letters to the seven churches, and, continuing, he read of seals being opened and Four Horsemen, and seven trumpets, and the two witnesses. Some of it he understood readily, sensing in the letters to the churches, for instance, that they were representative of what so many modern religious institutions had become. However, so much of it was openly symbolic, and it was a symbolism that he, personally, could not begin to understand, even if Jeremy, obviously, could.

He was at Chapter Thirteen. He read, *"He also forced everyone, small and great, rich and poor, free and slave, to receive a mark on his right hand or on his forehead, so that no one could buy or sell unless he had the mark, which is the name of the beast or the number of his name. This calls for wisdom. If anyone has insight, let him calculate the number of the beast, for it is man's number. His number is 666."*

Jerry stopped reading and in his mind he could hear the voice of Jeremy Palmer during one of the many times they had talked before Jeremy and the others had disappeared, it was a voice that Jerry Westfield remembered so well, and he was saying, *"This is real, Jerry! Some day this man the Bible calls the Antichrist will appear on the scene and become a powerful world leader, so powerful and charismatic that the whole world will follow him!"*

Jerry Westfield remembered that conversation and the fact that for days afterwards that phrase had clung to the forefront of his mind. *"The whole world will follow him...The whole world will follow him..."*

Jerry bent forward and looked closer at the page. There, next to verse 18, the verse about the number 666, was a note in Jeremy's hand. Eagerly, Jerry bent to read it.

"Six is the number of man," the note read. *"God's number is seven. Do three sixes equal man's trinity; three men joined for some unholy purpose? Or, is it the mark of the man who pretends or claims to be God?"*

Jerry's mind reeled

What does that mean? Man's trinity? Who's pretending to be God? Yes, I remember all that number stuff from Hebrew School – God's number; man's number. But, what does it mean here? Jeremy, what did you know? What were you trying to say? And, where did you and Kathy go? I wish...I wish you were still here. I want so much to talk to you.

Slowly, Jerry Westfield closed the book, shut off the desk light and crossed to his bed. As he lay back and tried to clear his mind, he found it a difficult task. He had so much to think about; so much to sort out; so much. Besides what was happening each day in his life, he now had to contend with God and Angels and Prophets and Demons...

He could only imagine what kind of dreams he would have tonight.

*   *   *

Jerry was in that half-real fog, just before sleep pulls its warm blanket over the conscious mind, when the sound came. At first, he actually struggled to make sense of it, but shortly, his consciousness restored and flooding in upon him, he recognized a gentle tapping at the door to his room.

"Yes," he called out, clearing his throat and swinging his legs over the side of the bed, "Who is it?"

"It's Jacob," came the familiar voice, "I need to talk to you."

"Come in, Jacob. It isn't locked."

The door opened, and Jacob Klausman stood in the frame, taking up most of the space.

"I'm sorry for waking you up..."

"That's all right, Jacob," Jerry quipped, "I had to get up to answer the door anyway."

"Well...then...what do you mean?"

"A joke, my friend! A very poor joke, it seems."

Something was wrong, of that Jerry was certain. He had seen Jacob Klausman in many moods over his stay at Jacob and Sarah's home, but this was something that ran deep. This was something that Jerry was certain Jacob could not shrug off with a wise crack or slap on the back or an enigmatic grin.

"It's all right, Jacob," Jerry stated calmly, "I wasn't asleep yet, honest. What's going on?"

For a brief moment, Jacob stared at the floor, then his eyes rose to meet Jerry's and Jacob asked, "Would you mind taking a walk with me, Jerry? I always feel better if I can walk and talk at the same time."

"No problem, Jacob. It's a beautiful night for a walk. I'll just get some clothes on, and..."

Jacob Klausman nodded once, turned and left the room, leaving Jerry with a half-finished sentence and an abiding sense of concern.

"...and..." Jerry concluded to the silent walls, "...I'll meet you downstairs."

*   *   *

It was, indeed, a beautiful night. Jacob and Jerry strolled for a while, overcome by the cloudless sky that allowed the dance of the heavens to be spread out before them in myriad points of flashing starlight. Jerry embraced the grandeur of it all, breathing in the night air greedily and joyously. Jacob walked quietly beside him, his head bowed. Neither man said a word.

It was Jacob who spoke first.

"Jerry," he said, "for the last three nights, I have had a dream. It's always the same dream. It starts out with all of us – you, me, Sarah, the kids, Ruth – all of us, and we are standing in a crowd of thousands of people – people pressing in on us from every side. These people are happy, Jerry, and they're cheering and laughing. We are standing on the steps of the rebuilt Temple, and we're listening to someone who is speaking.

"Then, suddenly, for some reason I don't know, there is a panic, and everyone is running and trying to get out of there. There's pushing and shoving and yelling and screaming, and many fall and get trampled – children and old people – and there is crying and blood. Then I hear the gunshots. I look up, and I see soldiers shooting at the people! First, they fire over the heads of the crowd, but the people won't stop, and then the soldiers are shooting directly at the people who are trying to run away! There's more blood...blood everywhere!

"We, that's all of us, we make it. We escape out of the city and suddenly, we are in the desert, avoiding the soldiers...just barely avoiding them, but we do make it.

"That's...that's where the dream ends..."

Jerry had no idea of what to say to his friend. His feet kept walking while his mind sought desperately for some words that would fit.

Finally, Jerry muttered, "So...you don't know who it is who's talking...you know, giving the speech, in your dream?"

"The first night," Jacob answered, "I couldn't make out who we were listening to. I could see the form of a man, you understand, but I could not see his face; could not make it out. But, on the second night and the third night -- then I could see his face clearly; very clearly...."

The night wind picked up in a small, cool gust and then was quiet.

"It was Strapollos." Jacob said flatly.

137

Jerry stopped walking and turned to face his friend whom he could see quite clearly in the pale but brilliant moonlight.

"Strapollos?" Jerry repeated, taking a step closer. "Jacob, please, help me to understand. Exactly what are you telling me, friend? What is it that you think this dream means?"

"I…I'm not altogether sure, Jerry, but the third night I had the dream, I saw an angel, and this angel was protecting us as we ran. I saw this angel leading us, along with thousands – yes, thousands -- of others, through the desert as a great army chased after us. Then, all at once, a great sand storm came up behind us, and the army was…was… just… swallowed up. The storm cleared, and they were gone!"

Jerry's breath was coming harder now, and his mind was racing. He managed to say, "Jacob…that's so…so incredible…and…bizarre…I don't know…could you, could you hear what Strapollos was saying in your dream?"

Jacob hesitated for a moment and then began walking again. Jacob's step was quicker now, more urgent, and Jerry found himself pushing just to keep up.

Jacob cleared his throat and spoke tersely, "Yes, I could."

Jerry didn't dare to ask. He just waited, and in a moment, Jacob was ready to speak again.

"He was saying," Jacob said with what seemed to be a great deal of control, "that he was greater than God!"

Jacob stopped and turned to face Jerry Westfield. Jacob's face was lined with sadness, and in the light blue moonlight, Jerry could not help but shiver.

"He even called himself…God," Jacob continued. "It was terrifying. The fear in the faces of the people was so real. I could hear them screaming!"

Softly, Jerry asked, "Do you know why everyone was running away?"

"No, and what made it even more insane was the fact that thousands of people were clapping and shouting their approval for this man. Then, as we were trying to leave, some of them were getting in our way, yelling and cursing, trying to strike out – at us, Jerry – at us!"

Jerry could not accept it all at once; could not fully believe what he was hearing, and his stomach was beginning to knot as his temples pounded. He had to deny it, and yet he could not. This was something very much like what he had just finished reading in Jeremy's Bible!

Suddenly, Jerry Westfield could see that Bible, and his mind, in an action it had rarely performed before, an entire page of the book was identically before him, so he could see every word. Jerry could do nothing else but read.

"The beast was given a mouth to utter proud words and blasphemies and to exercise his authority for forty-two months. He opened his mouth to blaspheme God, and to slander His name and His dwelling place and those who live in heaven."

From the edge of his understanding, Jerry recognized that Jacob was talking.

"God is speaking to me, Jerry. To us. We need to seek Him."

"What?" Jerry snapped back to full consciousness, shoving his hands into his pockets so Jacob would not see the trembling. "What do you mean 'Seek Him!'?"

"We need to pray and ask God to show us more, so we can understand His purpose for these dreams."

"Pray?" Jerry was beginning to sweat, and the night air was cool on the wetness around his collar and under his arms. "Jacob, my friend, you know me. I...I don't pray. I wouldn't even know where to start. I...I mean, you seem to be doing all right on your own, right? You don't need me to help you, do you?"

The look that Jacob Klausman returned to Jerry Westfield in the blue moonlight told everything, and Jerry knew that his friend was very serious – very serious, indeed!

"Jerry," Jacob sighed as he placed a massive hand on Jerry's shoulder, "I know this probably sounds crazy to you, but this is not the first time I have had a...what would you say?...a spiritual dream. Ever since the so-called 'disappearance,' I have been having dreams about the Lord God, and in these dreams (don't judge, Jerry, just listen) His angels have been telling me about future events."

Jerry was getting colder by the moment. He swallowed hard and asked, "Have you told Sarah about these dreams?"

"Yes. I have told Sarah about some of them, but not all. I...I don't want to alarm her beyond what she must already endure."

"Jacob, I know how much you love your God..."

Jacobs grip on Jerry's should tightened just a bit, and the fingers began to message, not too strongly, but definitely, strongly, unquestionably there.

"OUR God, Jerry! The Lord God is your God, too!"

Slowly and purposefully, Jerry removed Jacob's hand from his shoulder and held it in his own grip. He turned and looked deeply into Jacob's eyes.

"I see how much you love the Lord God, Jacob, but I can't just start praying out of the blue. Please...please, give me some time to think about it, OK?"

"I suppose," Jacob sighed in resignation, "that a few days..."

Jacob let the thought trail off. For the first time on their night walk, he looked upward at the sky. Then he turned and began walking again at a brisk pace.

"A few days?" Jerry laughed, trying anything to lighten the tension of the moment, "I'll need more than a few days, don't you think?"

But Jacob was already several yards ahead of him, and Jerry's smile faded into the dark as he jogged just to catch up to his friend.

"Jacob?" Jerry asked when he had come apace, "seriously, please. What do you expect us – you and me – to do about this dream?"

Without realizing it, they had walked almost full circle and they found themselves just a dozen or so feet from the house.

Jacob stopped there, and he turned on Jerry.

"Strapollos is evil, Jerry," he said, "very evil. I don't have all the answers, and I'm not going to say anything to anyone else until God shows me more, or I can figure out what He has already shown me.

"I know this much, however: Strapollos is no Messiah. And you, Jerry, had better be careful from here on about what you say, especially to that 'friend' of yours, that Ken person. I don't trust him or any of his people!"

Jerry licked his lips. He took his time, carefully formulating the words he was about to say.

"Jacob, you know how much I have come to respect you in these past months, but...please understand, my friend, I ask out of love, love for you and your family...do you really believe that these dreams are from God?"

Jacob's head rose slowly until his eyes were on a level with Jerry.

"Don't trust anybody, Jerry," Jacob said softly. "And, Jerry..."

"Yes, Jacob."

"Start thinking about learning how to pray."

140

CHAPTER SIXTEEN

Fourteen May: The Day Before

WHEN JOSHUA ZIMMER HAD SETTLED HIS CONSIDERABLE BULK as comfortably as possible behind his desk at the headquarters of Rabbi Michael Eissen, he reached out a pudgy finger and flipped over the page of his day-to-day desk calendar. The legend, 14 MAY, presented itself before him in extremely bold type.

Zimmer smiled and leaned closer to read the note he had personally hand-written on that page months ago.

It read: *"One Day To Go!!!"*

* * *

After more than two weeks of increased anxieties, unbounded preparations, and shameless promotions, the day for the Temple Celebration was almost at hand. It was the morning of May 14, and as Jerry Westfield sat down to write his column and to update his Web site, it occurred to him that he must have caught a touch of that racing fever. He found himself, at that moment, anticipating the event and musing about what his own part in it would be; could be.

Jerry's column was earning him wide acceptance throughout the world, with an ever-growing audience. His opinions and comments were quoted frequently on top radio and TV news programs, and he took a silent pride in hearing his name used to prove a point. Not even he could deny that Jerry Westfield was fast becoming a celebrity in his own right. Moreover, he was writing with more passion now than he had ever known. Whether it was his new-found home or his relationship with Ruth or the influence of Jacob Klausman and his family, something was changing him, making him – what? – better, perhaps, more rational and clear-sighted...

at least in contrast to the world around him that seemed to be growing madder by the day.

With a deep breath, he folded the sleeves of his shirt up to his elbows and turned his attention to the keyboard.

*   *   *

WESTFIELD TO CHRONICLE – WESTFIELD TO CHRONICLE
– COPY FOLLOWS
DATELINE 14 MAY, ISRAEL:

In Jerusalem and in Tel Aviv today, this country is busily making last minute preparations for an event which, most people are saying, will be the most momentous day in the history of Israel – the long-awaited placement of the cornerstone which will initiate the construction of the Third Temple.

To fully understand the passion in the streets and the significance of this event to the average Israeli citizen, one must look at a history that is both glorious and foreboding. Although the precise dates are somewhat disputed by scholars, it is safe to say that the First Temple was built and dedicated by Solomon around 950 BC. Solomon began to build the temple on the second day of the second month of the fourth year of his reign, only to have that work destroyed by King Nebuchadnezzar of Babylon in 587 BC, during the siege of Jerusalem. After the return of the exiles from Babylon in 536 BC, Jerusalem was rebuilt and the Second temple constructed and finished in approximately 408 BC. That lasted over four centuries until it was completely destroyed by the Roman Empire in 70 AD.

This Third Temple would, therefore, be the representation of more than nineteen hundred years of wandering and waiting for the Jewish people. That, in itself, would be more than enough for the rebirth of nationalism and the outright joy one sees here on every corner.

There is, however, much more going on here than a religious renaissance in a small country in the Middle East. On the wide screen, we see a world leader emerging from a sea of nations and spawning many questions as he comes. Is this the dawning of a new age or the sunset of the era of individuality and privacy? Will this New World offer us new opportunities, or new conformities?

Of course only time will completely provide those answers, but anticipation runs high. With the UN approval yesterday of the "Cashless Society Proposal," it is only a matter of time, perhaps only months, before the nations of the world ratify the agreement and begin the process of establishing a one-world digital currency.

To many, perhaps most, this is the first step on the golden road to Paradise. To others, admittedly in the minority but vocal and growing, it is the opening of the gates of Hell. The future begins, more and more, to take on the shape of a giant question mark.

In the coming months, we are certain to see many changes, some of which will be judged good and others will be called bad. For me, there are still many questions that have gone unanswered. Chief among them is this: At which moment did we suddenly change our course, and at what point did disaster decide to come calling? Gone are the headlines that so shocked and startled a sleeping world only seven short months ago, proclaiming the disappearance of millions of people, vanished from the face of the earth as if vaporized by some unknown force.

Maybe we have chosen to forget. It is true that the cataclysmic events of the past months have not permitted us much time to think about such things.

But I refuse to be drawn into that trap. I believe that these events are somehow linked together. I cannot forget my friends who are no longer with me, and I will continue to search for the truth of what really happened to them.

I find it disconcerting at the very least that most of us seem to be able to go about our business as if nothing had happened at all. Is it merely coincidence, chance, a roll of the dice, that we are here at this point in history? Possibly, but I choose not to think so. Do you?

On this eve of one of the greatest events in Israel's history, I invite your comments. E-Mail me at my Web Site and let your voice be heard.

Until tomorrow, this is Jerry Westfield reporting for The Chronicle *live from Israel. Let me hear from you, and have a good day!*

-- 30 --

END TRANSMITION – END TRANSMITION – END TRANSMITION

* * *

As a tall man, Demetrius Strapollos found ordinary elevators uncomfortable. This one was different. He had specified enough upper space to accommodate his six foot, four inch frame with plenty of headroom to spare. He though about that now and half-smiled as the machine came to a smooth and noiseless stop and the doors opened to a well-lighted, gray corridor before him. He was a full two stories below his mansion in the Brussels suburb of Nivelles, but temperature and humidity, carefully controlled, would have given the uninitiated no clue of their whereabouts whatsoever had they not known.

He stepped out of the elevator and walked down the hall, each step echoing off the tall, painted concrete walls, until he came to a large, gray, reinforced steel door. He placed the thumb of his right hand on the electronic scanner just below the small keypad on the wall and his right eye over the retina scanner.

A computer-generated voice responded. *"I.D. confirmed. Please enter the proper code at this time."*

Strapollos' fingers punched swiftly at the keyboard and the wall clicked and whirred as the automatic door unlocked. It swung open on noiseless hinges, and as it did the familiar sound of people at work, typing on keyboards, exchanging information, and even the hum of the machines themselves, began to filter through.

Demetrius Strapollos entered the room. It was a huge place, with a fifteen foot ceiling. On one wall there was a very large screen ten feet in height and twenty feet wide which could display whatever video feed Mr. Strapollos deemed important. Over 150 other large Plasma screens were scattered throughout, displaying not only words and numbers, but images ranging from quiet street scenes to meeting rooms to what appeared to be private living rooms. Strapollos smiled, for he knew that these were monitored by a select group of extremely loyal professionals who worked in eight-hour shifts, 24 hours each day. He also knew that not one of them was allowed to leave this room. These men and women not only worked here, but they ate and slept here – in short, for however long it would take, they lived here.

True to his word, Ken Mailer had covered the planet with satellites. Not someone else's, of course, but with Mr. Strapollos' very own spy satellites which were state-of-the-art and nothing less. They contained superior cameras with superior resolution, all very neatly tied into a wealth of extremely fast computers loaded with the latest software, most of which had been written by Ken Mailer and his staff over the last two years. All had been designed to produce detailed images with a clarity that rivaled the very best photographs from *National Geographic.*

There was nowhere – nowhere – that anyone could hide from his eyes now, Demetrius Strapollos mused. From here, from this room deep beneath his home, he could keep track of the whole world.

Big Brother has not only arrived, he thought, *but he has his shoes off, his feet up, and he is about to take over control of the world!*

Ken Mailer burst on to the scene from one of the many offices that lined the upper level of the control room. As he walked along the steel catwalk and down one of the metal staircases, he greeted Strapollos warmly.

"Good morning, Mr. Strapollos! It's a pleasure to see you, sir! We are fully prepared to demonstrate the capabilities of this system whenever you are ready."

Strapollos sat in his specially constructed, high-backed, black leather chair, positioned strategically on a three-foot high platform in the center of the room.

Strapollos said, "Proceed, Mr. Mailer. Let's see what you've got."

"Yes, sir! Yes, sir! Yes, sir!" Ken exclaimed as he bounced to his control panel. At that moment, it occurred to one of the computer analysts nearby that Mailer was very much like a kid trying to impress his father with what he could do.

"Before you, on the large screen," Mailer said in now even tones, somewhat akin to a bus driver presenting a tour, "we have a shot of the Mid-East from one hundred miles up. We will now increase magnification to present a view of Israel from five miles up."

On the screen there appeared a shot of Israel from the coast along the Mediterranean Sea across to the Dead Sea and from the Negev to the Golan Heights. The clarity was of a brilliance nothing short of amazing. Some of the people in the room who were seeing this for the first time, actually gasped in amazement.

Ken Mailer continued, "As you can see, this allows us to view the entire region. Now, we will zoom in further and tighten focus on Jerusalem."

From his black leather chair, Strapollos could clearly see the whole city of Jerusalem with both the old city and the new being very evident. He could see automobiles moving along the roads, and he could identify trucks and even people working around the Temple Mount. The resolution was incredible.

Strapollos kept a tight control on his growing delight as he turned to Ken Mailer and stated, "Very good. I am impressed with the quality. The real question, however, is how close can we actually get?"

Ken grinned, and it was all he could do to keep from giggling. He had been waiting for that question specifically.

"Please, watch this, sir," Mailer smiled.

Turning to a technician, Ken commanded, "Full amplification on target Temple Mount."

The technician typed at the keyboard, and the large screen blinked gray and white for a moment before resolving into the picture of a large clock, the face and hands filling the screen.

"What's this?" Strapollos asked. "That looks like one of the clocks in a large cathedral or town hall in mid-Europe."

This time both the technician and Ken smiled. Ken nodded, and the man pulled back slightly and adjusted the focus. As the picture on the screen backed down from maximum zoom, it became obvious that the picture was not that of a cathedral or town hall clock at all. It was, it became obvious, the wristwatch of a man that Ken Mailer had positioned for this experiment, sitting on the steps of the Temple Mount.

In spite of his control, Strapollos let out a yelp that rang through the room and wrapped around the steel pipes and grating.

"A good job, gentlemen," he stated with enthusiasm, "a good job! Can you do that anywhere in the world?"

"Anywhere you like, sir," Ken beamed proudly. "Anywhere you like! What's more, I have a little surprise for you."

"A surprise?"

"Yes, sir," Ken Mailer stated, "and when I say surprise, I mean just that!"

* * *

They had moved into one of the offices around the great viewing room. Ken could not sit, he was simply too excited, and Strapollos looked at him blankly.

"Give me your surprise, Mr. Mailer," Strapollos commanded softly.

Mailer began to pace as he said, "Very well, sir. Two years ago I met with a Mr. Brad Wallace, the CEO of Teleview Link, Inc. We had an interesting conversation concerning a new software package I had written that would enable him to market his company's new teleconferencing equipment ahead of everyone else, securing him a very large market share and, incidentally, saving his company from bankruptcy.

"In exchange for this technology, he offered me quite a substantial piece of the company, which I told him I would consider. It was at that time you and I met, sir, and after our first business meeting I realized that working for you made any money I might be offered, shall we say, no longer an issue. After that meeting with you, I went back to Mr. Wallace and told him that I would, indeed, supply the software in exchange for a small favor."

Strapollos eyed Ken Mailer and then sat, stretching his long legs before him.

"Continue," was all he said.

"You see," Ken smiled slightly, "I told him I wanted to place within the program a small instruction that would allow me to remotely engage the program and, in effect, turn on the camera at my discretion. After a brief hesitation, he agreed.

"Since that time, as you well know, sir, Teleview Link has become the standard for teleconferencing in both the business and private sectors. Needless to say, this gives us a virtually unlimited view of all sorts of things."

Strapollos' eyes grew wider and wider as Ken Mailer spoke. The possibilities were flooding his mind; raging through at crushing speed.

"How do you know," Strapollos asked at last, "which cameras you are turning on and what you're looking at?"

Mailer replied, "As with any software package, each unit has a registration number, but unlike some, this software cannot be activated and used unless it is properly registered first. The list is undated daily, and all I have to do is access the list from the secured server at Teleview Link, and I can activate anyone on that list at any time.

"Because the registration number is part of the activation code, I know exactly who it is I am tuned to."

Demetrius Strapollos closed his eyes, and for a long moment he did not open them. When he did, he fixed his gaze on Ken Mailer.

"Quite acceptable, Mr. Mailer," he said at last. "Quite acceptable!"

*   *   *

Back in the main viewing room where everyone could see, Strapollos took Ken Mailer's hand in both of his and shook it vigorously. Considering that the Temple dedication was now less than a day away, and considering what he had just witnessed in this room and privately with Ken Mailer, he appeared remarkably calm.

"I love technology!" he said to Ken. "Mr. Mailer, you have outdone yourself this time. You will, of course, come with me tomorrow for the dedication in Jerusalem. I will need my 'right-hand-man' at my side. My private jet is leaving at eight in the morning. Meet me here at seven, and Walter will drive us to the airport. We'll have coffee and something to eat on the plane. I believe I can promise you a most exhilarating day. You know how I like to start things off with a bang, as the expression goes.

"I'll see you in the morning."

Then he was gone, leaving Ken in a state of near ecstasy. He was pleased with himself beyond all measure, and Ken slapped the technician who had helped him on the back with warm enthusiasm and headed for an upstairs office, wondering to himself about that last comment Strapollos had made.

Shortly, however, he dismissed the thought. Now was not a time for wondering.

This was a time for celebration!

End of Part Two

PART THREE:
The Day

"I am come in my Father's name,
and ye receive me not:
if another shall come in his own name,
him ye will receive."
John 5:43

"...do not worry about tomorrow,
for tomorrow will worry about itself.
Each day has enough
trouble of its own ."
Matthew 6:34

CHAPTER SEVENTEEN

In the Morning

ON FIFTEEN MAY, THE SUN ROSE RED AND ORANGE, brilliantly and majestically over the cities of Jerusalem and Tel Aviv. After anguish and discussion, after fear and unbounded joy, after months of work and preparation, and with every story angle finally exhausted, the day for the "celebration" had come at last.

Directly in front of the Temple Mount, a temporary platform had been constructed by an army of workers, and microphones and cameras had sprung up everywhere like some eerie garden of mechanical flowers.

The order of events had been argued, set, and passed out to everyone who needed or wanted to know. At one o'clock the cornerstone was to be brought to the site in a procession of singing and rejoicing, and it would be placed on the exact spot where Solomon had placed the original cornerstone more than 3000 years ago.

At that time, Mr. Demetrius Strapollos was to address all those in attendance.

At the close of the ceremony, there was to be a concert by the National Israeli Orchestra with further singing and dancing.

Of course, there were also large and small gatherings planned throughout Israel, and the entire affair would be broadcast live via a world-wide TV hook-up.

Even the world-weary, world-hardened camera people seemed to relax a bit. Word had spread among camera techs and journalists and TV reporters and even the vendors who had been lucky enough to attain a license to sell – this wonderful, this marvelous, this day of days had been planned to perfection, and nothing -- they all knew – nothing could go wrong.

At least not today…here in Israel.

*   *   *

President Pedro M. Arano of Spain, as was his habit, studied his image in the small mirror beside the door of his office before he stepped out into the corridor which led from his executive suite to the long, gold and white staircase. That staircase, in turn, led to the great foyer and the door that brought him to his private limousine. Once outside his office two men dressed in dark suits, his personal bodyguards, joined him, one on each side.

Once downstairs in the foyer, President Arano waved to friends and workers in the reception area, stopping at one desk to ask a secretary if her child's fever had gone down. This familiarity was not forced. It was his normal custom, and he was well-liked by those who worked in and around the President's Offices.

The two bodyguards walked through the double glass doors and held them open for Pedro Arano. Much later, some of those present would say that they heard what they referred to as two "pops," while others would claim to have heard nothing but the rumbling sounds of morning traffic. In any event, Pedro Arano, President of Spain, stepped through the doors and instantly stopped and seemed to look upward into the slightly cloudy sky before collapsing backwards into the arms of one of his bodyguards, a bright red stain visible on the breast of his suit jacket.

Within minutes, police cars were everywhere, their red lights flashing off the polished steel and glass of the building. An ambulance screamed its way through a mob of cars and screeched to a halt directly before the palace. Three white-coated medical personnel jumped out and made their way feverishly up the stairs and into the foyer.

It was, of course, too late. The President was quite dead and beyond human attempts at resuscitation.

Guards and Police and camera people and reporters and secretaries and receptionists ran everywhere, some with a purpose, but many without any idea of why they were running at all. Soon, the sound of helicopters could be heard overhead. In addition, all surrounding buildings were being searched vigorously from top to bottom and room by room.

All this would be to no avail; would do no good.

No weapon; no cartridge; no shooter would ever be found.

*   *   *

In a small café just a few minutes from the Capital Building, Manuel Cisco, President of Portugal, was enjoying a casual breakfast with several businessmen of his acquaintance. The place had been secured for this purpose, and no other patrons would enter or even come close to the café this morning.

The meeting was well under way, and the men laughed and joked as they ate. A smiling President Cisco had just started on his second cup of coffee when a cell phone began to play its electronic tune. One of the secret service agents reached quickly into his jacket pocket and took the call. From over the rim of his cup, the President watched the man's face drain of color as he listened. The agent looked up and caught the gaze of Manuel Cisco.

"Tell me," ordered the President, immediately becoming the serious head of state..

"Sir...President Arano has been assassinated!"

President Cisco reached over and took the cell phone from the agent's hand.

"This is Cisco," he spoke into the phone. "Tell me what has happened."

The voice on the other end of the phone began to report what details were known of what had taken place just minutes before. As he listened, Manuel Cisco's stomach began to knot and grow sour, for he knew, full well, what was happening. Somehow, Strapollos had found out.

He would be next.

Although it was not particularly warm in the small restaurant, a fine line of sweat broke out on Manuel Cisco's forehead and across his upper lip. He handed the phone back to the agent.

"Gentlemen," he announced to all present, "I am afraid we will have to cut this meeting short. There's been an emergency, and I must leave immediately. I'm sorry, but I know you understand."

He motioned to his bodyguards, pushed back his chair, and rose from the table. It was the last physical act President Manuel Cisco would ever carry out.

The huge black and red fireball burst with a ferocious, angry roar from the kitchen area while almost simultaneously another blast directly under where they were all sitting ripped out the fabric of reality, twisting it into a living nightmare.

In less than five seconds, the small café had transformed into a steaming, groaning, wavering pile of rubble where the individuals who, moments before, were enjoying breakfast could not now be distinguished from the broken plates and the tortured, melted silverware that had furnished their table.

*   *   *

Special Agents Luis Alvarro, David Reasor, and Darren Willis sat close together in their hotel room in Tel Aviv, going over every detail of the operation one more time and one more time. With them were two swarthy Israeli men, men whose names they never used, much less knew, who eagerly awaited their opportunity to end Strapollos' plans along with his life. They wore long, Arabic garments to conceal their automatic weapons, and both understood that most likely, they would not be returning to their families alive. The two sat together and apart from the Special Agents. They knew that they would give their lives for what they believed in. Their hearts were right – unlike these hired guns who had enlisted them.

Luis Alvarro rose and switched on the TV.

"Maybe we'll get to see Strapollos arrive. They should be covering it."

Alvarro reached for his coffee cup just in time to see the screen go blank and the words, *"SPECIAL REPORT,"* flash on.

"There is shocking news, just in," the reporter said in a voice that attested to his words. "There appears to have been a dual assassination of President Manuel Cisco of Portugal and President Pedro Arano of Spain!"

Luis Alvarro choked on his coffee. Sputtering, he turned to the others.

"Are you guys getting this? We've got problems!"

The others jumped to their feet and surrounded the television as the story unfolded.

The TV reporter continued: "President Pedro M. Arano of Spain was assassinated just moments ago as he left his office building here in Madrid. Some eyewitnesses claim to have heard two sounds like shots, possibly from somewhere across the street. In any case, the assassin's two bullets hit the President in the chest, directly in the heart, and he immediately collapsed, to be pronounced dead only moments later.

"So far, government officials have not been able to locate the assassin, although we are assured that a massive investigation has been launched, and security around the city is tight.

"President Arano was the only one shot, and it appears that there were no other injuries.

"We now go live to Roberto Sanchez, our correspondent in Lisbon, for the latest there. Roberto…"

The TV screen faded to the picture of a young man standing in front of what might have been the remnants of Berlin at the end of World War II. Hearing his cue, his eyes rose to the camera, and he began.

"President Manuel Cisco was killed just a short while ago along with at least six others while attending a breakfast meeting with prominent local businessmen here in the city of Lisbon. The bomb exploded at the Café Comida in the section known as the *Bairro Alto*. You can see behind me the remains of the café. The names of the other men who were killed have not yet been released. We are assured that a full investigation is underway, but there are no suspects or leads at this time."

Luis Alvarro grabbed the remote and turned down the volume. David Reasor and Darren Willis looked at each other and then at Alvarro. They knew, without words, what had to be done.

David Reasor turned to the two Israelis and said, "Gentlemen, you know what you have to do. Good luck. Remember, there is to be no more contact. You must never try to find us, is that clear?"

The two men shook their heads and without any other words, they turned and headed out the door.

When they were gone, Luis Alvarro asked, "Do you think he knows about us?"

David Reasor reached in his pocket and checked his automatic weapon as he answered, "I'm not sure, but we need to be ready, and we need to get out of here, now. Luis, make sure you have our tickets."

Alvarro immediately checked his briefcase, and they were there, three first-class tickets to New York City. He held them up and then replaced them. Silently, the three men loaded their briefcases, checked the room to see if anything had been missed, and left, turning off the lights and television as they went.

The three men got off the elevator on the main floor and walked through the lobby that was filled with people moving in all directions.

David Reasor, with his eyes looking straight forward, was the first to break the silence.

"Forget about the car," he said flatly. "It may be rigged, and we can't afford to take chances. We'll catch a bus to the airport."

* * *

The three men walked through the doors of the hotel just as the bus from the airport pulled up. They waited as the people got off, and their eyes continued to scan the street, the lobby of the hotel behind them, the sidewalk, the bus driver, and everyone who emerged from the bus no matter how innocuous the individual might appear.

Finally, when everyone had cleared the vehicle, the three men got on. They sat in three separate seats, heads forward and eyes continually on the move, and it took them very little time to realize that they were the only ones on the bus.

Darren Willis sat in the seat directly behind the driver and asked, "Isn't it a little unusual to be so empty on the way to the airport?"

The driver never turned around, but he answered in a friendly if tired voice, "Most people are coming *in* today, sir – you know, for the Celebration."

Inside himself, Willis sensed that the driver was telling the truth, but he was still suspicious. He sat back, apparently relaxing, but his eyes remained awake and active and his mind raced and raced.

The bus driver checked his watch and pulled away from the hotel, making a large turn that would take him to the airport. Willis should have felt safer. They all should have.

They didn't.

Luis Alvarro looked out the bus window by his seat and wondered if the two 'zealots' they had enlisted would be able to complete their mission. His reverie was broken by a beeping sound that he instantly recognized as the radio beside the driver's seat. Alvarro looked up in time to see the driver answering, although what was said could not be made out.

The driver signed off, and at the next traffic light, he turned the bus in a direction away from the airport.

"Hey! Where are you going?" David Reasor snapped.

"The road up ahead is closed, sir," the driver answered wearily. "It seems that the military shot and killed two armed crazies trying to enter a secure zone. Don't worry, sir; we'll be all right. We're not going anywhere near that place. Also, we won't be any more than five minutes behind schedule."

Reasor looked at Alvarro and Willis. He knew they were thinking the same thing he was; that whoever was behind this was extremely good or extremely lucky. Darren Willis rose from his seat and walked to a place where the two others could hear him.

"What do you think?" he asked. "Should we stay on the bus or get off now?"

Luis Alvarro said, "I think we should get off and split up! We might stand a better chance if we…"

"Enough!" Reasor snapped, and he was swiftly standing beside his fellow agents. "We stay together, and we stay on this bus, understand? We'll be fine, and we'll be at the airport in a matter of minutes. Just get a hold on yourselves, and do it now!"

Nothing more was said. The three men turned their backs to the driver and checked their weapons one more time.

Then they sat back and waited.

* * *

The bus pulled in to the airport and screeched to a stop at the airline entrance. The three men got off without a word to each other or the driver and entered the building, continually scanning the crowd, always suspecting everyone. They checked the board and headed at once to the boarding gate for the New York flight. On the way, all three noticed a great deal of commotion off to one side.

It was such a stir, in fact, that they could not avoid looking.

Because of his height, they could easily make out Demetrius Strapollos surrounded by a crowd of energetic reporters and camera people. Beside Strapollos, they could just make out a dapper Ken Mailer and another figure, dressed in black – Rabbi Michael Eissen.

There was a literal sea of security agents around them, many of whom the three men recognized from former assignments or security dossiers they had read. There was no need for them to strain to hear, as the scene and the audio accompanying it was flashed on virtually every monitor in the airport.

"Mr. Strapollos," one struggling reporter shouted, "have you heard about the assassinations?"

"Yes, I have," came the replay from a very somber Demetrius Strapollos. "I heard about them on the Cable News Network while we were in flight from Brussels. I cannot imagine any more terrible news. These were two fine national leaders as well as very dear and personal friends of mine. I tell you, this is a shocking blow to the European Community, and I, personally, will not rest until their cowardly murderers are found and dealt with accordingly."

"Sir! Will this postpone today's celebration?"

Strapollos turned to the reporter and his countenance changed ever so slightly. The TV cameras showed a face of total benevolence.

"No, absolutely not," Strapollos answered in warm, reassuring tones. "This nation has waited long enough for this day, and it will be delayed no longer. We must go forward, as those two brave European leaders would have wanted us to do. This tragedy today only makes us all the more determined to establish true unity and peace throughout the world.

"Please, that's all for right now, ladies and gentlemen. I must be going, as I know you all understand. Thank you all so very much!"

Reasor, Alvarro, and Willis watched as the entourage moved on. For a moment they stood motionless, seeking each other's gaze. Then they turned and began to head for the boarding gate at a strong pace.

They had taken perhaps five steps when all three of them stopped. Each man had suddenly felt something, as if a rope -- a bristling, cutting rope -- had been thrown around their chests and pulled tight. They stood for a second, breathing with difficulty, gulping in what air they could. Then, as if on command, they turned together and looked back the way they had come.

About a hundred feet behind them, their eyes locked with those of Michael Eissen. The Rabbi looked at them with eyes that pierced each one and seemed to strip him naked before the gaze of the man in black. Slowly, the red lips framed by the black beard formed themselves into a smile, a smile not of mirth or of happiness, but something else... something one might have expected on the face of a gladiator of ancient Rome whose opponent lay blood-still in the dust.

Then, as swiftly as it had happened, the Rabbi turned and walked away. The chests of the three men loosened, and they breathed freely once more, taking in great gulps of precious air.

They turned without a word and hurried to the gate. They did not speak as they boarded the flight; they did not speak as they strapped themselves in separate seats; they did not speak as the plane lifted without incident and banked its way toward New York. They did not speak at all, for each man was busy within his own mind; within his own heart. Each was experiencing something with which he had lived before but never truly experienced, never truly seen naked and uncontrolled until this moment.

A growing, snarling, raging beast...called fear.

* * *

Jerry Westfield stopped at a traffic light on his way to pick up Ruth Cowen. Instead of their normal and now almost daily noon lunch, today it would be brunch at ten, because today, Jerry would meet and interview Demetrius Strapollos on CNN's live satellite TV and Internet hookup. Ruth had taken the day off so she could go with Jerry and be on the set with him during the interview.

Such an extraordinary event would dominate most men's thoughts every waking hour, but Jerry Westfield had more on his mind. His grandmother had once told him that if he had many problems, he should find a small stone and place it in his shoe. After a while, she had counseled with a smile, that stone will be all you will think about, and your other problems will fade into the background. Well, lately, he had been thinking very seriously about one particular stone known as his future. The popularity of his column in print and on the Internet had brought him new status and with that, more money. Even so, he had no children to spend money on, his ex-wife had remarried, and he, personally, never stayed in one place long enough to enjoy it.

No, this was definitely not about fame and fortune, this was about...something else.

He made a quick left and then a right and pulled up in front of Ruth Cowen's apartment building. Jerry had barely pulled to a halt before Ruth burst through the doors of the place with her usual energy and walked briskly to the car. Jerry jumped out just in time to open the door for her.

"You know," he smiled, "I really *can* park the car and come up and get you. You don't have to be waiting at the door all the time."

"What's wrong with that?" Ruth laughed as she settled herself in the seat. "Are you afraid someone will steal me on my way down?"

Jerry got in behind the wheel and answered, "Very humorous! I just...I just feel funny about it, that's all."

Ruth leaned over and kissed him on the cheek.

"So, let's go eat," she continued. "Is 'brunch' mainly breakfast or mainly lunch?"

"Depends on how hungry you are," Jerry answered. "How hungry are you?"

Ruth's face darkened a bit as she said, "Not very. I've been up for a while watching the news channel. Those assassinations were horrible! What's going on in this world?"

"I don't know," Jerry sighed, "but I don't think it's going to get any better in the near future. On my way over here, I heard that two armed men were shot and killed not too far from here, almost directly in front of Rabbi Eissen's headquarters. This should prove to be an interesting day, to say the very least."

"Are you all ready for your big interview tonight?"

"As ready as I'll ever be. You know, I never did get an interview with Eissen; his office claimed he was 'too busy.' I sent in questions and got back a list of those I could use and an agenda. I don't like TV that much. I'd rather sit and write."

Ruth took his hand and said, "You mean to tell me that the world-famous Jerry Westfield is shy?"

"Only when I'm with you, Miss Cowen – only when I'm with you!"

They both laughed, and Jerry pulled out into the traffic.

$$* \quad * \quad *$$

Jerry parked the car and he and Ruth walked hand in hand into the Little Café, the place they had lunched almost every working day since they had met. They sat at a favorite table by a window overlooking the street, and Jerry ordered coffee for the both of them.

When the waitress had gone, Jerry leaned over the small table that separated them.

"Ruth," he began, "it's only been three months that I have known you, but they have been a glorious three months for me. I had forgotten what it was like to be alive. You know, you keep going and keep going, and you call it life, but it really isn't. I realize now that I was just existing, working day and night so I wouldn't have to think about my own life and how really empty it was.

"I...I look forward to these lunches we have every day...and the times we get to go out together at night. I really...well...I know everything changes sooner or later, but I...I don't want any of this to change. Am I making any sense?"

It occurred to Jerry that Ruth's eyes were particularly bright this morning, as if she held sunlight behind her eyelids.

"Why should it change?" she asked. "It doesn't have to change if we don't want it to."

Consciously, Jerry tried to control his breathing that was coming faster and faster in spite of himself.

"No," he answered, "it doesn't, does it? Well, I want to make sure that it never changes."

Jerry straightened himself in the chair and spoke directly to Ruth.

"I am fifty-four years old, and if there is anything I know at all, it's that what you and I have is incredible; it's better than anything I have ever known. Ruth, I don't have the slightest idea as to what is going to happen in this world in the next five minutes, but I am certain...certain that...I love you.

"Ruth, I wake up thinking about you; I think about you all day; I think about you as I fall asleep. You are what I look forward to every day, and I want you to be with me for the rest of my life."

His eyes remained on her as his hand dug and fumbled in his pocket, finally producing a small, black box which he snapped open to allow the sunlight to catch the facets of the diamond ring he set on the table and gently pushed towards Ruth.

"Ruth," Jerry Westfield said. "Will you marry me?"

For a few seconds, Ruth said nothing. Some of the sunshine her eyes had held a moment before, brimmed over and tumbled down her smooth cheeks. Her hand met with Jerry's.

"I love you, too, Jerry. You're a very special man, and I feel I have been waiting for you all my life. I would love to spend the rest of that life with you.

"Yes, I will marry you!"

Usually calm, urbane, and cosmopolitan, Jerry Westfield sprang to his feet, brought both arms above his shoulders like an athlete who has just taken the gold medal, and bellowed, "Yes!!!"

Every head turned, and Joseph Moss, the proprietor who had known Ruth and Jerry from the first time they had lunch, began to bustle over.

"It's OK!" Jerry shouted to everyone. "We're getting married!"

The laughter erupted everywhere, and the patrons broke out in spontaneous, heartfelt applause.

The owner beamed at them and said, "Jerry, I see you and your young lady in here every day, and I know it is something special. Today, you have no check. Congratulations!"

"Thank you, Joseph. You are very kind!"

Ruth was glowing. She was going to marry Jerry Westfield. She never would tell Jerry that she already knew all about him before they ever met. She wanted to start off on equal ground to see what kind of a person he was without all the press clippings and ceremony. The man she had found was the man she was now to marry. An avid reader, she had always loved his work, and now she loved the man, famous or not.

They continued to talk and plan and laugh until Jerry checked his watch and it was time for them to leave, although nothing short of today's historic event could otherwise have moved them. Jerry dropped off Ruth at the Klausman's so that all of them could watch the event together.

Jerry did not go inside with Ruth for several reasons. He knew that Ruth and Sarah would definitely want to "talk," and he was scheduled to meet Ken Mailer at the hotel at twelve thirty, where he would join the entourage and be introduced to Demetrius Strapollos. From there, they would all be driven to the Temple Mount for the starting ceremonies at one in the afternoon.

Therefore, when Ruth left the car, Jerry just waved and drove off. As he pulled away, he glanced in his rear-view mirror and could just make out Sarah Klausman running to greet Ruth in the street, jumping up and down and dancing…dancing… dancing!

He never felt better…nor more alive!

*   *   *

Michael Eissen hung up the phone, walked over to Demetrius Strapollos, and whispered in his ear. The hotel suite was bulging with dignitaries from a myriad of nations, all of whom talked and laughed and did their best to look impressive, all at the same time. Eissen and Strapollos smiled at their guests as they walked into the bedroom part of the accommodations and closed the doors. They sat across from each other at a table in the room that boasted a huge fruit basket in its center with a card that indicated that it was compliments of the hotel.

Eissen spoke first.

"Everything is set. Both murders will be traced back to the three agents. We made certain that there is plenty of evidence, circumstantial but incriminating, pointing directly at them. It wouldn't surprise me if they had a small welcoming party waiting for them when their plane lands in New York."

Strapollos was obviously pleased.

"Very good, Michael," he said. "Now for the work at hand. This Jerry Westfield person is due here shortly. Understand that I want him on our side. He could make things much quicker and easier for us with a series of favorable reports in his newspaper and on his website. Mr. Westfield has developed a very large audience over the last year, and I see no reason why we should not capitalize on that fact."

Eissen stared at Strapollos.

"There are plenty of other reporters who would love to work with us. Jerry Westfield could be…well…difficult. Are you certain you want to get involved with someone like him?"

"If we are to attain the goals we have set," Strapollos answered, "we need public support, at least for right now. Jerry Westfield is a trusted commodity; the people believe in him, and that's what we need. When the digital currency is in place, and we are in power, well...then he can be your personal diversion, whatever you would care to do with him. Until then, we walk slowly and methodically."

Rabbi Eissen nodded his head, and without a further word, the two of them rose and joined the chaos in the living room.

CHAPTER EIGHTEEN

On Temple Mount

WHEN JERRY WESTFIELD WALKED THROUGH THE LARGE GLASS DOORS and into the busy lobby of the hotel, Ken Mailer was waiting for him. It occurred to Mailer that Jerry looked every bit the highly professional, popular newsman and journalist he had become. Jerry's fine dark blue suit, sky-blue tie, and the black-leather briefcase he carried bespoke a man of confidence who could be trusted and believed.

Just the kind of person we can use, Mailer thought, *if I can get him to co-operate a bit with Mr. Strapollos.*

What Ken Mailer said aloud was, "Jerry! Hey, Jerry! Over here!"

They exchanged greetings in the middle of the lobby and headed for the bank of elevators at the rear. When the doors closed and the machine began to lift them upwards, both men stood in a moment of silence. It was Ken who spoke first.

"Thanks for coming, Jerry. Believe me, we have all looked forward to this day with the greatest anticipation!"

"Thank you for the opportunity," Jerry said with a smile, aware that this was nothing but small talk. "It should be a very interesting day, don't you think?"

And what do you mean by that, Westfield? Mailer thought. He didn't say anything, however, for he really had no idea of what to say. Jerry looked…different, somehow, more confident…or something. What it was, exactly, Ken Mailer could not say. Whatever it was, Ken was not comfortable with it.

The elevator doors opened at the top floor, and Ken Mailer and Jerry Westfield walked out into a short hallway, smiling at each other.

They maintained their smiles as they were scanned and verified by four armed guards and finally let through the double doors and into the suite.

As they entered the room, Jerry immediately spotted Demetrius Strapollos in an animated conversation with the Prime Minister of Israel. Strapollos turned and caught sight of Mailer and Westfield across the room. Jerry watched as Strapollos turned to the Prime Minister, indicated the area where Ken and Jerry waited, patted the man on the shoulder and began to make his way across the crowded floor. He was smiling broadly as he approached.

Ken Mailer became even more enthusiastic than he had been in the lobby.

"Mr. Strapollos, may I present my personal friend, Mr. Jerry Westfield."

Demetrius Strapollos stood before Jerry Westfield and smiled warmly. At six feet four inches, he was an imposing figure as he stood peering down at Jerry with his coal-black eyes. He extended a firm, strong hand, and Jerry shook it.

"I am delighted to have you with us today, Mr. Westfield. Frankly, I am looking forward to our interview this evening."

"It is my pleasure, sir," Jerry replied. "I, as well, look forward to tonight."

In his mind, Jerry thought, *Keep giving those firm handshakes and those steely stares, Mr. Strapollos, but I've met greater and stronger than you, and they haven't scared me either.* Outwardly, he continued to ooze extreme pleasantness.

Ken Mailer could feel sweat running down the back of his neck. He was becoming uncomfortable, and he didn't exactly know why.

"Jerry," Mailer broke in, "we have not allowed any camera crews or reporters to travel in the cars with us, so that means you will have the full exclusive!"

"Thank you, I really appreciate that," Jerry stated. Then he turned to Demetrius Strapollos.

"Mr. Strapollos, Do you think it might be possible to ask you just a few questions before we leave for the ceremony?"

"I believe that would be fine. Let's make ourselves comfortable over there on the couch. We have about five minutes before we have to go."

Jerry followed the tall figure of Demetrius Strapollos across the room and sat down next to him.

"What would you care to know?" Strapollos asked with a friendly smile.

"I know what others are saying," Jerry began, getting right to the point, "but do you consider yourself to be the actual Messiah?"

Strapollos did not hesitate, and it was obvious that this was a question he had anticipated. "I have always felt a strong allegiance to Israel. My father was a rabbi, and he always believed that he was of the tribe of Judah. I have no proof of that, you understand, but I accept it as fact.

"I'm sorry, I'm wandering, am I not? Let me answer your question more directly.

"Yes. The Messiah is said to be a deliverer, and I believe that I am that deliverer. That is why I signed the peace accord, and that is why I am here today."

"Do you plan to oversee the building of the Temple, and are you in favor of restoring animal sacrifice?"

Again, there was not a second's pause before Strapollos answered.

"I will oversee the building of the Temple in the sense that I intend to make sure that Israel has all the help needed to complete the task. I, personally, will only be there when necessary. To answer your other question, yes, I do support the restoration of animal sacrifice. The Law of Moses requires it, and it is my wish and purpose to fulfill the Law."

Jerry was distracted for a moment as, across the room, Ken Mailer stood and announced to everyone that it was time to leave. Throughout the room, people began to lay down drinks and *hors d'oeurves* and pick up briefcases and file folders, heading for the door. Jerry noticed the security agents on their feet and circulating as the group made their way to the elevators.

Suddenly, Ken Mailer was there, and he was saying, "Jerry, you'll ride with Mr. Strapollos, Rabbi Eissen, and myself in the last car, all right?"

"And, if you'd care to do so," Strapollos added, "we can continue our conversation in the car."

Jerry smiled and nodded agreement, but before he could say a further word, they were all on their feet and being ushered into an elevator by the silent guards.

During the descent, Jerry found himself looking forward to the ride. He had tried to meet Rabbi Eissen but had been put off. Now, Eissen would have no choice. He would not concentrate on the man, however, for he had to concentrate nor only on this afternoon, but the interview he would conduct this very night. Instinctively, his hand touched his jacket at the pocket where the list of approved questions for the interview were stored. At the same time, his mind went over several *other* questions.

Those un-approved questions that only he knew.

* * *

When they reached the lobby, the first thing that was obvious was that the crowd of people in front of the hotel had grown significantly over the last half hour. From the front door of the hotel to the black limousines parked at the curb, a troop of soldiers had formed a human corridor, holding back the flood of people who pressed in for a closer look.

Demetrius Strapollos walked out of the hotel with Ken Mailer and Jerry Westfield slightly behind, and the volume of the crowd rose to overwhelming heights of intensity. Here and there, Jerry could spot someone with a raised fist or a sign condemning Strapollos or quoting from Scripture. Even as he watched, however, Jerry saw one of these people disappear into the surrounding humanity as if absorbed into quicksand. He did not see the man emerge.

The vast majority of the people, however, shouted, screamed, and poured out a support that was at once breathless and total, wide-eyed and adoring, visceral and all-consuming. All of it was directed at the man who now raised a waving arm to the crowd, and graciously allowed Ken Mailer and Jerry Westfield to enter the sleek, black limousine before him.

Jerry was settling himself in the leather seats, when he became aware of, felt rather than saw, an overwhelming presence that made him feel, well…uneasy. He raised his eyes and found himself looking directly at Rabbi Michael Eissen who was, in turn, gazing at Jerry from under the brim of his wide black hat.

"Rabbi Eissen," Jerry said, extending a hand, "how do you do, I'm Jerry Westfield."

Eissen withdrew a pale hand from under his black robe and shook the fingers of Jerry's hand.

"Mr. Westfield," Rabbi Eissen said softly.

"I'm sorry!" Ken Mailer fluttered nervously, "I was under the impression that you two had already met!"

Ken Mailer knew that Rabbi Eissen did not care to meet Jerry Westfield at all – in fact distrusted Jerry and wanted nothing to do with him. He also knew that the two had not previously met, but he was trying to keep things going well. He was trying desperately. Part of Ken Mailer wished the day were over.

Jerry Westfield bent forward and asked, "Rabbi, I understand that you are interested in the rebuilding of Babylon in Iraq, is that true?"

Ken's heart was beating like a rabbit caught in a steel trap. He couldn't believe what he was hearing, and he jumped in with, "Where would you get an idea like that, Jerry? I assure you…"

Rabbi Eissen held up a hand.

"I see that you are well-informed, Mr. Westfield. Yes, I have some interest there. It was a fascinating civilization, and I believe that there are many advantages to rebuilding such a culture."

Jerry, following his reporter's instinct, saw an opening and plunged into it immediately.

"Tell me, doesn't that pose any problems for you? I mean, a Jew, especially a Rabbi, involved in an Arab endeavor such as that?"

Rabbi Eissen turned slightly, looked straight ahead, and replied, "I suppose it would, to some. I believe that we are entering a time of peace between our nations, and such a treasure should be available to all the people on earth. Don't you agree, Mr. Westfield?"

"I see your point, Rabbi Eissen," Jerry replied, "but peace has proven to be an elusive dream throughout the ages. I think I'll have to wait and see."

Michael Eissen smiled, if you could call it that, and folded his hands across his chest. He leaned back, and his dark, unblinking eyes continued to engulf the reporter who sat across from him in this richly appointed limousine on this incredibly historic day.

Without willing it, a thought leaped to the forefront of Jerry's mind.

He makes my skin feel as if a hundred scorpions were crawling on it.

The door opened, and Demetrius Strapollos, having placated the crowd as much as possible, entered and sat. With a gesture of his hand, he indicated the people lining the walk and the roadway, wildly cheering, as their vehicle slowly pulled away.

"This is what I hope to bring to all people, Mr. Westfield. Do you see the peace? Do you see the peace and unity? Do you see Peace *through* Unity? I am committed to it, fully.

"Now," he continued, "I need to take some time and go over my speech. We will be arriving at the Temple Mount in a relatively short while, and I would appreciate it if you would hold off on any more questions until later."

How convenient, Jerry thought, and he wanted to say, *what an easy way to get away from any questions not 'officially approved' by the*

Rabbi. Instead, he nodded his head, and aloud he proclaimed, "Of course, sir. No problem."

Jerry sat back and began to jot down notes on what had been said and what he had personally observed. He knew, felt in his heart, that all this was somehow important – extremely important, and he was determined that not one word would fall through the cracks.

Not one word.

* * *

During the next twenty minutes of the drive, Demetrius Strapollos and Ken Mailer went over a plethora of agendas and speeches, Rabbi Michael Eissen continued to maintain an unblinking stare straight ahead, and Jerry Westfield gazed out the tinted window as Israel passed by outside the car.

The caravan continued along Highway One, climbing gradually into the hills of Judea and up into the city of Jerusalem. At first, the road signs made it look like any other city. They were not, as he had once fancifully mused, engraved in gold, nor did they radiate a special glow. Even so, there was, without doubt, something special – something magical – about the name – Jerusalem. So many people had yearned, with eyes filling with tears, for this city, the very heart of the Promised Land. So much weeping by so many; so much discord and strife; so much blood, Jew and Arab; and now, so much ceremony and uncertainty. *And,* Jerry mused, *I wonder what promises will be made this afternoon. I wonder if they'll be kept.*

The procession slowly made its way to the Temple Mount. Jerry Westfield, looking out the window, saw it first, and was struck by the incredible scene that was a strange mixture of Twenty-first Century technology and the artisan perfection of Old Testament Times. The platform directly in front of the Temple Mount was surrounded by well-armed Israeli soldiers, with others stationed at strategic locations throughout the area. High above the crowd, strung from poles and cranes, was a state-of-the-art speaker system that would melt the heart of any rock concert promoter. Camera crews from more than a dozen news networks formed an array across a platform that was, because of spatial necessities, only twenty-five feet square. Screens were set up in strategic locations so that the thousands of people present could feel a part of this ceremony no matter where they stood.

This holy and sacred area had never witnessed anything like this. To the left of the speaker's platform sat the cornerstone that would not be taken from the huge, flatbed truck where it now rested until it would be actually placed on the Temple Mount. That, in turn, would only take place by the order of the Master Builder and his specially appointed craftsmen.

The line of black limousines rolled to a slow stop, and the soldiers and special agents descended upon the vehicles like a swarm of khaki-colored bees and secured the area, creating another human corridor between the cars and the platform.

The doors of the limousines opened, and dignitaries and their guests began to make their way to the stage area amid shouts of joy and scattered applause from those fortunate enough to get close to the proceedings.

At length, an armed guard opened and held the door of their vehicle, and they emerged into the bright and gleaming sunlight.

Usually, Jerry Westfield was in the background at events such as these, digging up little known facts or looking under rocks for side stories, and now he could not help feeling very strange as he walked among the cheering and adulation of the crowd.

He reached the platform and sat down between Ken Mailer and Rabbi Michael Eissen. As he leaned back, an uncomfortable thought, the second within the hour, clawed its way into his consciousness. He wondered if he, Jerry Westfield, was being used as another 'decoration' by Mr. Demetrius Strapollos. That bothered Jerry, and his stomach involuntarily squeezed. It was not enough, however, for him to give up this chance to learn about the man who was the center of all that was going on today.

Besides, Jerry knew there would come a time when he would have his chance to speak his mind about the one this crowd was now naming in a chant that ran on and on, the same words flowing in an almost endless mantra.

Messiah! Messiah! Messiah!!!

* * *

There were the usual, and rather expected, opening remarks and introductions. Finally, the podium was given over to Abraham Ben David, Israel's newly-elected President. Although far from personally convinced of Demetrius Strapollos' Messianic nature, he was, nonetheless, acutely aware of tremendous political pressure and the crushing weight of that master of all politicians, public opinion. He knew, therefore, precisely how he had to proceed. As he spread his arms to embrace the audience, the crowd began to quiet.

"Men, women, and children of Israel," he began in a deep and steady voice, "we are gathered here today to celebrate the long-awaited presentation of the cornerstone of the Third Temple!"

The roar from the crowd was like a gigantic wave building and crashing with unleashed power on some tortured, rocky shore. It was followed by two full minutes of applause and cheering and screaming.

"It has been nearly two thousand years," Ben David continued when he could, "since the Temple of the Lord has stood on the Temple Mount. It has been over three thousand years from the time Solomon began to build the first Temple of the Lord here on Mount Moriah, where the Lord appeared to Solomon's father, David, on the threshing floor of Araunah, the Jebusite, the place provided by David.

"God, it seems – who is Jehovah Jireh, the one who provides -- has also provided for us a man. He has provided an extraordinary man who has promised to protect the interests of Israel and see to it that the Temple of the Lord is completed in accordance with the Law and the ordinances of King David.

"That man is with us today, and it is my privilege...yes, and my honor...to introduce to you the President of the European Community and the staunch defender and 'Friend of Israel' – Mr.! Demetrius! Strapollos!"

Sixty, perfect snow-white doves were released and danced ecstatically against the clear azure sky. Deep-throated horns began to sound and rumble everywhere, and the crowd responded with a din and roar that all but blocked the sound completely. Banners unfurled, catching the afternoon breeze, and people everywhere began to chant the words those banner proclaimed.

"Messiah has come! Messiah Has Come! MESSIAH HAS COME!"

Far off to one side, a group, a much smaller group of perhaps two dozen men and women, shook their fists in the air in defiance and tried to initiate their own chant, but to no avail – it could not be heard and faded away into the afternoon. They were, quite simply, swallowed up in a crowd firmly enthralled with Mr. Strapollos.

Demetrius Strapollos stood slowly, uncoiling both arms into the air, waving to the crowd. For well over three minutes the deafening, pounding roar of approval continued unabated. Finally, a smiling Strapollos approached the podium, and the audience quieted sufficiently to allow him to begin.

"I thank you," Strapollos began. "I thank you very much. I rejoice with you today, for today is a time that will long be remembered and that history will record as a day of destiny; a point in time where peace and unity began to reign..."

Again the noise rose to unspeakable heights; again the chanting began, *"Messiah! Messiah! Messiah!"*

Demetrius Strapollos left the bank of microphones and began walking across the front of the platform and back again, his hands in the air, like some prizefighter accepting the title belt.

Jerry Westfield sat uncomfortably, observing and becoming a part of the spectacle that unfolded its grandeur before him. To Jerry it had become surrealistic, and he felt as if he were part of a dream. He could not fully take it in, nor could he fully believe what was happening. For what he believed to be the first time in his entire life, even he was being effected by the total euphoria of the people...of the moment...of the day.

Now Strapollos walked back to the display of microphones and raised one hand. The crowd calmed instantly to allow him to continue. They were his.

"It is my wish," he said, "to bring unity to all the people of the world – to Muslim; to Christian; to Jew. It is time to beat our swords into plowshares and enjoy a new millennium of peace and prosperity. I say let it begin with us; I say let it begin now, and I say let it begin here – in Jerusalem!"

The crowd, the applause, and the chanting of "Messiah!" mounted even louder than before if such a thing were acoustically possible. The sound echoed through the Temple Mount and down the sun-drenched streets. It rang from the stone walkways of Old Jerusalem.

In the middle of it, Jerry Westfield could well believe that there was nowhere...nowhere in the entire city...that you could hide from it; *not* hear it. Even, he understood amid the din that wrapped him like a second skin, were someone totally deaf, with no hearing whatsoever, the sheer, thudding, consuming vibration of it would possess him from feet to brain in one massive bear hug of tumult and elation. It was as if there was a rush of new and hot blood coursing through even the oldest and most tired of veins.

It continued unrestrained for five solid minutes.

Strapollos turned and looked at Rabbi Eissen and shrugged slightly while his lips curled into a smile, and he mouthed, 'What more is necessary?' Eissen merely nodded his head. He understood what Strapollos had said...he understood well.

Indeed, there was only one thing left this day – one final necessity, and that was something most believed only the Messiah -- the true Messiah -- could do or would do.

With the crowd still chanting and screaming with eyes wide and wild, and the cameras still recording every second of it, Demetrius Strapollos held his hands high and shouted into microphones that had been cranked to top volume and beyond.

"TO...THE...TEMPLE...MOUNT!"

Strapollos turned and, with the strongest of military bearings, began to walk down from the platform, with Rabbi Eissen following close behind. The other dignitaries and invited guests on that stage were frozen for a moment of inaction, not knowing what to do or how to proceed, since this was definitely not a part of the stated agenda. Jerry Westfield took less than a half-second before he quickly jumped to his feet and followed Strapollos, with Ken Mailer close behind. If something were going to happen, Jerry wanted to be right in the middle of it.

Most people there knew what this walk meant, and those who didn't followed anyhow, like sheep desperately in need of a shepherd.

Now, there was no doubt left for anyone who knew about the Temple and the prophecies. By the action he had just taken and what, Jerry knew, would invariably happen once they reached the Temple Mount, Demetrius Strapollos was *de facto* embracing the sacred title of 'Messiah' for himself. What's more, he was doing so without saying a word of self-proclamation, to the delight of the multitude and the horror of a few.

Now, Strapollos had reached the steps to the Temple Mount, and with Rabbi Eissen at his side, he began the long assent. This was, literally, his crowning moment, and he basked in it. Even from a distance, that was obvious.

No one dared to stop him now.

The special agents assigned to protect Strapollos and Eissen had been caught off guard, but they had quickly reformed and moved now with the pair as they climbed the steps of Temple Mount, the crowd following him, now chanting and cheering and glorifying his name.

When he reached the top, Strapollos walked to the open area over the Dome of Tablets which was mounted over "*Even Shetiyah,*" the foundation stone where the Ark of the Covenant rested in the First Temple built by King Solomon.

His hands held high, Demetrius Strapollos stood at the apex of the rejoicing multitude.

A helicopter hovered high overhead with a television crew from Cable News Network capturing every moment.

It was broadcast live throughout the entire world.

*   *   *

Jacob Klausman slammed one huge fist down on the arm of his chair. He knew what was happening.

"What does he think he's doing?" Jacob shouted, far louder than necessary. "He is no more the Messiah than the Devil, himself!"

Jerry had offered to use some influence and get them prime seating at the actual event, but Jacob had politely refused for himself and Sarah, and Ruth opted for staying out of the massive crowd and with her friend. Now, from their seats in front of the TV set in their living room, the Klausmans and Ruth Cowen had an unobstructed world's-eye view of the entire proceedings. Sarah held her husband's hand and stared, half shocked and half mesmerized at the incredible spectacle playing out before her.

Intrigued by Jacob's outburst, Ruth asked, "What do you mean, Jacob? I guess I'm not that well-informed about my own culture, but what is it you see in this that I don't?"

Jacob took a deep breath and turned to Ruth. For a moment, the anger was gone from his eyes, and he was the compassionate teacher with the bright pupil, but as he spoke, it was with growing passion.

"Ruth," Jacob said, his voice filled with conviction, "in 1967, on 7 June, we captured Old Jerusalem, and the Temple Mount was restored to Israeli hands. A great General of that war, General Moshe Dayan, came to that very spot you just saw – the Temple Mount, and he and his aides walked *around* the place. You heard what I said, Ruth? *Around.* When asked why he did not walk up the steps to stand on the Mount, this General, this man of War, was shocked, and General Dayan told the reporters in very clear terms that he would not dare to do such a thing. You see, that action belonged to the Messiah, and the Messiah alone! This is not a story, Ruth; it's history. I even know someone who was there and witnessed it.

"You see, Ruth, there is such a thing as Rabbinic Tradition, and according to that, only the Messiah, when He comes, can lead His people to set foot on the Temple Mount. Do you understand? Only the Messiah."

"But, Strapollos just did that. He led the people up the steps and on to the Temple…" She stopped in mid-sentence, and her eyes grew wide with understanding.

"Exactly," Jacob nodded, finishing Ruth's thoughts.

"He…he's saying that he is the…the…"

"The Messiah…Yes, that's exactly what is happening. Oh, yes, it is tender, it is moving, I have no doubt it is well-planned, and even the most devout students of the Law are beginning to believe that Demetrius Strapollos is the promised Messiah. And, it is one thing more, Ruth."

"Yes, Jacob."

"It is also an abomination!"

Ruth and Sarah drew nearer to each other and held hands as the fever of the crowd, bursting from the TV set, grew ever hotter, ever more consuming.

In his chair, Jacob Klausman sat with his head lowered, his arms folded, rocking slowly back and forth; back and forth.

"Oh, God!" Jacob prayed. "Have mercy! Have mercy upon the nation of Israel this day!"

* * *

It took over half an hour before the soldiers could clear a path through the crowd to the limousines. When they finally reached the vehicles, Demetrius Strapollos and Rabbi Michael Eissen got into the first in line, while Jerry Westfield and Ken Mailer were escorted to the second gleaming, ebony car. *I'm certain*, Jerry thought as he approached the vehicle, *they must have a great deal to talk about that they don't want me -- or anyone else -- to hear.*

They got into the limousine and for a moment all Ken Mailer and Jerry Westfield could do was to try to catch their breaths. Ken was extremely animated, and it looked to Jerry as if Ken were having a hard time just sitting still

Like an over-excited two-year-old, Jerry thought.

"Well," Jerry said aloud, "that was quite a display of emotion out there, don't you think?"

Ken was completely overcome by the moment, and that was more than evident. His eyes caught the afternoon light and literally sparkled. Every muscle in his body was moving.

"Amazing!" Ken Mailer exclaimed. "That's what I'd call it! I've never been in the middle of anything like this before – anything! It's…it's exhilarating! Jerry, we are at the beginning of a new age! This is incredible; absolutely incredible!"

Jerry Westfield, his breath now coming regularly, and his heart beat down to a semblance of normalcy, looked directly into Ken Mailer's flashing eyes and asked, "And, what age would that be, Ken? The Age of Aquarius?"

It was as if a switch had been thrown somewhere in Ken Mailer's brain. The sparkling eyes turned cold and hard in a moment; the animation ceased and solid stone replaced the excited flesh of a moment ago. If it were not so frightening, Jerry mused, it would be fascinating to watch.

175

Mailer's dark eyes whipped around Jerry's face, and he snapped, "Can't you be serious for even a minute? Didn't you feel it out there? Don't you realize that this man...this man is soon going to rule the world!"

The words flown from his mouth and become irretrievable, and Ken Mailer would have spent a fortune to take them back. He knew that Jerry Westfield missed nothing, and this would, most certainly, be no exception. He would not have to wait long for a reaction.

"Rule the world?" Jerry repeated instantaneously as he leaned closer to Ken Mailer, his eyes now boring into Mailer's own. "What do you mean, 'Rule the world'?"

Mailer's eyes were flipping back and forth outwardly as inside he searched desperately for some answer he could give to Jerry Westfield. He knew it would be impossible to talk his way out of this one. There followed about four seconds of silence.

They seemed interminable.

"I mean, Jerry," Ken said at length, "that...well...you can see it, you know? He has the answers for the economy...for peace and unity. I mean, some day...you know, I wouldn't be surprised...I mean, you never know..."

Jerry could hardly believe all that he had just heard in this back seat of an official limousine. Perhaps he would ask Mr. Strapollos about the statement later, in some discreet place – like on world wide TV!

Ken Mailer was turning ashen, and sweat discolored his shirt and even the underarms of his light blue jacket were becoming dark. If Mr. Strapollos heard of this, what would he do? What would he *not* do? It was not a very pleasant thing to contemplate.

He turned his attention to Jerry Westfield and asked, "That was just talk, you know? Off the record. Nothing official here. Just two old friends...you know. Like... talking out loud, right?"

Jerry thought for a few seconds. He suddenly saw, reflected in Ken Mailer's eyes, the smallest shadow of what might happen to Ken if what Ken had said in haste ever got out.

"I'll tell you what, Ken," Jerry said. "I'll just keep all that in the back of my mind for now. OK? But, since we are speaking, as you say, off the record, tell me something."

"Anything, my friend," Ken managed to smile as hope crept back into his life. "Anything."

"Then tell me," Jerry said in a flat, moderate tone, "did your boss have anything to do with the assassinations that took place today?"

Jerry might as well have stuck Ken with an electric cattle prod.

176

"Absolutely not!" exclaimed Mailer as he began to bounce in his seat. "Those men were his associates, not his enemies!"

"So, you're saying that he only kills his enemies?"

"No! That's not what I meant, and you know it!"

Ken was sinking fast. It was becoming more and more difficult to breathe, and he knew this day had been too much for him. He wished desperately that he were home, in his bed, with one – perhaps two or three – of those wonderful, dream-filled pills Mr. Strapollos had so kindly insisted Ken have available in abundance.

"I don't know, Ken," Jerry continued. "There seem to be an awful lot of unanswered questions and loose ends surrounding this man. And, why do I have the feeling that I'm not going to find out very much tonight, either?"

"Tonight?" Ken brightened. Now, at last, he could change the subject.

"Oh, yes, about tonight. There are a few things we need to go over. Let's see, I would like you to be at the studio in Tel Aviv by seven o'clock. That will give us an hour before airtime to go over all the details. Mr. Strapollos likes everything well-prepared and thought out. Do you want to be picked up, or will you drive over on your own?"

Jerry began to scribble in his pocket notebook as he said, "I'll drive. The studio is only fifteen minutes from where I'm staying. Also, as I told you earlier, I will be bringing someone with me."

"That's right!" Ken smiled, the perspiration finally beginning to cool on his forehead. "The woman you started telling me about..."

"Ruth, her name is Ruth. We got engaged this morning."

"Congratulations! This has been a big day for you. Listen, I'll make certain she has a good seat in the studio – something fit for a VIP."

This was better. This was something Ken knew about and could handle. If they could just stick to the pleasantries...

"I'd appreciate that, Ken," Jerry stated, reaching for the cell phone in his jacket pocket. "And that reminds me, I think I'd like to give her a call, all right?"

Ken said, "Certainly! Certainly! I'll just put my headphones on and listen to my meditation CD, I need to relax for a while anyway."

Jerry looked at him and said. "Meditation? Does that really help you?"

"Oh yes." Ken said, happy to be rid of any further talk of... him.

"It works well, very well in fact." *Especially when I have my little white pills with me.* Ken thought to himself.

* * *

When the call went through, it was Sarah Klausman who answered the phone with a simple, "Hello."

"Hello, Sarah, it's Jerry."

"Jerry!" she bubbled. "We saw you on the TV! You looked wonderful! Wonderful? What am I saying? Congratulations, Jerry! We're so happy for you and Ruth!"

In the limousine, driving back from history on the Temple Mount, Jerry wondered if his face could split from smiling.

""Thank you, Sarah, you little matchmaker. Is Ruth there?"

"Yes, yes, she is. Hold on."

Jerry could hear Sarah shouting to Ruth, and in a second she was there.

"Jerry? Hi! I saw what happened on television. That was wild. How are you doing?"

"I'm fine," Jerry answered. It was so good to hear her voice. It calmed and soothed him and brought a pleasure that poured over him like warm water. "Listen, I thought we might have a little celebration of our own tonight, after the interview. What do you think?"

"I'd love to. What did you have in mind?"

"Well, the interview is scheduled for broadcast from eight to eight-thirty. Why don't you call the *Forel* and make reservations for four at nine o'clock. I'm in the mood for some good seafood, and they say this place is the best. Oh, and tell Jacob and Sarah to leave their money home. It's all on me this time, I insist!"

At the other end of the line, Ruth laughed and said, "OK; sound's great. Do you think that will give us enough time to get there?"

"It'll be fine. The restaurant is only a short distance from the studio."

"When will I see you?"

"In about an hour, and I can't wait."

"I love you," Ruth said.

"I love you," Jerry answered and disconnected the call.

As the limousine that carried him and Ken Mailer rolled through the crowd, it occurred to Jerry Westfield that he had never been happier.

Never.

* * *

It was about three-thirty when the limo pulled on to Hayarkon Street and stopped before the Sheraton Hotel where Jerry had left his car. He shook hands with Ken Mailer, giving him an abrupt good-bye, got into his own vehicle and headed for what his mind called, "home." In reality, he had only one thing he wanted to think about, and that was Ruth. He could barely wait to get away from all the craziness of the afternoon and do something really meaningful, like maybe gaze into Ruth's beautiful eyes for ten or twelve luxurious, uninterrupted hours.

When he parked his car and walked up to the door of the Klausman home, Ruth was waiting for him, and they met in a long and loving embrace.

"I've said it often, but I've never meant it as much -- it's good to be back," Jerry said with a smile that refused to go away.

Then, they were all over him. Jacob was pumping his hand, and Sarah was jumping up and down, kissing everyone.

"Congratulations, old friend!" Jacob roared. "This is the best thing you ever did! I am very happy for both of you!"

"And, we'd love to go to dinner tonight," Sarah squealed. "Just one thing…"

"Yes?"

"If it's possible, could you not mention the name 'Strapollos' while we're eating?"

They all laughed, and Jerry pulled Ruth closer to his side.

"I'll try, Sarah," Jerry said, still smiling. "I promise I'll try."

But, there's still tonight to get through, he thought, even as he spoke. *I'll try not to involve that…person…in our lives. I'll try…*
If I can.

CHAPTER NINETEEN

The Interview

IT WAS 6:45 ON THE LARGE CLOCK IN THE LOBBY of the TV studio in Tel Aviv when the door to one of the dressing rooms was held open for Demetrius Strapollos. The two large men with him closed the door gently and took up guard positions outside, one on either side. The room itself was small, with a mirror edged with soft lights that ran the length of one wall. Before that mirror was a large leather salon chair and along one of the other walls was what looked to be a comfortable couch. The counter below the mirror supported numerous bottles and brushes and make-up items of all kinds. It also held a small color TV and a vase filled with fresh-cut flowers.

Demetrius Strapollos sat in the chair before the mirror and stared at his reflected image. He felt wonderful, something between what a mighty warrior and a conquering king must feel after a highly successful campaign, the enemy routed and returning to garlands of spring flowers and golden crowns. The power coursed through his very veins. He wanted to shout and dance, but he knew that this was not a time for reveling, but for continued planning and very careful execution

Today had been a giant step towards the total victory, but there were even more mountains to climb. He could wait. Once the digital currency was put into place, he would be able to do almost anything. The feeling was overwhelming and very difficult even for him to control. It was power -- very simply, power -- something which, according to anyone who ever attained it, was better, far better, than sex or drugs could ever be! What excited Demetrius Strapollos so much was the knowledge that it was he -- he who was now on the verge of that ultimate high – power…both absolute and complete!

There was a knock at the door, and Strapollos turned to it.

"Who is it?" he asked in what could only be called a kingly tone.

"Rabbi Eissen," the voice returned.

Strapollos voice softened considerably as he said, "Come in, Michael."

As he entered the room, Rabbi Michael Eissen was smiling, not the smile of happiness, but the smile Strapollos had seen on some childhood companions who delighted in pulling wings and legs from trapped insects.

"I want to show you something," he said as he reached over and snapped on the small TV set.

The screen came to life with a shot of Kennedy Airport, and letters superimposed on the screen proclaimed that it was 11:45 AM, New York time as the correspondent began her report.

"Just moments ago, here at Kennedy Airport, Federal Officials arrested three men for the murders of President Pedro M. Arano of Spain and President Manuel Cisco of Portugal. The men were arrested without incident as they disembarked from Israel's El Al flight twenty-three originating in Tel Aviv.

"Details are sketchy at this point, but some reports list these men as special agents assigned to the United Nations. As to what motivated the assassinations, officials aren't saying at present.

"To repeat: Three men have been arrested in the killing of President Pedro M. Arano of Spain and President Manuel Cisco of Portugal. We will have more details as they develop.

"This is…"

Rabbi Eissen snapped off the set and moved to the couch where he sat and looked triumphantly at Demetrius Strapollos.

"My, my," Strapollos said to his companion. "What *is* this world coming to?"

Both men laughed out loud, their mirth tumbling from the walls to such an extent that even the flowers on the counter seemed to tremble.

* * *

Jerry and Ruth drove alone into the parking area of the studio. Jacob and Sarah would join them afterwards for that late supper at the elegant *Forel* in celebration of the engagement. Right now, Jerry had an interview to conduct, and he wanted to show Ruth the inside of "the news."

Jerry found a parking space just as few yards from the entrance, and the two of them walked up the sidewalk, through the double glass doors, and into the reception area. Within seconds, they were being led down the hall and into the main studio.

This was Ruth's first time inside a TV studio, and her eyes swept every corner of the place. There were scores and scores of lights hanging from the tall ceiling; several cameras rested on booms and there was one hand-held in front of the platform; there were wires and microphones everywhere. On the platform itself, there was a large desk with a chair behind it and one to the side. The backdrop showed Old Jerusalem and the site of the Temple Mount.

There was also space for a number of red-backed audience seats, and all of them were vacant. Jerry had told her that for reasons of security and control, the network had kept the location of the interview a secret. Apparently, that secrecy had worked.

Jerry and Ruth continued through the studio to the dressing room, where the makeup crew began to prepare Jerry Westfield for the bright lights and cameras. Ruth just sat on the couch and smiled at Jerry's uneasiness as make up was applied to his features. She was enjoying every moment of it.

At 7:45, there was a call for run-through. Jerry walked into the studio carrying a bundle of note cards with his approved questions and a mind filled with inquiries no one but he had ever envisioned. From the opposite side of the studio, Demetrius Strapollos emerged from the shadows followed by Rabbi Eissen and Ken Mailer, their bodyguards taking up positions in the darkness of unlit corners.

Larry Sangler was the producer for CNN in Israel. He was known as a brilliant man in his late thirties who had produced shows for CNN all over the world. He also happened to be one of Jerry Westfield's biggest fans.

"Gentlemen!" he called as he walked briskly on to the stage area. "My name is Larry Sangler, and it is a pleasure to have you here tonight on *CNN Live*. I'm sure this will be a great show, and I'm glad it's not raining, because our ratings are going to go through the roof tonight. What we want to do now is to get you in place, so please follow me.

"Mr. Westfield, if you'll sit behind the desk, please, and Mr. Strapollos, will you please sit in this armchair to the side of the desk. Good. Now, Mr. Westfield, I'd like you to direct a question at Mr. Strapollos, and if you, Sir, would answer – it can be anything at all; our technicians just want to get a reading on the two of you and make sure their equipment is functioning."

Jerry took a breath, collected himself as best he could, and asked Strapollos, "So, how is your vacation going?"

There were several light laughs from the crew, and Ruth rolled her eyes in disbelief. Strapollos, himself, smiled and indicated Ruth Cowen with a graceful sweep of his well-manicured hand.

"Apparently, not as good as yours, Mr. Westfield."

The thought passed through Jerry's mind that they were like two heavyweight boxers feeling each other out, sparring verbally before a major title fight.

Jerry's phone rang, and as he dug for it in his jacket pocket, he stepped out from behind the desk and walked from the platform into a shadowy area of the stage.

"Mr. Westfield!" Sangler shouted after him, some frustration evident in his voice, "we have very little time!"

"A moment, Mr. Sangler. I'll be right there."

About ninety seconds later, Jerry Westfield, his face expressionless, put the phone back into his pocket and walked to the platform.

"Remember, " Sangler instructed them, "when you hear the music fade down, I will introduce you. Then, Mr. Westfield will welcome the viewing audience and begin the interview.

"Please, don't either of you mention where we are broadcasting from. No one knows the city or studio the program is originating from, and we want to keep it that way. We do not want thousands of people breaking down the studio doors, do we?

"You will have two commercial breaks. One will be at 8:10 and another at 8:24. That will give time for one final question and answer before we go off the air at 8:29

"The whole world is watching, gentlemen. Good luck."

Larry Sangler walked swiftly to a marked area beside the stage checking the studio clock and pushing the small receiver closer into his ear.

"Talk about cutting it close..." he sighed. "Gentlemen, we go in ten... nine...eight...

Jerry's hands were sweating. He had been on TV many times before, but usually he was the one answering questions, not asking them. And then, there was that phone call – that special phone call -- just minutes ago...

The music flared and then faded down, and Larry Sangler began to introduce the show and the guests. Jerry took one more look at Ruth as the camera zoomed in on him. Ruth's smile was puzzled, for she saw, or thought she saw, something in Jerry's eyes that she could not make out;

something sad yet determined; something distant yet ready to spill out riotously at any moment.

The director's long index finger rose and fell, pointing directly at Jerry.

"Good evening, ladies and gentlemen," Jerry Westfield said, "and welcome to *CNN Live*. I'm Jerry Westfield, and I'll be your host for this Sunday evening, May 15. Tonight, I will be talking to Mr. Demetrius Strapollos, President of the European Community as well as founder and leading proponent of the Digital Cashless Society, as it has come to be known worldwide.

"Mr. Strapollos, thank you for the opportunity to speak with you tonight on *CNN Live* which, as you know, is being broadcast live via satellite throughout the world."

"Thank you, Jerry. It is truly my privilege to be here."

Jerry could see the monitor and what was being fed live to the world. The TV camera was more than kind to Demetrius Strapollos. Even from his sitting position, his six foot four inch frame stood out boldly. His jet black hair and handsome face made him appear more a movie star than a politician. More like –yes – a king!

Jerry did not even notice his own image. With growing clarity, he was becoming aware that this was an opportunity that must not be wasted. With an effort of will, he blocked out everything and everyone except this tall, dark man sitting before him. Is was almost as if he felt his mind flex and tighten and bear down on his subject to the exclusion of all else in the room.

The first of the "approved" questions lay before him, and Jerry used it to begin.

"Mr. Strapollos, you have become a powerful world leader in what appears to be a comparatively short amount of time. In my introduction, I might possibly have added another title to your portfolio. I know our viewers would like to know more about what happened in Jerusalem today. Chants of "Messiah!" could be heard echoing throughout Old Jerusalem this afternoon, and those chants were aimed at you, Mr. Strapollos. How do you feel about that?"

"Jerry, I understand that according to the prophets, the Messiah is the one who brings peace to Jerusalem and the entire Earth; the one who initiates the rebuilding of the Temple and establishes Jerusalem as the capital of the world. I believe that destiny has brought me here to fulfill those very prophecies. Therefore, without apologies and without equivocation, I accept the fact that I am the Messiah."

Jerry Westfield looked down to the next approved question on the list.

"So, you believe that the prophets of old were speaking of you when they referred to the Messiah?"

"I can't say that with authority, but I do believe that I have been chosen to lead Israel, as well as the world, into peace and unity."

Next question.

"There are many experts who claim that three or four new military conflicts break out somewhere in the world each day. How do you plan to bring peace to a world ripped apart daily by violence born of inequities, suspicion, and greed?"

"Peace through strength – that's the answer. We need a world government with a law that has teeth rather than platitudes. If certain groups continue to cause trouble, then they must be dealt with. What we have now is a society run amuck. I believe that the people are ready for a New World Order; one that will bring peace and prosperity to all people. We are a global society, and it is time we were governed like one."

"Mr. Strapollos," Jerry read, "let me get back to the issue of the Temple. When will construction begin, and approximately how long will it take to finish a project of this magnitude?"

"Construction should begin on June first, which would be the fifteenth day of Sivan on the Hebrew calendar, and from what I am told, most of the materials are already in place. It is a bit more difficult to answer the second part of your question. The First Temple took Solomon seven years to build, while the Second Temple was finished in five years. The special craftsmen who have been assigned to build the Third Temple hope to finish it in a little over a year. They want to have it ready for dedication on the Feast of Tabernacles, which is the fifteenth day of Tishri, which would be in the first week of October of next year."

Without expression, Jerry moved to the next approved question.

"What is the significance of rebuilding the Temple?"

"As I am certain you understand, Mr. Westfield, the Temple is the center of worship for the Jewish people. Unlike other religions, the Jewish people can only have one Temple where blood sacrifices can be made, and that Temple must be in Jerusalem and built on Mount Moriah."

Jerry's jaw was beginning to work slowly, as if he were chewing his words, but he voiced the next prepared question.

"You talked about a one-world government. Are you prepared to lead such a government?"

For the first time in the interview, Strapollos moved, turning slightly to look directly into the camera rather than at Jerry. The monitors in the studio revealed what the home audience now saw -- a handsome, charismatic leader looking directly into the eyes of each individual viewer.

"I would accept the challenge gladly; with truly open arms. As I said before, I have the answers to the problems the world is facing today, and under my direction and guidance, I could lead the world into the next age. Too much individuality and abuse of freedom is what we have now, and that leads to chaos. Unity and direction under strong leadership lead to peace."

Jerry's eyes flared. Slowly, his right hand swept away the stack of cards with their prepared and approved questions as he leaned into Strapollos and held his gaze.

"Really?" Jerry began. "Well, Mr. Strapollos, I'm not so sure I believe you can have too much individuality. What you are saying reminds me of an old book by George Orwell called *Nineteen Eighty-four*. That was all about a dictator called, 'Big Brother,' watching over your shoulder and keeping an eye on all you did and said. Is that the kind of society you are proposing?"

Strapollos eyes widened a bit – perhaps a sixteenth of an inch -- but other than that, he gave no indication of being upset by the officially 'unapproved' remark and question.

"I am not familiar with that particular book," Strapollos said softly, "but I do know the only way you can keep a society in check is to monitor them. It brings security and order, and that's what is lacking today. There's looting and murder taking place right now, this moment, that would never happen in a closely monitored society."

Now it was Jerry's turn to look directly into the camera and, by projection, into the eyes of the world.

"You may think that way, sir," Jerry intoned, "but personally, it all sounds very scary to me. One world leader; one world government – when I think about that, there is a phrase that comes to my mind, a phrase I am sure you have heard before. *'Absolute power corrupts absolutely.'* Everyone should have someone to answer to. To whom would you answer, Mr. Strapollos, if you were that man? To whom?"

Demetrius Strapollos' chest began to rise and fall in ever quicker motions as he came forward in his chair until he and Jerry were at the edges of the desk that separated them, literally only inches apart.

"I answer to God alone for my actions, Mr. Westfield!" Strapollos exclaimed. "How about you?"

Jerry ignored the question and pressed further, the approved questions totally forgotten.

"You say you answer to God? Then I guess my next question would be, Mr. Strapollos, which god are we talking about?"

Before Strapollos could say a word, Jerry caught the director signaling frantically. Jerry gave an imperceptible nod to the man and addressed the camera.

"You're watching *CNN Live*. Don't go away; we'll be right back."

Immediately, Larry Sangler's voice boomed over the speaker system from the control room.

"Gentlemen, you are doing an absolutely phenomenal job. We are into a 90 second break; the director will cue you at ten seconds."

Jerry could not see beyond the cameras because of the bright lights around the platform. If he had been able to look beyond, he would have seen Rabbi Michael Eissen seated in the front row of empty seats, his eyes dark; his lips moving and curling.

In the meantime, Demetrius Strapollos leaned in to Jerry and, just above a whisper, said, "Playing hard ball are we, Mr. Westfield?"

The words struck Jerry hard, and he sensed his stomach go taut, but far from causing fear as might have been intended, they formed in Jerry a new resolve. He was face to face with an enemy. The gloves, as they say, were off, and he felt his jaw set hard.

He leaned over the desk and answered, "Strike one, Mr. Strapollos."

Wh*o is this, sitting across from me?* Jerry thought. *This is no ordinary politician or world leader with the usual gloriously self-serving plans. This is something else…someone who…who…*

Jerry's eyes closed momentarily, and there, in his mind, stood Jeremy Palmer, Bible in his hand. They were at Jeremy's home, safe and warm, and Jeremy was saying, *"A world leader will rise up out of Europe and become very powerful. He will do whatever he pleases, even to the point of declaring himself equal with God. He will be the Antichrist…He will be the Antichrist…He will be the Antichrist…"*

Why do I think of you now, Jeremy, Jerry pondered. *What are you telling me? Is it Strapollos? Is he the one you kept telling me about? It doesn't matter, because I'll keep going anyhow. The two men I trust most in the world, Jeremy – you and Jacob Klausman – believe this man to be evil. That's enough for me.*

The director yelled out, "Ten seconds!"

Jerry shuffled the cards on his desk, the ones with the approved questions. Now, he had a plan. The director continued the count down.

"Three…two…one!" Again the index finger pointed at Jerry.

"Welcome back. Thank you for joining us tonight as we continue our discussion with Mr. Demetrius Strapollos.

"Mr. Strapollos," Jerry continued, reading from the approved list. "You have been instrumental, to say the least, in the adoption of the UN resolution to create a one-world currency. Could you please elaborate on that for our audience?"

Strapollos visibly relaxed. They were back to rehearsed questions; as long as it stayed that way, it would be all right.

"I would be glad to, Jerry. The economies of every nation have been under extreme stress even before the cataclysmic natural events of the past six or seven months. Therefore, my staff and I put together a concise and all-inclusive plan that will give all people of every nation a secure and convenient way to transact their business, while at the same time placing everyone on a level playing field. No individual, no matter where he lives in the world, will have to worry about a failing or devaluating currency system draining his resources and threatening his family's well being. What he receives for a day's wage will *spend* like a day's wage when his family goes to the store.

"With the Digital Cashless System in place, there will be considerably less identity thefts, resulting in less overall crime. There will simply be no cash to steal. If a person's card is stolen or misplaced, they can call the system anytime from anywhere in the world without cost to them. The system will be available twenty-four hours a day, seven days a week, and within seconds, they can have that lost or stolen card rendered inactive."

"When will this system be in place and ready for use?" Jerry continued.

"Our goal is to have the system in place by the first of the year. It is a large undertaking, and it will require full cooperation from all fronts. The European Community and the Middle East Region will be up and running first."

There followed a pause of about one second. During that amazingly short span, it was as if a shift of some kind had taken place in the fabric of Jerry's mind. All at once, everything seemed amazingly clear. Everything Jeremy Palmer had told him about the 'Antichrist,' all the anger and worry that Jacob had poured out were forming and reforming in his consciousness. The prepared questions before him blurred and seemed insignificant and trivial.

"Mr. Strapollos," Jerry asked, looking directly at his subject. "You just said that with this new system there would be less identity theft. It seems to me, sir, that if we still have credit cards, or 'new smart cards' as you call them, identity theft would still be a very real issue. How do you plan on dealing with that?"

Strapollos moved his head slightly and gradually changed his sitting position to face Jerry straight on.

"There are solutions to every problem Mr. Westfield."

Jerry could feel the mood changing and his pulse increasing, still he continued on.

"That leads me to my next question, Mr. Strapollos. I understand your people are experimenting with a certain means of identification for this cashless society. Are you willing to tell us anything about that tonight?"

"There are always new developments on the horizon," Strapollos answered carefully, leaning back in his chair. This was not an approved question, and it was not something he cared to discuss.

"Technology is constantly changing and challenging us, Jerry," he answered. "We must be ready to embrace the future, whatever it brings our way."

Looking directly into a camera, Jerry said, "I guess that's a 'No,' folks."

Jerry continued, "Come on, Mr. Strapollos, will this work? Can we live as one people, with one currency, with little or no national ties?"

Demetrius Strapollos folded his hands in his lap and began to exude all the charm he could muster. He realized that the 'script' had departed, but he only had minutes to go.

"We were created as one people," he said, "and through the ages we have been scattered into many fragments. It is time for the world to unite and join together to help each other. It is the only way we will survive these stressful times, and the only way that we can hope to prosper. Of course it will take time to get used to, but the advantages will be great. In a sense, we are rebuilding the fabled Tower of Babel."

Jerry put his left elbow on the desk and rested his chin in his hand.

"I am certainly not a Bible scholar," he remarked smoothly, "but I seem to remember that God wasn't exactly one of the chief cheerleaders of the first Tower of Babel. Why should he be in favor of this one?"

Before the answer, whatever it might have been, the director motioned for Jerry to call a break.

Jerry addressed the camera and said, "We will continue this interesting discussion and ask Mr. Strapollos one final question when we come back. Please stay with us."

The director yelled, "We're out for 90 seconds!"

Jerry stood and stretched himself. He didn't want to say anything to Strapollos except on television. Stepping down from the platform and crossing to Ruth, he kissed her tenderly on the cheek.

"You're doing fine," she smiled up at him. "Here, Jacob gave me something earlier that he said to give to you, so here it is."

She hugged him as tightly as she could and whispered, "I love you! The hug was from Jacob for you; the words are strictly mine."

"And, I love you," Jerry said as he hugged back.

He left Ruth and started back to the platform when he was suddenly aware of Rabbi Eissen standing next to him.

"It would be very unwise, Mr. Westfield, to ask a question that would embarrass Mr. Strapollos."

"I'm not looking to embarrass anyone, Rabbi," Jerry said as he brushed by the solid figure in black, "I just want the truth."

Eissen grabbed his arm as he went by and whispered, "The truth just might scare you, Mr. Westfield."

Jerry pulled his arm back and took his place behind the desk.

"Ten seconds!" the director yelled.

This was the home stretch, and Jerry knew it. No prepared script; no approved or disapproved questions. Truth…just truth, scary or not.

The director gave Jerry his cue.

"Welcome back, everyone. Just before the break, Mr. Strapollos and I were discussing the Tower of Babel. I had made the comment that God hadn't approved of the Tower of Babel the first time, and I speculated as to why He should change His mind now? Your comment?"

"I was speaking, Mr. Westfield, in a figurative fashion, in the sense that we are all God's children and, in effect, one people. It is time to put aside our racial and ethnic differences and beat our swords into plowshares as the prophet Isaiah prophesied would happen."

"Mr. Strapollos, would you also beat your swords into plowshares, or would that just be for the rest of us to do?"

Strapollos locked into Jerry's eyes and two seconds passed slowly. Then, Demetrius Strapollos smiled slightly, his eyes turning sad, his countenance falling in one of the best counterfeits of sorrow Jerry had ever seen.

"You…you seem very suspicious of me, Jerry," Strapollos asked, almost with a quiver in his voice. "May I ask you why? What have I done to make you feel this way?"

Although hidden in the shadows, Rabbi Eissen began to smile. This was better. Now Strapollos would turn the tables on Westfield.

Jerry's heart was pounding faster and faster. He knew exactly what Strapollos was doing with this bid for sympathy, but Demetrius Strapollos had no idea of what Jerry had learned on the phone just prior to going on.

Now was the time. Yes, now was the time for the knockout blow.

"Mr. Strapollos," Jerry asked smoothly and evenly and with every ounce of sincerity and control he could dredge up, "did you have anything to do with the assassinations of President Arano of Spain and President Cisco of Portugal?"

Ruth's mouth actually did drop open. Rabbi Eissen almost fell from his seat, and grabbed on to his black hat with both hands. Strapollos coughed once, his eyes darting from Jerry to the desk to the 'approved' questions that would not be used the remainder of this night.

In the control room, the crew was stunned, and Larry Sangler just shook his head and said, "Take notice, guys! That is Jerry Westfield. You know it's coming, you just don't know when!"

Although it seemed an eternity, less than three seconds went by before Strapollos, as much in the throes of iron-willed self-control as anyone had ever seen him, said, "That is quite an accusation, Mr. Westfield, something very close to slander, I believe. You seem to know more about this than I do. At this point, all I know is that their deaths were a terrible, terrible tragedy. Just before we went on the air, I was made aware that the United States has made three arrests in New York City related to the murders. I have not been able to confer with my sources, because, as you know so well, I have been here with you.

"Now, really, Sir, I would like to hear your reason for asking me that scandalous question."

Jerry looked directly at Strapollos, his gaze never wandering.

"My sources tell me that the three men who were arrested today deny even being in those countries at that time. What they do admit, sir, is being hired by President Arano of Spain and President Cisco of Portugal in a plot to assassinate you, Mr. Strapollos…you. They claim you discovered the plot and had them killed instead."

By now, Larry Sangler was all but dancing on the control room walls. Bringing his hand down again and again on the panel, he said to the control room personnel, "He is incredible! He must have connections all over the place to get this kind of information! Wow! I can't believe it; this guy is unbelievable!"

For the first time in the entire interview, several beads of sweat oozed through the makeup and stood out on the forehead of Demetrius Strapollos. He was beginning to show signs of wear.

"I don't have any idea in the world of what you are talking about, Mr. Westfield! Where in the world do you get such information?"

He had to be careful not to call Jerry Westfield a liar, since Westfield obviously would not have started this were he not confident to make such a statement on live television, which meant that the three jailed agents in New York were beginning to talk. Strapollos was furious that he had not known of this in advance.

"As far as my involvement in this matter, I assure you I know nothing about it. If, in fact, there were an assassination attempt aimed at me, I assure you that I will get to the bottom of it. I'm afraid I cannot comment any further on this issue without more information."

Strapollos hand slapped down unexpectedly on the desk top, and even Jerry Westfield blinked.

"I will say, however, that I do not appreciate you accusing me of murder in front of the whole world, Mr. Westfield!"

"Need I remind you that I am not your accuser, sir," Jerry countered. "I am only reporting what has already been stated and giving you the opportunity to respond to your accusers."

The director was again signaling, and Jerry knew they were running out of time. Still, Jerry could not resist one final jab.

"You must admit, sir, that people seem to disappear when you're around."

"Millions of people disappeared last year, Westfield," Strapollos snapped back. "Perhaps you would like to blame me for those, too?"

Now, the director was jabbing wildly in Jerry's direction, and he knew that he must end the show now…right now. He raised his head and looked directly into the camera's lens.

"The Book of Proverbs states, *'When the righteous triumph, there is great elation; but when the wicked rise to power, men go into hiding.'*

"We all must stand the test called time, even men of power like Mr. Demetrius Strapollos. Time will tell us where we are going, as it tells us where we have been.

"I thank Mr. Strapollos as well as CNN for the opportunity to be with you tonight. This is Jerry Westfield talking to the whole world – Good Morning; Good Afternoon; and, Good Night."

* * *

The director yelled, "Cut! We're off the air!"

Strapollos rose slowly from his seat, and his deep, fire-filled eyes looked directly at Jerry.

"You set me up, Westfield ," he said softly. "I won't forget that."
Jerry glared back with a fire of his own.

"You set yourself up, Strapollos. I was just doing my job."

"A job you may not have much longer," Strapollos added.

Rabbi Eissen appeared at Jerry's side and whispered, "I warned you, Mr. Westfield. Do have a pleasant night, and do be careful; so much can happen out there on the streets."

Then the Rabbi turned and followed Strapollos out the door, followed by the two silent bodyguards.

Ken Mailer had not uttered a sound during the entire interview, but now he was literally coming apart. He did not know what to do with himself. He stood in the middle of the almost empty studio, fidgeting – straightening his jacket and fixing his tie over and over again.

He turned quickly and approached Jerry, speaking rapidly as he came.

"I don't think you understand what's going on here, Jerry! You can't just do this kind of thing and get away with it! Do you have any idea at all of whom you are dealing with?"

Jerry placed his hand on Ken's shoulder with an incredibly somber look on his face and said, "I'm afraid I do, Ken, but what worries me most is that you don't."

Abruptly, Ken tore away, ripping his jacket from under Jerry's hand. He turned and, huffing and mumbling, stormed out the studio door.

Ruth came up and placed her arms around Jerry's waist, looked up at him and said exactly the right thing, "Let's get out of here."

Jerry had reached over, picked up his notes and was headed for the door with Ruth when Larry Sangler stopped them.

"Jerry Westfield, that was one of the most incredible interviews I have ever witnessed. How did you know about the three guys implicating Strapollos? It's just hitting our newsroom now."

"That call I received just before we went on the air," Jerry answered, "was from Bob Lewis, my boss at the *Chronicle*. He filled me in with some information he got just that moment, red hot from one of his sources close to the story."

"That was great! I get to do a lot of news shows, but most of it is the same old stuff; no surprises. But this…this was reporting! Thank you for reminding me why I got into this business in the first place. I hope to see you again."

Jerry shook the man's hand, and they exchanged a few more pleasantries, but Ruth still had Jerry by the waist, and she gave a gentle tug at his belt.

Smiling, the two of them walked out of the studio and on to the streets of Tel Aviv..

*   *   *

It was 8:45 PM, and the *Forel* was only a ten-minute walk from the studio. Ruth and Jerry left the car in the parking lot and headed out hand in hand.

It was a beautiful night, with a slight breeze blowing in from the Mediterranean. They strolled the wide sidewalks of Dizengoff Street, watching the stars twinkle at them through the leaves of the trees that lined their way.

"Thank you," Jerry said. "Thank you for being there. It meant a lot to me."

"It did?"

"Sure. I mean, how often does a guy get engaged, interview the Messiah, and get his life threatened all in the same day?"

Ruth looked at him seriously at first, then Jerry gave her one of his crazy faces and they both started laughing, locked in each other's arms, spinning around on the street like two kids in love for the first time, ignoring other couples who stared but couldn't help smiling themselves.

"Come on!" Jerry laughed. "It wasn't that funny!"

Ruth held him close and breathed, "I love you, Jerry Westfield!"

Jerry saw himself reflected in her eyes, and he bent and kissed her – kissed her as if the entire world depended on it.

After a few minutes they began walking again. They passed the Gavish Jewelry Store, with its window filled with imported and hand-made jewels, where Jerry had bought her engagement ring. He told her of how nervous he had been in the store and how this old jeweler had been understanding and helped him.

They turned down Frishman Street and in a moment they were at the door of the restaurant. A waiter brought them to the table where Jacob and Sarah were waiting.

Jacob Klausman said, "Well, you made it. Ten minutes late, but you made it!"

"Oh, Jacob," Sarah scolded, "leave him alone. He's had a bad day."

Ruth and Jerry smiled and sat with their friends.

"Waiter," Jerry proclaimed, only a little regally, "bring us a bottle of your best champagne. Tonight, we are going to celebrate!"

"Very good, Sir," said the waiter as he faded away.

Jacob placed both of his massive hands on the table, leaned forward, and said, "I have to say it and get it over with – you were great tonight. The way you handled him was brilliant!"

"I only did what I had to do," Jerry replied. "I don't think it made me too popular with the pro-Strapollos crew."

Jerry looked around. Some of the people in the restaurant were beginning to recognize him and talk among themselves in excited whispers.

Jacob said, "Don't worry about it. I think you'll be surprised; not everyone is ready to declare him 'King of the World.'"

Sarah turned to Ruth and asked, "So tell me, what was it like being there? It must have been amazing!"

"It was…it was tense, Sarah, very tense," Ruth answered. "In person, 'that man' seems larger than life, and he's very…charismatic; almost mesmerizing. Oh, and this Rabbi Eissen! He is just plain evil! After the interview, he threatened Jerry. I don't even like calling him 'Rabbi;' he's not worthy of the title."

Jacob's gaze snapped to Jerry.

"He threatened you? What did he say?"

"He was just blowing off steam," Jerry laughed. "Forget about it; I have. That's not the first time someone has threatened me about something I said or wrote."

Jerry locked eyes with Jacob. He really had not forgotten about it, nor was he about to, but he didn't want to upset Ruth any more than she already was. Without words, Jacob understood what his friend was doing, and he went along.

"Ah, you're probably right," Jacob half groaned. "I imagine he was beside himself with the way things went. You put a flea up his nose, that's what!"

Sarah saw the waiter coming back to the table with the champagne, and she changed the tone by asking, "So, is everybody hungry?"

"I'm starving," Jerry pronounced. "I haven't eaten a thing since breakfast. What are you going to have, Jacob?"

"Sarah and I love the broiled sea bass here. They cook it just the way we like it."

"Yes," Sarah interrupted, "why don't we start with that famous mixed antipasti!"

The waiter who had finished the amenities of pouring the champagne took down their orders and turned to Ruth.

"And for Madam?"

Looking at the others, Ruth said, "On the way over, Jerry and I were talking about the trout stuffed with garlic and eggplant."

Looking up at the waiter, Ruth smiled, "I hear you're famous for it."

The waiter nodded, "Oh, yes, Madam. I believe you will be very pleased. It is exquisite."

"Good!" Jerry exclaimed. "Then bring us two of your exquisite trout dinners. Jacob, are you certain you and Sarah won't join us?"

Jacob raised one eyebrow in Jerry's direction and said, "I don't think so. No offence, but you have…that. We'll stick to today's house special, the delicious broiled fish."

When the waiter was gone, Jacob raised his glass and said, "I propose a toast. Here's to Ruth and Jerry, may your hearts always be one as they are today. And, may the Lord God be with you always and be your light on the path before you."

They lifted and touched their glasses over the candle in the middle of the table, and they drank together.

Jerry and Ruth kissed.

This day was one they would never forget.

And, although they did not know it at that moment, neither would the days that were very soon to come.

End of Part Three

PART FOUR:
Flames

Place me like a seal over your heart, like a seal on your arm;
for love is as strong as death, its jealousy unyielding as the grave.
It burns like blazing fire, like a mighty flame.

Song of Solomon 8:6

CHAPTER TWENTY

Birth of Horror

IN THE ALMOST FIVE WEEKS THAT HAD PASSED from the eventful night of the interview, both Jerry Westfield and Demetrius Strapollos had been kept very busy. At first, Jerry spent some time wondering about the vague threat implied by Rabbi Eissen, checking to see if there were any strangers about Jacob's house at night, looking over his shoulder as he strolled the streets, eyeing the rear view mirror more than usually as he drove, feeling there was 'someone there' and turning to find an empty room. In time, however, the increased pressures of his column for *The Chronicle*, his growing web-site, and the offers that poured in asking for articles and TV appearances took up so much of his daily routine, that his major worry became finding time to spend with Ruth. He had little time for the ravings of some camp-follower in black, and his concern gradually faded and became relegated to the status of an unpleasant memory to be stored as far back in the mind as possible.

For Demetrius Strapollos, Michael Eissen, and Ken Mailer, it was a month spent much like a troop of frantic masons working on a crumbling wall -- plugging holes and fixing cracks. In actual fact, Jerry Westfield had caused some damage, but not that much – certainly not irretrievable. Those who believed still believed and with glowing, growing strength. Those who were shaken were either persuaded with golden words or just – persuaded. Whatever it took, it had worked. Jerry Westfield had been a momentary bump in an otherwise smooth and flawless road.

In fact, there was only one thing – one item – that steadfastly refused to go away, not under logic or gold or threat, and they were in a Federal Holding Facility in New York City. It was Monday, twenty June, and the three agents arrested for the murders of President Pedro Arano of Spain and President Manuel Cisco of Portugal were awaiting a hearing which was scheduled to begin on Wednesday. While it was possible to forget words spoken during a TV interview or even the burning symbolism of leading a march on to the Temple Mount, it was impossible to ignore the insistence with which the frenzied news media filled the airwaves with the story on a continuing basis.

Even now, from the screen of a large Plasma TV in an opulent mansion in a fashionable suburb of Brussels, an attractive young woman dominated the screen and held forth on the subject.

"...in the world waits to hear the stories of the three men accused of the assassinations of President Arano of Spain and President Cisco of Portugal. Are their accusations true? Was Demetrius Strapollos somehow involved in the deaths of these world leaders? According to our own CNN news pole, the vast majority of people, some 73 percent, believe that Mr. Strapollos had nothing to do with this tragedy, and that the stack of evidence against them clearly indicates that these three agents are the ones responsible for the brutal slayings. Most people questioned also favor the death penalty for these three if they are proven guilty in a court of law.

"We will know more as the week goes on.

"For CNN News, this is Ellen Thompson reporting live from New York."

* * *

He pushed the button on the remote that shut off the TV, which at the same time concealed it with his favorite beautifully framed oil painting. He then slammed the remote control on the desk in his study, cracking its shell and sending component parts scattering. The over-sized black leather desk chair, specially built to accommodate his height and frame, swung around violently.

"What are we doing about this?" Demetrius Strapollos all but screamed. He was furious, beyond fury it seemed, and his eyes flared and burned at his lone companion in the room.

"I don't want them at that hearing on Wednesday, do you understand? And, I don't want them talking to any of those morons from the UN! Some of them are ready to believe anything said against me, and I will not give them a chance to oppose me!"

Strapollos stood and rose to his full height and glowered down at the man who sat in front of him.

"You should have taken care of this in Tel Aviv! None of this would have happened if they weren't alive to get on that plane!"

Rabbi Michael Eissen listened placidly to all the ranting and raving and vocal shrapnel that flew about him. When Strapollos had exhausted his anger, Eissen said, "Will you, then, allow me to take care of it permanently this time."

Demetrius Strapollos sank back into his chair and turned around to his desk, turning his back on Michael Eissen.

"You understand," Strapollos said, his voice calmer now, completely under control, "that we cannot simply have them gunned down for all to see. I don't want a large dirty mess turned into a larger, filthier one before the entire world."

From behind him, Rabbi Eissen's voice came softly, "I have my ways, Demitri, the special ones that only you and I know of. This is the time to use them, and I will not let you down. Consider that this is a short side trip on our path to victory; don't let it take away your breath.

"I'll see you tomorrow, but in the meantime, I'd keep my eye on Mr. Mailer. He's showing signs of instability -- cracking up, as some would say. Too much stress. I believe you can relate to that."

Demetrius Strapollos pushed himself up from his desk and slowly turned around, saying, "Stress! Do you wish me to tell you about stress..."

He stopped abruptly.

The room was empty.

* * *

Luis Alvarro, David Reasor, and Darren Willis were asleep on their individual bunks in three side-by-side cells in a Federal Holding Facility in New York. It was just a few seconds before midnight, and the only light in the cells came from a small light bulb in the hallway ceiling.

Together, earlier in the day, they had decided to tell every detail of the operation to anyone who would listen in a hope of convincing someone of their innocence. If that meant talking to District Attorneys or UN Councils or CIA investigators, then that is what they would do. Enough of the tale had been leaked to the press that there was interest everywhere, but now, somewhere along the path that would follow from their day in court tomorrow, they would tell the entire story and let the world take it from there.

For now, they slept.

At ten seconds to midnight, the three closed circuit TV cameras that kept constant watch on the cells simply ceased working. The guard on the desk with the bank of monitors noticed that the screens had gone blank, and he knew he would have to look into it and possibly phone in a report. It was, however, only five minutes until his next required personal observation of the three prisoners.

He would check on it then.

David Reasor was the first. He felt the chill mist, cold and wet and unfriendly, enter his cell, and he instinctively reached for the blanket at the foot of his bed. An agent trained to sleep lightly, he caught a movement from the corner of one half-opened eye and was immediately sitting at the side of his bunk.

His trained eyes swept the cell, and there was nothing there. Nothing except...

A shadow, darker and deeper than any caused by man-made light, lingered in one corner of the cell, and for a fraction of a second, Reasor had the feeling he had known this shadow before. It hung, rather than rested on the brick and concrete walls, and it had a dimension to it, a depth that beckoned and warned, together and at once.

"Who are you?" Reasor whispered. He had meant to shout, but a whisper was all that he could manage, because he was beginning to gasp for air. It was not as if someone were choking him; he felt no pressure on larynx or throat. Rather, it was as if the air in the room itself were being slowly drawn away. He heard a sound and realized that it was his heart pounding frantically; he was aware of large drops of sweat running down his face. In the cold light from the corridor, his hands were beginning to take on a bluish caste.

Because, in essence, he truly was a brave man, his last conscious act in this world was to throw himself at his attacker. This he did, only to fall through the floating, chilling blackness to end, curled up and lifeless, in the corner of his cell, where the guard would find him five minutes later.

Luis Alvarro was next, followed by Darren Willis. Alvarro was awakened by a foul odor like that of decaying flesh that permeated the air, and Willis came to consciousness with the feeling of something cold and wet creeping on his chest. Like Reasor, both men saw the deep and formless hanging shadow just before the air was withdrawn from their lungs. Like Reasor, both men fought back against the intruder, hurling themselves at the dark presence. Like Reasor, both men lay dead in their cells seconds later. Alvarro was found still clutching to the bars of the cell door, while Willis lay on his back on the floor, his face contorted in fear, the frozen mask of someone who had seen something mere men were never meant to view.

When the shadow finally disappeared, it was four minutes after midnight.

*   *   *

The headlines and lead copy in the morning edition of *The Chronicle* said it all:

ACCUSED ASSASSINS FOUND MYSTERIOUSLY DEAD

Early this morning, guards at the Federal Holding Facility in New York City found Luis Alvarro, David Reasor, and Darren Willis dead in their cells. The three men, accused in the assassination of Presidents Pedro Arano of Spain and Manuel Cisco of Portugal, died of apparent suffocation.

Federal officials, as of this time, have no comment on how such a thing could have happened. According to a Federal Marshall, the cells in the facility are visually checked every half hour. Moreover, surveillance cameras located in the hallways and entranceways show no unauthorized individuals going in or out, but were disabled for a time prior to the three men being found, apparently by some sort of system overload.

A full investigation is presently underway.

*   *   *

Jerry Westfield got his cell phone from his pocket on the second ring.

"Hello," he answered. "Westfield."

"Jerry? This is Bob Lewis. Is everything all right?"

"I'm fine, Bob. Why do you ask?"

"Have you heard the news?"

"About what?"

"They found those three agents dead in their cells this morning."

"What! How...how could that happen?"

"Nobody seems to know. The report is that they suffocated to death."

"Suffocated? Unbelievable! Was it suicide?"

"Our sources at the Medical Examiner's Office say it couldn't have been. Maybe it was someone on the inside? Like I said, no one knows."

Jerry was silent for a few seconds, then he stated softly, "Perhaps Mr. Strapollos could fill us in. I think he managed to get to them."

"There's more," Bob Lewis continued. "You know the driver and the body guard these three guys told about – the ones they were trying to find to corroborate their story?"

"Let me guess. They're dead, too."

"You got it! They found one of the bodies, the guard, after it washed up on the shore in Peniche, about fifty miles north of Lisbon. The driver showed up in the trunk of a car in some old warehouse outside of Madrid. All very neat and very clean!"

Jerry stood and began to rub his forehead as he circled his room.

"Do the authorities have any leads?"

"No!" Bob Lewis said disgustedly. "Not one. No clues; no leads – antiseptic, as they say. Listen, Jerry, I'm worried about you. Between that interview last month and those articles you're writing, I've been getting a lot of heat. Scarcely a day goes by without someone of political or financial position pounding the desk in Mr. Finch's office, pressuring him to shut you down!

"'Now, Mr. Finch is a very powerful man, and he's owned this paper for over thirty years, and so far he's not budging, but he lets me know about it, Jerry, he lets me know.

"Please be careful. This guy, Strapollos, is not going away. Despite everything going on around him, he is still growing in power and influence. He has an approval rating of over seventy percent. Presidents don't have figures like that!"

"Come on, Bob, Strapollos has got bigger fish to fry than me," Jerry laughed, hoping that Bob Lewis would believe that lie, even if he didn't. "I'm just a very little fly in a very big jar of ointment."

"Just the same, I want to make sure your wings aren't pulled off. Jerry, I'd like to bring you back here for a couple of months; wait things out; let it all settle down a bit. Bring Ruth with you, of course. We'll pick up the tab. What about it?"

"Thanks for your concern, Bob, but I don't think so. I mean, Ruth just can't walk in to her boss and tell him she's leaving for two months, and she'll see him later. She's the Assistant Manager. Besides, there's too much going on over here for me to be leaving now, and I think you know that.

"Sorry, Bob. I'm staying right here."

"You always were pigheaded. All right, I'll do what I always do for you, cover your rear end! Promise me you'll be careful."

"Yes, Mommy!" Jerry laughed. "I promise I'll be careful. And, by the way, I don't think it's politically correct to call a Jew 'Pigheaded.'"

"Very funny. Ha, ha – that's me, laughing. Look, I know we haven't asked you to check in every day like we used to, but…well, I want you to start checking in every other day, OK?"

"Yes. Yes, I can live with that. Thanks for calling, Bob, and thanks for worrying. I'll talk to you in two days. 'Bye."

Jerry Westfield placed his cell phone back into his jacket pocket and leaned back in the desk chair in his room in Jacob and Sarah Klausman's home and thought about what Bob Lewis had just told him. He could still hear Rabbi Eissen's oily voice saying, "I warned you, Mr. Westfield…"

It was different now. He had been shot at before in certain hot spots around the world as well as during the LA riots; and threatened on various other occasions as well. But, that had always been just him. Now, he had to think about Jacob and Sarah and the kids, and, of course, Ruth. The thought had crossed his mind of moving out, but when he had broached the subject to his friend, Jacob, as he expected, would not hear of it.

He made up his mind that if things got any worse, he *would* get his own place. For now, however, he would just follow Bob Lewis' advice.

He would be…careful.

*　*　*

One of the many benefits of living in the Klausman home was the privacy Jacob and Sarah afforded their guest. Therefore, when the door to Jerry's room swung open without a knock and Jacob Klausman stood framed in the opening, Jerry knew whatever message Jacob carried was not good.

"Turn on the news, quick," Jacob snapped.

Jerry reached over and turned on the small TV set he had purchased for his room.

"Jacob," Jerry said, "I know about what happened to the three agents in New York. So, if this is about…"

"That's not it," Jacob interrupted. "You have to see it for yourself."

The screen came to life. They picked up a newscast in midstream, since Jerry kept the set permanently tuned to CNN, and it was not difficult to soon grasp the full horror of what they were seeing and hearing.

A young woman dressed in jeans and a bulky top, obviously not prepared to go on world TV, stood on some balcony holding a microphone, her hair whipping wildly in the wind. Behind her was a roof-top view of a city. There was movement in the streets below, you could tell, but it was all but impossible to make out exactly what was taking place.

"…stands in shock today," she was saying, "as reports come in from surrounding areas. The size of the device is not yet known. All we know for certain at this point is that a thermonuclear device – what most of us would call an A-Bomb or H-Bomb – has exploded in Delhi, India.

"I have some statistics here. Delhi has a population of…"

Several streaks of static crossed the screen, and the picture changed to a studio set with Cathy Wells, well-known anchorwoman of CNN seated behind a desk.

"Karen," Wells said, "sorry for interrupting, but we are now getting reports from Russian and US authorities, telling us that it was a ground level detonation. According to one US official at NORAD, initial yield estimates remain at fifty kilotons, which, they say, could level an area a half mile in diameter, with more damage down wind.

"We are speaking with CNN's Karen Hallahi, our correspondent in India who is currently on assignment in Delhi. Fortunately, Karen was several miles upwind of the area of the blast.

"Karen, this is Cathy Wells, can you hear me?"

"Yes…yes, Cathy, I can hear you! Go ahead"

"Karen, you were about to tell us some population figures?"

"Yes, Cathy, I have those stats. Delhi has a population of over five million, and if you include the surrounding metropolitan area including the suburbs, the number reaches nearly eight million. The amount of people killed and injured certainly will not be known for some time, perhaps weeks, but there is certainly the obvious potential for hundreds of thousands of casualties.

"You mentioned the wind, Cathy? The wind is now blowing from the southwest towards the northeast. I don't know if we can pick it up, but I can see the infamous 'mushroom-shaped cloud' moving away from us – from where I am. People are being told to move upwind, towards New Delhi and south."

"Karen," Cathy Wells interrupted, "you say the wind is blowing towards the northeast? That would take it across the border and into…let's see…China. Is that correct?"

"Yes, it is, Cathy. At this time, I can hear emergency vehicles roaring to the scene. As you can imagine, fires are burning out of control all around the blast site. I have with me now, one of the fire fighters on the way to the scene.

"Sir, thank you for giving us a moment here. What have you been told at this point?"

The man whose face now filed the screen was obviously uncomfortable. When he spoke in heavily accented syllables, his uneasiness was apparent.

"We...we have been...told...to enter the area with...caution, and to stay...upwind. If the wind...if it shifts...we are to get out...leave...as soon as possible...because of the...you know...radiation..."

"How about damage? Have you heard anything about how much damage there is?"

"Madam...I am sorry...I have to go now. I have...to leave..." the man said, and he was gone from the screen. The camera turned back to Karen Hallahi.

"As you can see, everyone is getting ready to move in, but with extreme caution.

"I must say, I can hardly believe it myself, standing here looking at clouds of smoke billowing up into the sky, all overshadowed by a very large, mushroom-shaped cloud, which you may or may not be able to see, breaking up and slowly moving away from us."

"Karen, for those who may have just joined us, would you tell us again what it felt like when the bomb went off. From your position, I mean, which was about ten miles away."

"It was a horrific explosion, Cathy, that seemed to continue and continue for at least five minutes. It was unlike any explosion that I, or any one of us here, have ever experienced. You could feel the air moving around you, first one way and then another. When we looked outside and saw the mushroom, the fear was overwhelming. As I watched that huge cloud climb upward, my legs just froze in place. I had read so much about the bomb and its effects, but to actually see it was...terrifying!"

"Karen, we're going to break away for a while to cover some other stories emerging from this tragedy. We'll be back to you as soon as we can."

The picture switched back to the studio set and Cathy Wells.

"Reaction from the government of India can only be described as outrage. Members of a militant group known as "The Judgement," currently based in Pakistan, have taken credit for the bomb. The Pakistani government denies any knowledge of the group, and world leaders are currently pleading with India not to retaliate with nuclear weapons. India and Pakistan developed nuclear capabilities in the mid-Nineties and have seriously threatened each other on several occasions. This unthinkable deed, however, could bring devastation not only to India and Pakistan, but to the entire world.

"We'll be back with some questions for our resident experts right after we look at these reactions from citizens throughout the world..."

Jerry Westfield stood to his feet and began rubbing his forehead in tight, hard circles.

"Some fools actually did it!" he exclaimed to Jacob. "Oh, those poor people!"

"The real horror will be with the survivors," Jacob said, his eyes staring straight ahead. "The burn victims are the worst. I don't envy those rescue workers. I remember going into a building that had been fire-bombed, and there was this burned child...and...and... Jerry, what they are about to see, they will see in their nightmares the rest of their lives.

"What's worse, Jerry, is that I think this is just the beginning. The demon is out of the bag now."

Looking puzzled, Jerry asked, "What is that supposed to mean?"

"It's an old phrase we used among ourselves in Special Forces. It was a common belief that once somebody used the bomb, used it against people for the first time; once 'the demon' was out of the bag, others would soon follow."

"Oh, Jacob," Jerry said, staring into his friend's eyes, "I hope you're wrong. I would hate to think that we were in for more days like this one."

Jacob Klausman took a deep breath and said, "Believe me, Jerry, I want to be wrong! With all my heart, I want to be wrong! It's just that...I sense the darkness growing, day by day."

Jacob placed a hand on his friend's shoulder and quietly, confidently stated, "I know the Lord God has a plan. We just need to trust Him."

"I'm beginning to believe He's the only one we can trust," Jerry said.

Jacob mustered up a slight smile and said, "Coming from you, my friend, that's progress."

They turned their attention back to the newscast.

*   *   *

"Repeating the top story – A militant group, based in Pakistan, calling themselves "The Judgement," has detonated a nuclear device in Delhi, India. The blast is estimated by authorities at NORAD to be in the fifty kiloton range. The exact number of casualties is not known.

"We are fortunate to have with us, US Army Major (Retired) Thomas Greene. Major, you worked with NORAD for the last ten years of your career. How do you go about measuring this type of explosion?"

"Well, Cathy, first you must understand that these are only estimates based on satellite imagery. The initial blast creates a huge amount of heat, you see, and by measuring this output of heat and the residual heat emissions, we get a general idea of the size of the device."

"Major, do you believe the Pakistani Government when they say they knew nothing about what happened?"

The Major sighed and looked into the camera.

"At this point, you have to go with the story they are giving. There has been no follow up, that is, no troops rushing over the border, so it doesn't appear to be an attack of any kind. And, as to where the bomb came from, well, let's remember that there are a tremendous amount of Russian nuclear weapons unaccounted for, and many of them have been traced to that region of the world."

"Major, this is a question I hate to ask, but I feel I must. Could this happen again, somewhere else in the world?"

"Let me give you a blunt answer. Of course it could. The United States and other countries have been tracking the movement of nuclear weapons out of Russia for some years now, ever since the break up of the Soviet Union. A number of convoys have been stopped and materials confiscated on their way to countries like Iran and Iraq. However, there is no way of knowing how many devices there were, and how many are now missing. The Russians themselves have lost track of their own inventories. When certain weapons made their way into the black market, that created another source for those with money to obtain weapons of mass destruction.

"I'm afraid what we have here is a product of fifty years of the cold war."

"That doesn't sound too hopeful for the human race, Major."

"Situations change – history teaches us that. I believe that things have a way of working out in the long run. People have the power within themselves to initiate change. I think we can re-write our destinies; we just have to put our minds and hearts to it."

"Major Greene, thank you for being here with us, and let's hope you are right. Let's hope that people from all over the world will learn from today's terrible disaster, so it will never be repeated.

"We'll be right back with more reports live from Delhi, India, and comments from European Community President Demetrius Strapollos. Please stay tuned."

* * *

Jacob Klausman folded his hands behind his head and looked up at the ceiling.

"You know," he said, "if I were a betting man, I'd wager Strapollos says he is coming to India. And, I wouldn't be surprised if he involves himself in some type of negotiations between India and Pakistan. Wouldn't that be a pretty feather in his cap, especially with all the bad publicity he's gotten over the past month? He needed a good crisis to solve right about now, and – guess what? -- he got it."

Jacob looked over at Jerry and added, "Kind of makes you wonder, doesn't it?"

Jerry's eyes went wide.

"Jacob, you can't think…No, I can't believe…I can't conceive of anyone being that evil, even Strapollos. Besides, as much as we might want to, we can't blame him for everything bad that happens!"

Jacob stared at Jerry with dark, piercing eyes.

Jerry added, "You don't really think that…do you?"

"You know something of my connections," Jacob answered, his gaze softening a little. "I found out a bit of information that I think you will find very interesting. I'll tell you after this next news segment."

Jerry shook his head and commented, "So, you're going to leave me hanging?"

Jacob merely motioned to the screen.

*　　*　　*

"Welcome back to CNN's coverage of the nuclear explosion in Delhi, India. We go live, now, to our correspondent, Karen Hallahi, who is now air born over the city of Delhi. Karen, are you there?"

Through the static, the picture emerged of Karen Hallahi, now wearing a flight helmet and securely strapped into a seat. The picture was filled with static and none too steady.

"Yes, Cathy, I'm here. My cameraman and I were able to board a military helicopter. Apparently they need to send live pictures showing the damage to experts in the US and elsewhere who will soon be on their way to the scene. I guess we were at the right place at the right time. At the moment, they are scanning the area for survivors. The pilot is being very careful to stay upwind of the area to avoid any contact with fallout."

The camera swung from Karen's face to peer over the side of the open portal of the helicopter.

"The area that you can see below us used to be a large, five story building complex. As you can see, there is nothing left to indicate that now. The area all around ground zero is glowing hot. We have to be very careful not to be directly over that area, because the heat is tremendous and the air is extremely unsettled."

"Karen, this is Cathy Wells. You mentioned fallout. We have not yet been able to get an expert with us to discuss the fallout. Have you been able to learn anything on your own so far?"

"I'm certainly not an expert, Cathy, but I have been able to speak with some of the military personnel, and they tell me that fallout is radioactive particles that attach themselves to dust and other fragments. Fallout can be either air born or the residue of an explosion on the surface.

"Now, from what I've been told, nearly all of the fallout from this explosion has drifted northeast. The prevailing winds are from the southwest at about fifteen miles per hour. If the wind direction does not change, it will carry the cloud over the Great Himalayan mountain range that is approximately one hundred miles from here, and into China – fortunately, over a sparsely populated area of China."

"Karen, can you see how big the area of destruction is?"

There was a pause as viewers saw Karen Hallahi confer with the pilot and then turn to the camera.

"It's hard to say right now, because we can't fly over all of it. According to our pilot, and this is only a guess, it appears to be about three-quarters of a mile or so in diameter."

"Are there any signs of survivors?"

"No...no, not yet. We are adjusting our position now to show you some large fires to the north. Buildings are..."

All at once the camera and the helicopter were shaken. On the TV screen, the pictured jumped, but it still showed Karen being thrown violently against her restraints, her helmeted head smashing into the bulkhead behind her. There was a roaring, deafening sound, and black smoke began to pour into the cabin through the wide, open portal. The pictured rocked and blinked and finally blackened like the smoke.

"Karen! Karen! This is Cathy Wells, back at the studio. Karen, what's happened? Karen!"

The picture on the feed from the helicopter sputtered back to flickering life. An obviously shaken Karen Hallahi, her face smudged with the ashen residue, faced into the camera, her eyes wide.

"An explosion! Explosion from down there. Maybe a gas line, or one of the buildings. We're heading back to the base!"

"Well, Karen, you certainly had us worried. Thank goodness you're all right."

"Cathy, the smoke! The smoke from that place! It's all over us! I hope we haven't been contaminated!"

The picture and the transition cut off sharply, and the studio set appeared once more, showing Cathy Wells seated at the desk, wearing earphones.

She hesitated only a second.

"As you can see, it is just an awful, awful situation at this time. Our thoughts and prayers go with you Karen and all those who are now dealing with a...a... monumental disaster. Hopefully we will be able to get back in touch with Karen again later on.

"Right now, we have with us, from our studios in Brussels, the President of the European Community, and a rising star in the world political arena, Mr. Demetrius Strapollos.

"Mr. Strapollos, thank you for being with us on such short notice."

"Not at all, Cathy," Strapollos answered with just the right mixture of concern and affability. "I am just as horrified at this terrible incident as, I am certain, is the rest of the world."

"Mr. Strapollos. What do you think can be done to stop this kind of terrorism?"

"Well, Cathy, as you know, I am for a controlled society, where all weapons such as this would be sought out and destroyed. There is no need for these weapons in a controlled and peaceful society such as I would like to create."

"Mr. Strapollos, are you planning on going to India?"

"Yes, I am. As soon as my people tell me it is safe to do so, I will examine the site and talk with the people. We want to help in any way we can. Perhaps I will be able to talk to both India and Pakistan, who knows? The European Community has already contacted the government of India, and we will be sending our nuclear experts as well as much needed medical supplies and personnel."

"Thank you, Mr. Strapollos, for your time and efforts.

"This is Cathy Wells for CNN..."

*   *   *

"Listen to him!" Jerry exploded as he snapped off the set, "Thousands of people are dead, and all he can do is campaign! A controlled society, all right; controlled and dominated by him!"

212

Jacob glanced at Jerry and asked, "I trust you heard the part about him going to India and maybe having a friendly little talk with both nations?"

"Incredible!" Jerry sighed. He walked to the window and stood looking out over the Mediterranean.

"OK, Jacob," Jerry said, "so tell me the really interesting news *you* have."

Jacob Klausman sat back as far as he could, and this time he folded his hands over his stomach.

"As you know," Jacob began, "I maintain some contacts in military intelligence, and I did a little investigating on our friend, Strapollos.

"His father was not a Rabbi, but he was studying to be a Rabbi when he fell in love with a woman from Athens and eventually married her. She was not a Jew, and she did not want to become one. So, although he kept his faith, he was ostracized by the Jewish community there. Although it may sound romantic, that ostracism broke his heart, and he died, according to many, well before his time.

"After his father's death, his mother raised little Demetrius with a great measure of bitterness towards the Jewish people. In his early years, he would often boast that he would get back at 'those rotten people' for what they did to his father."

"Come on, Jacob," Jerry stated, "Do you really think that all this is an elaborate – and I'd have to say, a 'very elaborate' – setup to crush Israel and its people?"

Jacob turned to face Jerry, and his eyes were fixed and solemn.

"No," Jacob answered, "but I do believe it is a part of it. Some of Strapollos' father's old friends who had deserted him began dying off very soon after he began coming into his own in Greece. Strange accidents took place along with fatal heart attacks in healthy men.

"My point is this: What have we seen so far, what with the assassinations and murders, that is new for this man? Don't call him anti-Semitic, Jerry; he doesn't just hate Jews; he hates everybody!

"Now, are you ready for this? According to my sources in Military Intelligence, Strapollos is in the process of creating his own 'Special Forces' group; highly trained men whom he will probably use to enforce all his 'new ideas' if and when he finally gets the chance!"

"What can we do, Jacob?" Jerry asked. "Do you want me to start exposing these things to the public?"

"You know what would happen if you did that," Jacob responded. "Nothing would happen -- nothing, except that you would most likely lose your job and your life, probably in that order."

Jacob leaned closer to his friend and placed a hand on Jerry's shoulder.

"Jerry, I know you don't want to hear this, but we need to pray. Nothing else is going to stop this man, not all the articles you could ever write. It is up to the Lord God to show us what to do."

Jerry did not respond to Jacob, but inside he felt a stirring he barely recognized. He had to say something before that feeling grew. He turned to his friend.

"You know," Jerry stated, and was amazed that there was a tremor in his voice. "I know it sounds terribly selfish, but I finally find someone I want to spend the rest of my life with, and all hell breaks loose."

"Jerry," Jacob said, "you have money, and your boss, that Bob Lewis fellow, he would help you as well. You and Ruth could just run away to some island or some other safe place and live the rest of your life there."

There was a slight pause before a thin smile drew itself on Jerry's face.

"What?" Jerry exclaimed. "And give up show business?"

Jacob stared at Jerry for the briefest second, then threw back his head and roared. Jerry joined him, and the two friends fell into each other's arms.

Even in the midst of horror, Jerry always knew how to get a laugh out of Jacob.

It was a sort but needed emotional release, as many have said, there is a fine line between laughter and tears.

CHAPTER TWENTY-ONE

Contact

ALTHOUGH IN THE FEARS OF MANY IT WAS EXPECTED that the nuclear blast in India would be but the prelude to other such cataclysmic devastation around the world, time crawled onward and nothing happened. Demetrius Strapollos went to India and, in a move broadcast throughout the world by every news agency, was single-handedly responsible for bringing India and Pakistan to the bargaining table and emerging with a signed peace treaty. Some claimed he had used what amounted to political blackmail and even threats drawn directly from his own power, but most cared little how it was done. For most, it was enough that the feared era of nuclear destruction had been averted, thanks to one man and one man only – Demetrius Strapollos.

The summer in the Mid-East came and went without conflict or even threat of confrontation. The construction of the Temple began and was now well underway, with the voices of the Arab nations protesting virtually at the laying of every stone. Demetrius Strapollos made regular trips to Iraq, Iran, Egypt, and Syria, managing peace here and there by appointing members from each of these governments to his new extended Parliament and making promises of open commerce and prosperity for all.

With all this going on in the world, and the positive excitement it engendered, the story of three United Nations agents found dead in their cells at a Federal Holding Facility in New York was soon relegated to the back pages of every newspaper. Finally, and not very long after, it did not appear at all, and no one seemed to notice or – for that matter -- even care.

At the same time, Jerry Westfield was kept more than merely busy chasing stories throughout the region. At times, his room in the Klausman home would go unused for days, and there even were periods, short though they were, when Ruth Cowen did not receive a daily phone call and slept fitfully through an anguished night wondering and praying for the man she had grown to love.

Chief among the reasons for Jerry's absence was his follow-up on Strapollos' new fascination with the reconstruction of the ancient city of Babylon. Indeed, Jerry became increasingly aware that Demetrius Strapollos and Rabbi Michael Eissen now spent considerable time in Babylon, assisting financially and politically with the rebuilding process there. Strapollos had, it seems, successfully convinced the Arab leaders that a beautiful and spectacular City of Babylon could once again become the capital of the entire region, bringing great trade and wealth – needless to say -- to all.

Now, it was mid-October. Jerry Westfield had poured forth article after article in which he tried to point out some of the behind-the-scenes machinations of Strapollos' political machine. Similarly, he had called to question the rebuilding of the Temple at the same time as the rebuilding of Babylon, where the children of Israel had spent such bitter captivity. All of this -- he had pointed out – all under the auspices of the same man... Demetrius Strapollos.

Although Jerry knew there were many who were far from supporters of the new "Messiah," there were far more who placed their trust in him, implicitly.

The India-Pakistan Peace Treaty; the rebuilding of Babylon as a uniting factor with the Arab nations; the construction of the soon-to-be-finished Temple in Israel – these alone seemed to be more than enough. People throughout the world marveled at the political prowess of a single man. People throughout the world looked upon him as a great man of peace. People throughout the world heaped honor upon honor on Mr. Demetrius Strapollos.

* * *

It had been almost a full year since "The Great Disappearance," as most people called it still; that moment when more than an estimated 600 million people, perhaps more, had vanished from the face of the earth, none of whom ever returned. It had proven to be a legal as well as an emotional nightmare. Now, settlements and the legal confusion concerning properties and monies left behind by those who had..."gone..." were finally being resolved; at last coming to an end. For the majority of families, there was, at last, a feeling of closure to a bizarre, painful and unresolved incident in their lives. Relatives were able at last to assume properties, belongings, and monies that had been hanging in some transcendent lawyer's limbo for nearly a year.

No real answer to the disappearance had ever been found or even propounded. The most common explanation, as outlandish and imaginative as it was, claimed that the disappearance was the prelude to an alien invasion. Sometime in the future, when the aliens invaded for good and all, all the people who were taken would return enlightened and ready to lead the world into a new age, where men and women would live forever in peace and an aura of cosmic tranquility.

There was a second explanation, but it was highly berated and widely rejected. This group claimed a more ominous reason for the disappearance. This "sect," as the media called them, believed that something supernatural took place; something they referred to as "The Rapture." Derived from a Latin word meaning to be caught up or plucked up by force. In their scenario, all those who were faithful followers of Jesus Christ were taken up to heaven and would return with Jesus at the end of seven years to reclaim the earth. In those seven years, however, they prophesized that great hardship and devastation would take place all over the world. This would culminate in a gigantic battle between Satan and God – a battle commonly known as...Armageddon!

This idea had, of course, been widely ridiculed and rejected by the mainstream media and by most people in general. Those who proclaimed such a belief became the target of mockery and satire, later followed by rocks, random gunshots, and, when found, a bombing of their meeting place. It was pointed out again and again that these people were those "born-agains," those Bible-quoting religious fanatics who, for the most part, were hopelessly and totally insane. Much like, as one columnist had ruefully observed, those who had disappeared just last year. But they were not alone in there belief, many Arab people had long believed in a final Judgment day, in which God would return to earth and separate those who were evil from those who were good. Yet the thought of Strapollos's world of great prosperity and peace had most people totally and completely enthralled.

* * *

In New York City, a small package was delivered to *The Chronicle, Attention Jerry Westfield.* Bill Foley signed for it and swiftly brought it to the office of the Managing Editor -- Bob Lewis.

"Excuse me, Mr. Lewis. This package came for Jerry Westfield. What should I do with it?"

"Is it ticking?" Bob Lewis asked with a half-smile as he looked up from his desk.

"No, sir...well, at least not yet," Bill answered, shaking the package slightly with a smile of his own.

"Then open it up."

"You want me to open it? You know, Mr. Lewis, Jerry might not like that too much. You know how he is about things like that. Once at his apartment, I opened a Reader's Digest contest envelope, if you can believe it, and he was all over me."

Bob Lewis put down his pen and starred at Bill Foley.

"Give me the package, Mr. Foley," he said firmly.

Bill handed him the package and waited while Bob Lewis looked it over.

"It's addressed to *The Chronicle*," Lewis said. "It might contain some urgent information, you know. In that case, Jerry would want to know what it was, and he'd want to know about it right away."

Bill Foley stood before Bob Lewis' desk and studied the ceiling with his eyes, trying unsuccessfully to suppress a small giggle.

"What's that, Mr. Foley?" Bob Lewis said with mock concern. "You think we should open this? We should open it for Jerry's protection? Why, yes, Mr. Foley, I quite agree with you!"

Lewis' large hands tore into the wrapping, and in short order the contents were exposed on his desk.

"Well, look at it," Lewis said to Bill Foley. "It's a video tape and a letter in an unsealed envelope. Mr. Foley, since it *is* unsealed, the sender certainly must have wanted us to read it..."

Not waiting for a reply, Bob Lewis removed the single sheet of neat, handwritten words, settled himself in his desk chair, and read the page aloud to himself and to Bill Foley.

Dear Mr. Westfield,

I am Kerri Palmer, Jeremy's sister. We met once at Jeremy and Kathy's place. It has taken us some time, but we were finally able to take ownership of the house and property. Thank you for your concern about Jeremy and Kathy's home. Although it had been broken into, it was not destroyed as so many others were in those first several weeks of looting after the disappearance. That's thanks to you.

While going through some of Jeremy's personal things, I found this tape that had your name on it, and I know that you and Jeremy were good friends, so I though you should have it. He gave me a tape, too, the same day that they vanished. I think he meant to give the enclosed tape to you at that time and on that same day, but he just never had the opportunity.

Mr. Westfield, I looked at my tape.

It has changed my life.

I only wish I had listened to Jeremy before all this. I hope it will affect you as it has affected me.

May God help us and strengthen us, Mr. Westfield, for all the dark days that lie ahead.

Thank you again.

Sincerely,

Kerri Palmer

"Come on," Bob Lewis said without hesitation when he had finished reading, "let's go to the video room and take a look."

"Do you think we should?" Bill Foley asked, hoping fiercely that they really would.

"I have a feeling this may have something to do with 'The Great Disappearance.' We need to see it."

"Hey, you're the boss!"

Bob Lewis raised his eyes to the ceiling and headed for the video room with Bill Foley close behind. As they walked down the corridor, Lewis thought, *I'm kidding myself. I've got to keep smiling; keeping it light, but I know what happened. I know – I just hope that maybe – just maybe -- I'm wrong.*

When the door closed behind them, Bob Lewis did something he would not do under ordinary circumstances. He turned and locked the door before putting the tape into the machine and pressing *PLAY*. Lewis and Foley sat down and watched the scramble of static from the lead-in tape. In a few seconds, however, a picture resolved itself on to the screen of the monitor.

Seated at a surface too cluttered and personalized to be anything else than a private desk in someone's home, sat a good looking man, clean shaven, with brown hair and eyes, who looked to be in his mid to late forties.

Bill Foley exploded out of his seat.

"That's Jeremy Palmer! Jerry's friend; one of the ones who disappeared. Jerry used to…"

"Will you shut up and sit down!" Bob Lewis barked. "I know who it is; I think I met him once, but I cannot, Mr. Foley – I cannot hear anything with your mouth going in high gear!"

Bill Foley, properly chastised, sat immediately.

With rapt faces, they both watched and listened.

* * *

Hi, Jerry! *(The figure on the screen began.)* How are you doing? I hope and pray that you never have to listen to this tape, but you're pretty hard-headed, so I figured I'd better make this for you. Actually, I planned on making something like this for a long time, my friend, but it always felt kind of – you know – stupid doing it. Then yesterday, Jerry, yesterday I felt this real…I don't know…urgency in my spirit, so I'm doing it, and I'm going to give it to you tonight or tomorrow, whenever I see you next.

If you followed my instructions, then the very fact that you are watching this means that you are probably in shock, wondering what happened to me and Kathy and the rest of us. Well, my dear, dear friend, I'm about to tell you.

Its happened, Jerry! Jesus has taken us home! And, oh, Jerry, how I wish you were here…

Excuse me, Jerry…I'm sorry…I promised myself I'd stay calm…

You'll need a Bible to follow all that I am about to tell you, Jerry. Believe me, it's not my intention to give you a long Bible teaching, but only to tell you some of the things that will now take place. I think you'll have to listen to this tape a few times to get it all. For now, just listen to what I have to say; then you can look it up in the references I'm going to give you, OK? Maybe you can use my Bible if you can find it.

Jerry, ancient prophecies have declared that there is a time of trouble coming upon the earth like no one has ever seen or will ever see again.

Look in the Book of Revelation, Chapter Six. It talks about Four Horsemen. I won't take the time to tell you how I know, but they are symbolic. The White Horse and rider is the Antichrist. He is the first to appear. Then, the Red Horse comes, and he represents war. Violence will increase a hundred fold, because, as the Scripture says, God will take peace from the earth.

This, Jerry, will be followed by more wars which will lead to the Black Horse, which is famine and pestilence, representing all types of diseases nurtured by wars. There will be great and violent changes in the weather with frequent and devastating earthquakes all over the world. Read Matthew, Chapter Twenty-four, Jerry – read all of it.

The final one is the Pale Horse, representing Death. Men will kill each other in a frenzy, for hate will grow and greed will prevail. Disease and hunger will kill many, because of the tremendous devastation and lack of food caused by wars and these natural disasters.

All this will happen, Jerry, but the most important part of all is this man on the White Horse. He will appear on the scene first. Think, Jerry; you've heard me talk about this before, but I don't know if you really ever listened. If not, please listen now, because it just might save your life.

Now, look in the Book of Daniel, in Chapter Seven. The angel is telling Daniel about the nations that will rule. In verses twenty-four through twenty-seven, he is telling Daniel about the last kingdom to rule the earth.

This is what the prophet says: *The ten horns are ten kings who will come from this kingdom. After them another king will arise, different from the earlier ones; he will subdue three kings. He will speak against the Most High and oppress His saints and try to change the set times and the laws. The saints will be turned over to him for a time, times and half a time. But the court will sit, and his power will be taken away and completely destroyed forever. Then the sovereignty, power, and greatness of the kingdoms under the whole heaven will be handed over to the saints, the people of the Most High. His kingdom will be an everlasting kingdom, and all rulers will worship and obey Him.*

OK, Jerry, this is what it means. The 'ten kings' are representative of the leaders in the European Community. For out of that kingdom will come a man who will either invade and conquer three of the nations, or he will assassinate their leaders, it is not completely clear. Once he is in full control, he will declare himself God and say terrible things about the God of gods. He will be successful and rule the world through great promises of peace that will only lead to more devastating wars and destruction- this will continue for three and a half years. Then, the Lord God Almighty will come back and establish His kingdom on earth.

That's the good news, Jerry; we will be back! Until then, my friend, you must listen to all of this tape and do what I tell you.

You must!

* * *

It was Bob Lewis who had taken up the remote and paused the video. He sat in the darkened room, staring at the image of the personable Jeremy Palmer, frozen on the monitor.

"What do you think about this?" Bill Foley asked.

"My grandmother…" Bob Lewis said slowly. "My grandmother used to…tell me…all about this stuff…years ago…my grandmother…"

But Bob Lewis was not speaking to Bill Foley. In his mind, he was back in his dream, the dream of his grandmother sitting in her large, overstuffed living room chair, stroking his hair as he sat in complete happiness at her feet – the feet of his dead grandma, his beloved grandma who had come all that way just to tell him something.

There was a presence just outside the door, and it was trying to get in, and his grandmother was saying, *"Trust in God, you hear? Trust in God, and never believe…that one!"*

That one? The Antichrist? The one on the White Horse?

Trust in God, you hear? Never believe…never believe…THAT ONE!!!"

Which one, Grandma? Tell me, please!

"Boss? Boss? Are you all right?" Bill Foley said as he shook Bob Lewis' arm, his face filled with concern.

Instantly, Lewis was himself again, his images of Grandma fading rapidly. He sat bolt upright in his chair.

"Of course, I'm all right, Foley," he said, his voice filled with power once more. "Just…just listen closely, and you might learn something!"

He aimed the remote at the monitor and pushed the *PLAY* button.

* * *

The video continued:

In Daniel, Chapter Nine, verse twenty-seven, it reads, *He will confirm a covenant with many for one 'seven.' In the middle of the 'seven,' he will put an end to the sacrifice and offering. And on a wing of the temple he will set up an abomination that causes desolation, until the end that is decreed is poured out on him.*

I believe that means he will sign a treaty of some sort with Israel for seven years. In the middle of the seven years, he will stop the people from making sacrifices in the Temple and worshiping God, and he will build an image of himself and compel the people to worship the image instead of God, until the Lord comes and defeats him.

Please, Jerry, read Chapter Thirteen in the Book of Revelation, and you'll see a great deal more.

Remember, Jerry, it's not a cliché. I know how you hate clichés, but if it's overused, it is simply because it's so true -- Jesus does love you. Please talk to Him as you would talk to anyone else – to Kathy or me. Confess your sins to Him, Jerry, and He will forgive you. He, and

He alone, is your Messiah; accept no one else, no matter what that person says or does. Trust Him with all your heart. Then, no matter what happens – whether you make it to the end or...or die trying – we will be together. We will be together with Him forever.

Jerry...of all the things I could tell you, I cannot stress enough the importance of accepting Jesus as your Savior and Lord. That's the most important thing of all. No matter what else I tell you, it just won't help without that. I tried to tell you last Monday night, while we were watching football, but I guess I wasn't convincing enough or you weren't too receptive. But I'll keep trying, Jerry, because I can't do it for you. Each person has to make his or her own decision – I'm very aware of that – but Kathy and I believe our prayers will be answered, even if you have to go through this terrible time that I feel is so close.

Jerry...it's...it's difficult for me...you know...to even say...this next part...

My friend, I hope and pray that you will be able to make it through this period of time...alive. Many will die refusing to follow and worship this man and his image. He will force everyone, common people as well as high officials, to wear a mark on the forehead or on the hand, and without that mark, you won't be able to buy or sell anything. I don't know what that will be, exactly, but it will probably be connected to that "Cashless Society" thing we keep hearing about and that you were telling me that friend of yours from college is working on.

Please be careful, Jerry, because anyone who takes this mark and worships the Antichrist and his system ... Well, he or she will be rejected by God and will suffer His wrath.

Jerry, please...you must remain strong.

If you must go through this, I pray that God provides you with a special friend to help you, someone strong and who becomes grounded in faith on whom you can rely. I have tried to be that friend to you, Jerry, but ...now you will need someone else.

Whatever you do, do not give in. It is not hopeless; not for those who will trust the Lord. When the seven year agreement runs out, so will his kingdom. Then Jesus Himself will come back with all His people and defeat the Antichrist and his armies at the battle everyone refers to as...Armageddon.

How I look forward to seeing you then, my friend.

Please, Jerry, trust Him. He said, *"I will never leave you or forsake you."* And again, He said, *"I will be with you even to the end of the age."*

God bless you, Jerry.

Kathy and I…we're praying for you

We're praying for you, and…

We love you…

I feel kind of foolish saying this now, but if in fact you're viewing this tape then I guess it's appropriate. Goodbye, my friend…till I see you again.

* * *

Bob Lewis pushed a button, and the screen went blank. The videotape began to rewind. The Managing Editor of *The Chronicle* sat in his chair, staring at the blank, dark screen, his face set, his eyes focused on something between the TV monitor and the end of the universe. He did not move; did not stir.

Bill Foley looked at his boss and had no idea of what to do or say. There passed an uneasy minute of silence…then two…then three. Finally, he managed a voice just slightly above a whisper.

"Mr. Lewis, do you want me to send it to Jerry?"

Slowly, Bob Lewis turned his head and stared at his companion. As if he were coming back from some distance, he slowly focused in on Bill Foley and, in an uncharacteristic monotone, said, "Yes. Send it special overnight mail. Don't forget to include the letter. I'll call Jerry and tell him it's coming."

"OK," Bill said, gathering the letter and hastily removing the tape from the player, glad to have any excuse to leave. "I'll get right on it!"

Without any other words, Bill Foley left the room.

Bob Lewis sat there, staring at the blank screen.

Staring and thinking…staring and thinking…

When his secretary came to find him over an hour later, Bob Lewis had not moved.

* * *

It was just slightly after two in the afternoon in New York when Bob Lewis put in the phone call to Jerry Westfield in Israel, where it was 9:03 PM. Jerry got it on the second ring.

"Hello, Westfield speaking."

"Jerry, it's Bob," the caller said in slow, precise, and measured tones.

"Hi, Bob! Hey, you sound a little far off. Are you OK? Is there something wrong?"

"A package came for you today…"

"OK," Jerry responded, "so?"

"…from Kerri Palmer."

The recognition was instantaneous, and Jerry's voice rose accordingly.

"Kerri Palmer! That's Jeremy's sister. I think I met her once…"

"Yes, she's Jeremy Palmer's sister."

"Well? Come on, Bob, what is it?"

"It's a video tape…"

"Bob, did you look at it?"

There was a slight pause, and then Bob Lewis said simply, "Yes, I did."

Jerry was getting anxious. There was something about Bob's tone that was unsettling. Instinctively, his grip on the cell phone tightened.

"Well? Come on, Bob! It's all right. I couldn't care less that you opened it, OK? What was on it?"

"Jerry, do you remember that conversation you and I had a while back, when I told you about those dreams I was having about my grandmother?"

Jerry put his mind to it, and the connection clicked.

"Yes," he answered. "Yes, Bob, I remember. She's passed on, but in your dream she comes back to warn you about something. Am I close?"

"Close enough," Bob answered. "Well, Jerry, that's what the tape's about. Only this one is from Jeremy."

"Jeremy?" Jerry said with a sharp intake of breath, and now he was sitting upright, every sense sharp and clear. "Jeremy is on the tape?"

"Yes," Bob Lewis confirmed. "Do me a favor. Call me as soon as you look at it, and tell me what you think. Jerry, I really need to know. I just had it shipped to you. You should have it by tomorrow afternoon."

Jerry was almost in shock. *A tape from Jeremy,* he thought, *a tape from Jeremy…*

from Jeremy…

"Jerry, are you still there?"

"Yes…ah…yeah sure," Jerry said, forcing his mind back to the conversation at hand, "I'll call you soon as I see it; I promise. Listen, Bob, do you know when it was made? Does he talk about the disappearance at all?"

"I think…I think you have to see it for yourself, Jerry. See it, then call me, OK? Take care."

"Yes, yes, all right. You take care, too. Goodbye, Bob."

Jerry sat back in his chair, the memories pouring in like a flash flood. Vividly, he could see Jeremy and Kathy sitting at the kitchen table, laughing and teasing him about the possibility of his ever getting married again. He could see himself vowing that there was no way in this world that would ever happen. Suddenly, Jerry was overcome with the wish that they could be here to meet Ruth; to get to know her; to talk and laugh with her.

They would love her, he thought.

Again, Jerry remembered the long talks they had together…about so many things, and of course…about God. The Palmers had such faith and love for God, and it couldn't help but spill over and touch Jerry a little bit.

He remembered a time when he was eating dinner with them almost every night. Kathy knew about Jerry's "sweet tooth," as she called it, and had made dessert after special dessert just for him, since both she and Jeremy ate rather lightly in the realm of sweets.

With his divorce raging about him then, it had been a terrible time for Jerry, and Jeremy and Kathy Palmer had given him something very special…hope. The memories were warm, and Jerry smiled as he leaned back his head and eagerly savored them with delight.

Without the Palmers' encouraging and reaching out to him, Jerry wondered, would he still be hanging out at Willoughby's with Bill Foley, losing the evening at the bottom of a glass and becoming more and more bitter about the divorce and his lack of family life? He truly liked Bill Foley, but he wondered if, together, they might not have sunk to the thick glass bottoms of those bar glasses and stayed there?

Jerry shook off the feeling and consciously turned his thoughts once more to Jeremy Palmer, whose tape would be in his hands in less than a day.

In less than a day!

He smiled as he anticipated seeing his old friend, Jeremy, again… even if only on videotape.

That, and hearing once more the voice that stirred his heart

*   *   *

Ken Mailer lay on his bed, staring at the television set without watching it, one leg twitching periodically. He had long ago moved from his princely apartment into this small room overlooking the control center located two stories below the Strapollos mansion in a fashionable suburb of Brussels. He worked long hours, sometimes twenty or more at a stretch, and he used drugs to keep himself awake. Then, when he could finally allow himself to sleep, and the rest he so desired simply would not come, there were other drugs to force a black vacuum to engulf him, if only for a while.

Every now and then, and more frequently of late, his fingers began to tremble or his leg began to twitch and spasm, and he had to place his hands into his pockets until the tremors passed or excuse himself and lock his body into a lavatory stall until the disobedient leg stopped its macabre dance.

He found food undesirable, and what weight he had and really needed began to melt from his bones.

Although Ken Mailer thought of it rarely, he was several steps removed from the man he had been just a few short years ago.

The phone beside his cot rang, and Ken answered it with a quick and nervous, "Yes! Mailer here!"

"Ken," came the smooth voice, "this is Mr. Strapollos. Meet me in the control room in fifteen minutes."

"Yes, sir! Fifteen minutes! Certainly, sir! I'll be there!"

Ken threw on a shirt and a pair of jeans that was lying beside his cot and dragged a comb through his dry and unwilling hair. He left his room and groped his way down the steel stairway, grumbling and exhausted. His reddened eyes scanned the vast open area filled with TV monitors and desks with computer work stations on them. It was like descending into a high tech...what?...jungle. That was it – it was a jungle; just as dark and just as dangerous!

I need to get some rest, Ken Mailer thought as he plodded onward, one step and then another. *I can't keep going like this. What does he want now? I need a few days to myself! Just a few days!*

By the time Ken Mailer got to his specialized area of the control center, the security door was gliding opening, and Demetrius Strapollos was gliding through them, headed directly for him.

"Ken," Strapollos began without preliminaries, "I need to know the status of the monetary system, and I need to know now. Who is ready to go on line, and who is not ready?"

Ken flopped down in front of a keyboard and monitor and reached for his mouse. On the screen, he clicked the icon marked "Cashless." The report began to unfold in white letters on a vivid blue background.

Slowly, Ken Mailer commented, "Well, sir. As you are already aware, the European Community has completed the three month trial period without a single glitch. The Mid-East Region is going on-line the first of next month, and Russia and the East European Regions are scheduled for the first of the year. Now, the United States has been dragging its feet lately, but the good news is that our sources in Washington tell us that we have made enough "friends," to insure that Congress will pass it just before they break for the holidays."

Demetrius Strapollos pressed forward.

"Once the Government clears it, how long will it take before the United States are on-line and ready to go?"

"Not that long, sir. You see, their technology is in place already. We could have them on-line and functional by June first of next year."

Kan Mailer paused and took a deep breath.

"China, however," he continued, "well, sir...China is a another story. I'm afraid they have their own ideas."

"That does not concern me," Strapollos half-smiled. "China is quite pleased with the progress they have made lately in world trade and commerce. They have learned to depend upon that revenue. If they wish to continue...and they most certainly will...then they *will* comply."

Ken scanned the monitor again and reported, "That leaves Central and South America. Actually, sir, those people are the most anxious to begin, and their governments have really been cooperative. Almost all of that region will be on-line by year's end, with just a few minor exceptions because of the extensive damage from the hurricanes and flooding, as I'm sure you understand"

"Yes, Mr. Mailer, I do understand, and I also understand that you have done a remarkable job here; an outstanding accomplishment. I am pleased.

"Now, make certain that I have a printed copy of this material on my desk by 9:00 AM tomorrow morning. You know how very important it is that we keep on a precise schedule."

Demetrius Strapollos moved closer to Ken Mailer and placed one large arm around Ken's comparatively diminutive shoulders. Strapollos' height now seemed to dwarf Ken who, with growing concern, was noticing that his hands were beginning to shake.

"You know, Ken," Strapollos intoned soothingly, "Rabbi Eissen is concerned about you again. He seems to think you're showing signs of stress that could lead to problems with your performance. Now, you seem to be all right to me, Ken. How do you feel?"

"Well, sir," Ken answered cautiously, placing his vibrating hands below the level of the computer console, "I am feeling a little...how shall I say...tired. I mean, I've been pushing the team and myself a lot, especially lately. A little rest is all I really need, sir. Maybe I could have...if it's all right...that's all I need...a little rest."

Demetrius Strapollos removed his arm and looked at Ken Mailer with eyes that turned from concern to the harshness of a stern teacher who is something less than pleased with his pupil.

"Now is not the time to rest, Ken," Strapollos said simply and without feeling. "This is, as the Americans say, the home stretch. We need to work harder than ever. Come here."

Strapollos embraced Ken Mailer in a gigantic bear hug, and Ken Mailer melted into it. In that embrace there was acceptance and warmth and security. In the grasp of those arms, Ken felt he could find the strength to do whatever this man wanted or required of him. He was so…wonderful. He was like a brother…a father…a god.

Strapollos's lips were close to Ken's ear, and he whispered softly, almost lovingly, "Do you have enough of those pills I gave you? They are your salvation, Ken. They will get you through."

"Oh, yes! Yes, sir," Ken whispered back, cherishing the warmth of his mentor's breath on his neck. "I have plenty."

The bear hug loosened, and Strapollos stood back, raising himself to his full height, still holding Ken loosely at arm's length.

"Good," the tall man smiled. He let go of Ken and took a step backward, somewhat like an artist admiring his latest creation.

"You will make certain those figures will be on my desk by nine, won't you?"

Without waiting for an answer, Strapollos turned and walked briskly out the room, the door easing shut behind him.

When the security locks finally engaged and the sound of the bolts falling into place had faded, Ken Mailer took a long, deep breath and leaned back in his chair, closing his eyes, trying to savor the praise of Demetrius Strapollos while at the same time waiting for his hands to stop twitching.

As he did this, it occurred to Ken Mailer, right-hand man to possibly the most powerful force in the world, that were it not for the approval of his mentor and the obvious prestige of his position, he was coming closer and closer to loathing the very life he had coveted so fiercely just six short months ago.

He shook his head and dismissed the thought at once.

CHAPTER TWENTY-TWO

Earth and the Fire Below

THERE WERE JUST A FEW LAZY WHITE CLOUDS gliding their effortless way east. Other than that, the sky was clear and cobalt and the temperature stood at an extremely pleasant sixty-two degrees as the wind oozed in from the west at about fifteen miles an hour. In short, it was the kind of day that was fairly typical for this time of year in Northeastern California.

It was early Saturday as the park ranger made his customary morning rounds in his rumbling park vehicle, checking facilities and roadways. Finding that everything was in order and all was well, he headed towards Lassen Peak. It occurred to the ranger that Lassen Volcanic National Park, established in 1907 as he often told groups of tourists, was a great place to work, with its many alpine lakes, vapor-emitting vents, hot springs, boiling mud pots, and lava formations. He particularly loved the park's main feature, the volcanic Lassen Peak itself, rising 10,457 feet into the rich, deep, blue sky. He sighed with contentment and could not resist the smile that now spread itself across his face. *Yes,* he thought, *it's a great place!*

As he approached the peak, the ranger suddenly braked and pulled his park vehicle to the side of the earthen road he traveled. Fumbling in the seat beside him, he removed a pair of powerful binoculars from their case and began to focus in, intently studying the magnificent natural structure before him.

Something was somehow different, and it took him a moment to realize what it was. The normally dormant volcano was emitting a goodly amount of steam and…he focused in a bit closer…yes, some volcanic dust as well.

He was, indeed, a good and dedicated ranger, as most of his co-workers attested, and he was well-trained as well. Immediately upon fully recognizing and confirming the activity, therefore, he was on the radio, calling in his findings.

* * *

Two members of the United States Geological Survey, or *USGS*, for short, were immediately assigned to investigate the diligent ranger's report. The men conferred for about twenty minutes, and they remarked that they had been recording slight tremors in the area over the last two weeks, tremors that had begun recently after a very minor quake had occurred along the fault line. It had been so minor, in fact, as to be barely noticed in the park itself.

* * *

That same morning, at precisely the same time the park ranger called in his observations, a nine-year-old boy was playing behind some old buildings in the Southern California community of Cathedral City, fifty miles south of San Bernardino and thirty-five miles north of Salton Sea Lake. The boy saw what appeared to be smoke, and his eyes went wide. It seemed that it was rising from the ground. He ran to look closer and found a crack in the earth, that was the way he would later describe it to reporters – he found a crack in the earth about ten feet long. A mist, much like smoke, rose from the small crevice, and the boy, smiling at his discovery, reached out an arm to embrace the cloud. He shoved it with enthusiasm into the curling vapor.

The heat was at once overwhelming, and he drew back his arm immediately and with a small cry, mainly of surprise. His hand and forearm were wet and red, and it felt like the time he had stayed too long at the beach, and Mommy had to rub down his back with the greasy, smelly cool stuff.

Because of that memory; because of the sudden redness of his skin; because he was, after all, nine years old, he began to sniffle and cry and suddenly run for home all at the same time.

His mother, brushing off the steps of their front porch, heard the child's wail from a block away.

Within minutes of the boy's sobbing story, there was a police car and a small group of concerned citizens surrounding the boy first, and then the phenomenon -- watching it grow to fifteen and then twenty feet in length.

The Police reported the incident to the USGS, and waited.

* * *

As Police and citizens observed the crack in Cathedral City, in the city of Merced, over three hundred miles to the north, another fissure was discovered. Fortunately, it was found by a local Police Officer on regular patrol, and there were no others around. This one was close to thirty feet long and spewing live steam and volcanic dust. Occasionally, hot rock fragments flew twenty-five or more feet into the air.

The Officer blocked off the area with his patrol car and immediately called in to his station.

Within minutes, it was reported to the USGS.

* * *

By late afternoon, six incidents of this nature had been reported. Dozens of small quakes were felt from San Francisco to Mexicali, Mexico. At USGS headquarters the mood was one of general uneasiness, and it was getting worse.

In the meeting room, with maps and charts covering the walls like some montage of modern art, a group of USGS officers waited. When the door opened, they immediately ceased all talk and all eyes turned to give their attention to the man who had just entered.

James Robinson, "Jim" to almost everyone who knew him, was the man in charge. His knowledge and authority were unquestioned by anyone who worked with him for longer than a day, as was his personal courage and dedication. He was in his early fifties, but remained lean and muscular of body – something he worked at constantly. He was a graduate of Ohio State, where he had once roomed with an up and coming student who was there on a football scholarship but had a mind that more than matched his athletic ability. A man named Bob Lewis.

"Ladies and Gentlemen," Robinson acknowledged, striding to the map board and getting directly to the matter. "As you can see by this chart, every one of these occurrences stretches northwest for about 1000 km -- that's 600 miles for those of you who can't be converted to metric -- from the Imperial Valley of Southern California to Point Arena on the Northern Coast. All, ALL, lie directly on the San Andreas Fault."

His dark eyes swept the room for a second before he continued.

"Folks, you know as well as I do what this could mean. It appears the whole Fault is about to move."

There was some mumbling from the gathering. In truth, many had suspected as much but hoped they might be mistaken.

"Now, how much or when it will move is difficult to say, but we have sent teams to all the locations showing activity, and I have issued a notice to close Lassen Volcanic National Park as well. This situation warrants caution, and due to the extreme geological activity of the last year…"

He paused as his eyes swept the faces of the people in the room.

"… I see no reason to be optimistic."

Robinson leaned forward, taking in every one of the individuals who had gathered to meet with him.

"We have a situation here," he said in a slow, level tone that emphasized its seriousness, "that may soon be out of control. As soon as we are out of here, I'm putting in a call to the Secretary of the Interior.

"Folks…" he said, and every eye lifted to meet his gaze, "we're going to need some help on this one!"

*   *   *

As the meeting at USGS ended and people scurried to individual tasks, at Lassen Volcanic National Park, things were heating up, both literally and figuratively. Smoke was now rising directly out of the cone of the volcano, and a helicopter dispatched from Sacramento had just arrived to get a look only it could provide, a look *inside* Lassen Peak itself.

"Attention Lassen Base," the pilot snapped into his helmet microphone. "This is USGS Helicopter A-6 reporting from Lassen Peak. Over."

At USGS headquarters, James Robinson, just out of his meeting, recognized the voice coming over the speaker, reached over and took the base microphone, speaking directly into it.

"Roger that, A-6. This is Base. Dave, this is Jim Robinson. What do you see? Over."

"Well. Hi there, Jim," came the response, somewhat punctuated with static, "I guess this has got to be something special if you're on the line. Let me see if I can help. Well, from what I can see, we have some increased activity. Our instruments…let me see…yes, they're registering high levels of carbon dioxide, hydrogen, carbon monoxide, and sulfur dioxide.

"Jim, listen, we're going to make one more pass, and then we are getting ourselves out of here. We count five people on the ground, and you really need to get them away from here right away, A-S-A-P. I tell you, Jim, this one could...LOOK OUT!"

Although no one at the base could see, a tremendous blast had shot up from inside the cone of the volcano in a violent, rumbling red and black eruption. The enormous energy loosed itself like a cannon blast, catapulting the helicopter, toppling and spinning, high into the azure sky, where it exploded in smoke trails of twisted metal. Steam and gasses rose in a murky cloud and large and small portions of lava shot upward from within the cloud, forming a fiery fountain of incandescent drops and fragments. Cinders and ash fell back in showers on the external slopes of the growing cone and into the seething crater.

"A-6! Come in, A-6!" Jim Robinson shouted, "Where are you, Dave? Come in! Come in!"

"Jim," said the base radio operator who was in separate contact with the five team members still on the ground, "...Jim, there's been a eruption...their helicopter was directly in the explosion...he's...he's gone..."

James Robinson lowered his head and said softly, "Notify the authorities to begin immediate...that's immediate...evacuation of anyone within one hundred square miles of the area."

"Yes, sir. Do you want me to..."

But Jim Robinson was gone; already on the way to his office.

He had a great deal to do.

*   *   *

Back at Lassen Peak, the dark, boiling cloud began to rise higher and higher in the sky. The three geologists and two park rangers on the ground dropped every piece of equipment they were carrying and bolted for their vehicles with a professional's knowledge that they were running against death and stood only the smallest chance of survival.

Even as they ran, the volcano screamed again and blew out the side of a slope, launching deadly pieces of the mountain vertically, like rockets, through the air. The two park rangers did not see the full grandeur of the spectacle, for they were hit by one of the first segments of rock and lay mangled and dead in the midst of red, roaring fury.

The geologists made it to their vehicle, which started immediately and began a break-neck ride down the road while flashes of lightning danced through the clouds heavily charged with dust particles which hung now behind and above the fleeing scientists.

Within seconds the lava rose in the cone and began to flow through the large crack in the once snow-capped mountain, creating an assault of water and mud rushing ahead of it. The sun was now blocked by the rising cloud, and night was falling in the early afternoon. Larger fragments of rock were now landing everywhere, exploding like bombs and mortar shells and demolishing small park buildings while starting fires that leaped to life on all sides.

The three men in their vehicle, wide-eyed and breathing in deep labored gulps of hot air, flew desperately down the mountain road. One of them wept openly while another moved his lips without words. The driver kept glancing in the side mirror, fretting and moaning, his nose running and his chin dripping saliva at the sight of the monster that relentlessly pursued.

A huge section of the mountain, falling like a fiery meteor, finally ended their agony.

And their lives.

* * *

By now, the media had mobilized and was in full gear, trying to get people into the area, not knowing that the real story was actually developing elsewhere.

The residents of Cathedral City and Merced looked with growing fear as the openings in the earth widened and began spewing scalding steam and hot rock fragments forty, fifty, sixty feet into the air.

"Oh, God!" shouted one awed witness.

And the growing crowd screamed in agreement.

* * *

When the phone rang at USGS headquarters, the clerk who picked it up barely had it to his ear before the voice at the other end of the line, filled with concern and authority, shouted, "This is an emergency! Let me talk to Mr. Robinson! Now! Right now!"

The call was put through in three seconds.

"Jim? Jim, this is Joel over at Cathedral City. Listen carefully, 'cause I'm not joking! I think we have a developing volcano on our hands!"

"Are you sure? Tell me what's happening."

"Remember the study we all read on the volcano at Paricutin in central Mexico in '43?"

"Yes, I remember! Do you think that's what's going on where you are?"

"Jim, listen to me for a second. In that study, the district around Paricutin had been shaken by earthquakes over a two-week period. Then, a vent was observed to open and emit scalding steam and volcanic dust, then hot fragments, and later molten rock. The eight-month eruption built up a cone about 1500 feet high. The accompanying lava flow was relentless, and it buried the village of Paricutin and several other nearby settlements.

"Now, the boy who discovered this fissure in Cathedral City told us that when he first saw it, it was much smaller and completely flat. Right now, I'm standing a couple hundred yards away from the activity, and from here I can see a definite cone developing -- definite."

"How high is the build up?"

"I estimate six feet."

James Robinson rubbed his forehead for a moment and then spoke slowly and deliberately into the phone.

"OK, this is what I want you to do. Evacuate everyone within a mile radius, you understand, then set up shop and don't take your eyes off it. I want a report every hour on the hour until further notice. We may have to evacuate more people, but let's take it one step at a time. And Joel..."

"Yes."

"Don't take any chances. I want no heroics here, got it? We've lost enough people already."

* * *

The report from Merced was somewhat different, but just as threatening. There, the crack was steadily growing longer, moving on a north and south axis at about two miles per hour. After several hours, however, observers blinked and checked their calculations to make certain -- the movement stopped.

Suddenly, and without precedent, it just stopped.

* * *

Shortly after the phenomenon at Merced had been duly noted and recorded, the phone rang at USGS headquarter, and James Robinson picked it up.

"Robinson!" he snapped.

"Jim, this is Joel at Cathedral City. The activity has stopped here. Don't ask me why, I don't know. It was going full steam ahead, and it quit without notice of any kind. All we have now is a small amount of steam rising from the cone."

"What's the height of the cone?"

"About eight feet."

"Joel, I think we have two scenarios. One, it's over. That would be the best explanation, because we're all in favor of that one, I know. The second scenario, however, is that the pressure is building between the plates, and we could be in for a very large earthquake. What's your feeling on this? And, don't tell me what you think I want to hear; tell me your gut feeling."

There was a second's pause before the voice came crackling over the telephone line.

"I don't think it's over," Joel answered. "I'm sorry, Jim, but I have an awful feeling that won't go away. I think the movement has only momentarily blocked the pressure from being released. If it doesn't manifest itself here, then it will – somewhere else along the fault line. What's going on at Lassen?"

"Satellite and aerial photographs show a cloud of ash and gasses rising nine miles. The blast has killed at least seven people that we know of, and in a thirty square mile radius, there may be hundreds of casualties, especially in Chester and Westwood, where they had very little warning. Beyond that, a vast area from Janesville west to Wendel near the Nevada border will soon be covered with ash and debris. The wind currents are carrying most of it eastward, away from the heavily populated areas. I suppose we can be thankful for that, at least.

"Listen, Joel. I want you to stay put for now, OK? Allow no one near the site. The National Guard is sending a small contingent of troops to assist in keeping order and to help prepare for possible evacuation."

"Well," Joel laughed weakly, "I hope they can get here before the news media does! It's not easy keeping the vampires away from something like this.

"Listen, Jim, I'll call in at the first sign of movement...I promise!"

* * *

The morning following Jim Robinson's directions to his man on the scene, at precisely 4:08 AM in Redlands, a town of sixty thousand roughly ten miles south of San Bernardino, the earth began to shake. At first, it was a slight rumble, disturbing none but the lightest of sleepers, but it grew in intensity and pitch, reached a peak, and stopped as suddenly as it had begun.

Minor damage was all that was reported. The heavier sleepers awoke with a jar, grasped the sides of their beds and waited only seconds before they lay themselves down once more and resume the important task of sleeping. A few cans fell from shelves in supermarkets, and pictures tilted on the walls of some homes. In short, damage was not much beyond the nuisance level.

In the parking lot of a twenty-four hour convenience store, however, a small opening appeared, cracking the asphalt and leaving a fissure measuring perhaps two and one half inches wide and about eight feet in length. Within a few minutes, a very small train of steam began to rise from the opening.

* * *

John Bebee, grumbling and anxious for his morning cup of coffee, drove his pick-up truck into the dimly lit parking lot of the convenience store and parked it directly over the seething crack. He was not aware of that fact, however, since his mind was engrossed in the injustice of his having to rise so early to work so hard for his 'daily bread.' He had just reached the store entrance when the explosion from the parking lot lifted and threw him into the place in a shower of glass from the window he had unwittingly passed through. John Bebee's pick-up truck became a rocket that was launched some two hundred feet into the air before returning by crashing through the roof of the small market and settling itself in the frozen food aisle.

Violently, and with enormous power, steam and rock fragments blasted open the small crack, turning the entire parking area into a war field of unguided missiles. A few seconds later, another earthquake hit, and this one rocked the foundations of all the surrounding buildings.

* * *

Machinery at the United States Geological Survey began to record hundreds of tremors all along the fault line. Los Angeles, already hit twice before, including the time that had interrupted Ken Mailer's address to the United Nations, was now visited by a third earthquake, powerful enough to be felt 1000 miles away. Mercilessly and systematically, it devastated that once great city. Fire raged out of control, and the death toll was beyond calculating. Even the outlying areas, the very fringes of the onslaught, looked like old newsreels of sections of London after the German V-2 rockets were done with them.

It was not that rescue vehicles were slow to come, they simply did not know where to begin.

* * *

In New York City, at the offices of *The Chronicle,* Bob Lewis watched the reports coming in from the west coast. He had read all the news service releases, and now he sat speechless as he listened to the anchor on CNN.

"Early this morning, about 4:10 AM, Pacific Time, an earthquake, now determined to be a massive 7.8 on the Richter scale suddenly and without warning struck Los Angeles and other parts of Southern California. It is still before dawn on the West Coast, and we will not know the full extent of the damage until sunrise, about two hours from now.

"This earthquake was preceded by a volcanic eruption at Lassen Peak in Lassen Volcanic National Park in Northeast California. Tremors are currently being felt all along the San Andreas Fault, stretching northwest for about 600 miles from the Imperial Valley in Southern California to Point Arena on the Northern Coast.

"We are told that this zone marks the boundary between the North American and Pacific tectonic plates. Earthquakes occur along it because of obstacles to the steady, even movement of these plates as they slide past each other.

"On January 17, 1994, an earthquake measuring 6.7 on the Richter scale struck northern Los Angeles, California, killing 57 people and seriously injuring more than 1500 others; leaving about 20,000 people temporarily homeless.

"Today's quake was much larger and far more damaging.

"With us now, via satellite, is James Robinson of the United States Geological Survey Office. Mr. Robinson, thank you for joining us; I know this has been a long night for you."

In New York, Bob Lewis' eyes went wide. There on the screen was his friend and Ex-Ohio State roommate, Jim Robinson. Lewis made a mental note amid a flurry of positive memories to get in contact with his college buddy, perhaps when all the turmoil was finally over – if it ever were.

"Mr. Robinson," the TV anchor was asking, "how powerful is a 7.8 earthquake?"

"Extremely…extremely powerful. Let's take the first of the three quakes that hit Los Angeles – the one in '94. That was 6.7 on the Richter scale. This one was ten times more powerful."

"Can you explain how that works, Mr. Robinson?"

"Well, seismologists have devised scales of measurement to describe earthquakes quantitatively. The best known is the Richter scale – named after the American seismologist, Charles Francis Richter – which measures the energy released at the focus of a quake. It's what is called a logarithmic scale that runs from 1 to 9. A magnitude 7 quake is 10 times more powerful than a magnitude 6 quake; 100 times more powerful than a magnitude 5 quake; 1000 times more powerful than a magnitude 4 quake – and so on."

"Do you think there will be any more quakes associated with this one?"

"There will probably be several hundred smaller tremors over the next two weeks. In all honesty, it's hard to determine exactly what will happen at this point. After all, I think you'll agree that we have had an extremely unusual rash of earthquakes all over the world this past year. Our main concern now is the people, we are doing everything possible to get to those in trouble."

The interview continued, but Bob Lewis wasn't listening.

An unusual rash of earthquakes this past year? Bob thought. *Jim, old Pal, we've had an unusual rash of just about everything – from the moment those people disappeared…*

Then, with the TV still playing, even if it did go unheard, Bob Lewis turned his thoughts to the tape made by Jeremy Palmer.

CHAPTER TWENTY-THREE

Fire in the Heart

JERRY WESTFIELD CLICKED THE REMOTE and shut off the CNN report featuring James Robinson. He leaned back into the yielding sofa, and gazed at Ruth Cowen with concern lining his eyes.

"I can't believe this is happening," he said, including the news story and the television in one wide and all-inclusive sweep of his hand. "It's like a bad dream, and you want to wake up so it will go away. Only you find out you're not sleeping, and what you thought was a nightmare is really the latest TV news!"

It was slightly after two in the afternoon in Jaffa, and Ruth, on one of her rare days of rest away from the bank, sat in her apartment with her arm around Jerry, watching TV and luxuriating in the joy of just being together with him.

"So much tragedy and heartache today," she said, shaking her head, her face somber. "Over this last year, it's just been a…a horror. You know, I can't even look at the news any more. Honestly, I only look at it with you, because you're such a part of it. Otherwise, I wouldn't even bother!"

Jerry smiled. He reached out his own arm and pulled her closer to him. His eyes sparkled in the abundant afternoon sunlight pouring through the windows.

"I'd be lost without you, Ruth," he said, "because without you, everything in this world stinks!"

He paused and blinked his eyes, adding with a laugh, "How's that for poetic language? Maybe we have a book here, you think? 'The Love Poems of Jerry Westfield,' or 'The World Stinks!'"

They laughed together, pleased with each other.

"Tell me, lady," Jerry said at length, "where did you come from anyway, Heaven?"

"I feel the same way about you," Ruth laughed. "I have bruises all over from pinching myself to make sure I'm not dreaming. Maybe you're the one from heaven? Do you have wings under that shirt?"

Jerry joined her laughter and said, "Oh, yeah, I'm from heaven all right! I don't think!"

Jerry looked into Ruth's dark eyes, reached out, and drew her even closer. He swept her deep ebony hair away from her face and ran the back of his hand over her cheek, his fingers lightly brushing her lips. They kissed in an embrace that was more than physical; more than the time or the place; that was the essence of what they had been, were, and would yet become.

After a moment, Jerry sighed and said, "I would give a lot if I didn't have to, Ruth, but I must go back to the house. I'm expecting a really important package from *The Chronicle* – special delivery from Bob Lewis."

"All right. I'll go with you."

"I...I don't think so," Jerry said reluctantly. "You stay right here in you beautiful apartment. I love you, and I want you with me, but I...well, I need to be alone for this one. It's a tape from an old friend."

"It's from Jeremy, right?"

Jerry's eyes widened. "How did you know that?"

Ruth leaned back, still holding his hand and smiled gently.

"You have that look you get whenever you talk about him. You know, it's weird, but I can even sense when you're about to bring up his name. Oh, darling, he must have meant a great deal to you."

Jerry looked away, out the window at the view of Jaffa spreading below, and Ruth leaned into him and took his arm, laying her head on his shoulder. For a moment, neither of them spoke.

"Listen," she said softly, "you go do what you have to do. I have plenty of work to catch up on. The new monetary system goes on line the first of the month, and I still have a lot to learn about it. Plus, I need to get ready for all those conferences we're having at the bank. I'll see you tonight. Now, we are going to the movies, right? That's still on?"

"Absolutely!" Jerry replied. "I'll pick you up at seven, and...you're right, Jeremy did mean a lot – he and his wife, Kathy. Sometimes, I'll just see something, and it will remind me of him...or I'll see a young couple across the street, and I'll think...

"Like that CNN interview we just saw and that Robinson guy from USGS. Did you see what he was wearing?"

"No, I didn't. Do you mean his clothes?"

"No, not his clothing. It was a sort of pin – an emblem he wore in his left lapel. It was the sign of the fish. It looked to be silver.

"The fish? What's that?"

"It's something I haven't seen for quite a while. Jeremy used to wear one, but his was gold or gold colored. It's the sign of Christianity. The Christians used it as a secret communication symbol during the days of the Roman persecution."

"How do you know so much about…"

Ruth paused and looked at Jerry with a slight grin.

"Never mind, I know. Jeremy told you."

Jerry smiled and gave her one more kiss. Another ten minutes, and he was out the door.

As he drove back to the Klausman home, it occurred to Jerry Westfield that he was very tired. He could barely sleep last night thinking about the tape, speculating as to what would be on it. He knew the package would probably be delivered around three o'clock, and he wanted to be there.

By the time he got home, that would give him less than an hour to work on his article for tomorrow's paper.

* * *

Jacob, Sarah, and the kids were gone for the day, visiting Jacob's parents. Until about nine this evening, therefore, Jerry had the place to himself. He gloried in that thought. And poured a large glass of juice in the kitchen, taking it upstairs to get to work on his article.

When the package had not arrived by three-thirty, however, Jerry began to become restless. He was looking up the number of the carrier, determined to see if there were some sort of monumental hold-up, when the doorbell rang. Jerry tumbled down the stairs to answer it.

"A package for you, Mr. Westfield. Please sign here."

Jerry thanked the delivery man and, in his excitement, slammed the door in the young man's face. Instantly regretting his hastiness, he opened the door, waved and apologized to the startled messenger.

Back inside, he tore at the wrapping, and when he had gotten to the contents, he placed the tape on the table, and immediately began to read the letter.

Dear Mr. Westfield,

I am Kerri Palmer, Jeremy's sister. We met once at Jeremy and Kathy's place. It has taken some time, but we were finally able to take ownership…

Jerry read slowly, savoring the message, allowing certain parts of the letter to take root in his mind

...I think he meant to give the enclosed tape to you at that time and on that same day, but he never had the opportunity...
...It has changed my life...
...I only wish I had listened to Jeremy before all this...
...May God help us and strengthen us, Mr. Westfield, for all the dark days that lie ahead.
Thank you again.
Sincerely,
Kerri Palmer

As swiftly as he could, since he found his fingers trembling, Jerry Westfield placed the tape into Jacob Klausman's VCR and sat down. The moment he saw Jeremy's image resolve on the screen, his eyes began to fill, and he was surprisingly overcome with a surge of hot and urgent emotion. Usually, he was very good at keeping his personal feelings under control, even with world leaders and Strapollos-types, but somehow this was different. It had been less than a year since he had last seen Jeremy, but suddenly, it seemed like ten – a hundred – the lonely ache of empty time.

Was it just a year ago? It seemed like it was another lifetime. The year between had been a time that had torn at the fabric of Jerry's heart and soul.

Hi, Jerry! How are you doing? I hope and pray that you never have to listen to this tape, but you're pretty hard-headed, so I figured I'd better make this for you. Actually, I planned on making something like this for a long time, my friend, but it always felt kind of – you know – stupid doing it. Then yesterday, Jerry, yesterday I felt this real...urgency in my spirit, so I'm doing it, and I'm going to give it to you tonight or tomorrow, whenever I see you next.

If you followed my instructions, then the very fact that you are watching this means that you are probably in shock, wondering what happened to me and Kathy and the rest of us. Well my dear, dear friend, I'm about to tell you.

It's happened, Jerry! Jesus has taken us home. And, oh, Jerry, how I wish you were here…

Jerry stabbed blindly at the pause button. That had been the last drop the reservoir could hold, and the dam shattered and splintered and loosed its penned up burden. Jerry began to cry, then to sob, and, finally, he was weeping uncontrollably. All at once, the truth that Jerry had been denying inside himself for almost a year washed over him with amazing force and clarity. Finally, it all made sense, and just as finally, once and for all, Jerry understood that the "Great Disappearance" had been the "Rapture" that Jeremy had been telling him about for the better part of five years.

Jerry Westfield amassed a formidable pile of used tissues before he could continue. He was glad, thankful actually, he was alone in the house, first, so no one saw his outburst and tears, and second, because it was like being with Jeremy once more…well, almost.

He pushed 'Play.' The tape continued, and for Jerry it was as if he were hearing everything for the first time and through new ears. There was no doubt in his mind now about Strapollos, or the Cashless Society, or the Mark of the Beast he had read about in Jeremy's Bible. There was no doubt in his mind about…about what he knew he would have to do.

He kept listening

Jerry…of all the things I could tell you, I cannot stress enough the importance of accepting Jesus as your Savior and Lord. That's the most important thing of all. No matter what else I tell you, it just won't help without that. I tried to tell you last Monday night, while we were watching football, but I guess I wasn't convincing enough or you weren't too receptive. But, I'll keep trying, Jerry, because I can't do it for you. Each person has to make his or her own decision – I'm very aware of that – but Kathy and I believe our prayers will be answered, even if you have to go through this terrible time that I feel is so close.

Once again, his tears began to flow, and he instinctively paused the tape. For perhaps the first time in his life, Jerry Westfield began to pray. He had no idea of what to say or how to say it, so, with gasps and sobs and sometime incoherent words that even he could not understand, he poured out his heart to the God he had denied, the one he could not see and only now had begun to feel.

Suddenly, Jerry Westfield sensed something. Whether it was a special presence in the room, or it came from within the cavernous depth of his own soul, he could not tell, but he understood the deep and abiding feeling of peace that began to well up within him like a flood and engulf him in its warm, and loving embrace.

His hand brushed the control, and the tape in the VCR continued.

How I look forward to seeing you then, my friend.
Please, Jerry, trust Him. He said, "I will never leave you or forsake you." And again, He said, "I will be with you even to the end of the age."
God bless you, Jerry.
Kathy and I...we're praying for you.
We're praying for you, and...
We love you...
I feel kind of foolish saying this now, but if in fact you're viewing this tape then I guess it's appropriate. Goodbye, my friend...till I see you again.

Although he thought he was exhausted of tears, Jerry found a new supply. Yet, even as it emptied him, he was being filled by something new; by a peace that would not go away; that refused to be lessened or quelled; a peace he could feel through his tears.

He clicked the remote. The tape stopped, but the feeling didn't. For a while, Jerry Westfield just sat there, bathing in this incredible presence.

After a few moments, he ran upstairs, a remarkable springiness in his legs, and got Jeremy Palmer's Bible.

Then, holding on to it as if it were made of diamonds and gold and contained all the secrets of every government in the world, he played the tape again.

* * *

By five o'clock that afternoon, Jerry realized that he needed to talk to Bob Lewis. With the seven hour time differential, it would be ten in the morning in New York City, and Bob would be there and alert. Jerry took the steps to the roof two at a time, his cell phone dialing as he ascended.

In New York, everyone including Bob Lewis was glued to the news coverage of the continuing and escalating disaster in California. When the phone rang, it was Lewis himself who answered it.

"Bob Lewis."

"Bob, it's Jerry."

"Jerry! What do you think about this terrible mess in California? Unbelievable, isn't it?"

"It's horrible. From what I've seen, it looks like Hiroshima after the bomb hit. By the way, I saw your old Ohio State buddy on the news today. You know, Jim Robinson of USGS."

"Yeah, I saw him, too. He lost a few men today, and that can't be easy. He looked pretty stressed out."

"Tell me something, Bob. Did you notice that silver pin he was wearing?"

"You mean the fish?"

"Yes, the fish. Do you know what that's about?"

"Sure I do. My grandmother had one."

"Bob, does it mean that your friend is a Christian?"

"If he is, Jerry, it's news to me. The last time I saw Jim Robinson, he was drinking like a fish instead of wearing one. But...I guess people can change. I've known that to happen."

Jerry swallowed hard. This was the opening he had hoped for.

"Speaking of change, Bob, I...ah...I watched Jeremy's tape this afternoon. I watched it a couple times."

There was a short pause before Bob Lewis asked softly, "Well, what did you think of it?"

Jerry Westfield took a deep breath of Israeli air and closed his eyes. Into the phone, he said, "I never believed that I would say this, Bob, but...I believe it. I mean, I really believe it. All of it."

There was an even longer pause before Bob Lewis all but whispered, "Me too, Jerry; me too."

Both men took a further silent moment to fully internalize what the other had said and meant. It was Jerry who broke the silence.

"We need to get together, Bob. Why don't you take a break and fly over here to Israel. It's beautiful, Bob. I'd love for you to meet Ruth! You can tell the bosses that I requested a personal meeting with you. What do you say?"

"Man! That...that sounds good, Jerry, but I don't know. I mean, things are crazy here now. Look, I'll see what I can do. And yes, you know I would like to meet your lady. I promise, Jerry, I'll try.

"Now, you take care of yourself. Things are going to get pretty tough from here on out. Even if Jeremy Palmer was only half-right."

"I will, Bob. I promise, I'll be careful. Tell Bill Foley I said hello. I'll talk to you next week."

Jerry snapped the phone closed and returned it to his jacket pocket. He spent the better part of the next hour reading the notes in Jeremy's Bible. By six o'clock, he realized he'd better take a quick shower and get moving if he were going to pick up Ruth on time.

Jerry closed the Bible, tucked it under his arm, and started upstairs.

* * *

In California, the nightmare continued. When the sun had risen and attempted to burn through the blanketing haze and smoke, what light there was revealed a catastrophe of unparalleled proportions. Fires burned out of control throughout Los Angeles and as far east as San Bernardino. Accurate damage assessment was impossible, but even the most vividly conservative estimates had at least 500 dead with attendant serious injuries numbering in the thousands.

In Northeast California, Lassen Peak continued to smolder, although the lava flow had slowed down considerably, the cloud continued to rise into the California sky, spreading the cloying, choking ash for hundreds of miles.

Government agencies, already overrun with urgent requests for assistance from Florida and throughout the Southeast due to the abnormal hurricanes and tornadoes that had lately plagued the entire region, tried desperately to respond to the unprecedented California crisis.

They didn't always make it.

* * *

In Washington, DC, the President of the United States sat in the oval office, staring out a window, mulling over the briefing and meeting he had just had concerning the devastating events in California. A phone buzzed on his desk, and, with a sigh, he picked it up.

"Yes."

"Mr. President, Mr. Strapollos is calling from Brussels and would like to speak with you, personally. Will you take the call, sir?"

"Yes, I will. Put him through."

There was a click, and a smooth, deep voice filled the receiver.

"Mr. President, I am so sorry to hear about this terrible tragedy in California. I wish to offer you my help."

"Thank you, Demetrius, I...that is, we...all appreciate your concern. It is, as you can understand, very early in the recovery effort to know exact specifics as to what is needed, but I do know that volunteer workers are at a premium right now. We would readily accept any workers you could spare, and be grateful for them. I realize there is still that mess in Delhi from the bombing, and some of our own people are remaining there, but..."

"We have plenty of people willing to help, Mr. President," Strapollos interrupted in a voice filled with sincerity and concern. "I will personally put things into motion immediately. My agency officials will contact your people as soon as possible. I'll see to it."

"Thank you, again, Demetrius. My staff will be prepared to assist them and provide whatever information they will need.

"Oh," the president continued, "by the way, I believe we have enough votes in the Senate to pass that currency legislation before the session adjourns for the holidays."

"Excellent!" Strapollos exclaimed mildly. "I will look forward, then, to meeting with you after the first of the year. If there is anything else I can do to help, please let me know. My phone is always open to you."

"Thank you," said the President. "Thank you so very much!"

As Demetrius Strapollos hung up the phone, a wide grin formed itself across his face. Slowly, he was becoming a living hero to millions across the globe.

Step by step, he thought to himself. *Step by step!*

* * *

Jacob Klausman poured two mugs of steaming, freshly brewed coffee, and, since both men took it black, slid one over to Jerry Westfield, who was sitting across from Jacob at the kitchen table.

"So," Jacob smiled, "how was the movie last night?"

"Not bad – a real tear-jerker, though. Any sweeter, and I'd need a shot of insulin. Ruth loved it!"

Jacob's smile widened as he said, "I see."

"How was your visit with your parents?"

"It was good," Jacob sighed, "except that my father loves to talk politics."

"I always wondered where you got it," Jerry commented with a pleasantly sarcastic grin.

Jacob ignored him and continued, "I tell you, Jerry, it drove Sarah crazy. I tried to steer the conversation away from it, but do you think that did any good? Of course not! Anyway, once the politics was over, the rest of the visit was just fine. They love to see the kids and hear about what they're doing. I tell you, Jerry, it does me good to see my children and my parents happy."

"You have great kids, Jacob. I'm sure that they give your parents a great deal of pleasure."

Jerry took a deep swallow of coffee and placed the mug on the table, turning his gaze to his friend.

"I received a tape from Bob Lewis yesterday afternoon," Jerry said finally. "I think it's…very interesting, Jacob, and I would like you to see it."

"Sure," Jacob replied. "Sarah left early to do the food shopping, and the kids are in school by now. So…let's go put it in the VCR. You know we hardly ever use this thing anymore."

Jerry hadn't expected such a quick response. Sooner or later, he had to tell Jacob, and it might as well be sooner. He hoped…he prayed… that Jacob would understand what had happened to him and why, although, in truth, he wasn't so sure how to explain it himself.

The two men walked into the den, and when the tape had been loaded, Jerry took the remote and said, "Jacob, maybe I should explain just a few little things before we watch the tape."

"What do you mean?" Jacob asked.

"This tape…it's from my old friend, Jeremy Palmer, the one I told you about. He made it the day before 'The Great Disappearance' last November. When you hear it, Jacob, you won't believe how amazingly accurate he is about all the things we've been going through."

"I'm interested already," Jacob roared "Will you stop talking and play the tape!"

Jerry sat back and pushed *PLAY*. The two of them sat in silence as the tape continued. At times, Jacob seemed to twitch and turn, but he never took his eyes off the screen. Now, it was Jerry who prayed, never wanting to upset his friend, Jacob, but knowing that there was no other way.

On the tape, Jeremy was saying good-bye.

How I look forward to seeing you then, my friend.

*Please, Jerry, trust Him. He said, "*I will never leave you or forsake you.*" And again, He said, "*I will be with you even to the end of the age.*"*

God bless you, Jerry.
Kathy and I...we're praying for you
We're praying for you, and...
We love you...
I feel kind of foolish saying this now, but if in fact you're viewing this tape then I guess it's appropriate. Goodbye, my friend...till I see you again.

Jerry snapped off the tape. For what seemed a time just short of eternity, the two friends sat in unmoving silence. Finally, Jacob spoke, his voice level and sincere, as if carefully choosing his words.

"This...this is a good man, this Jeremy. I mean, I can feel his sincerity when he speaks. The look in his eyes – you cannot fake that, Jerry – it is one of genuine love. Also, I want you to know that I respect... deeply respect...what he said...I do, but...but..."

Jacob Klausman turned to Jerry Westfield.

"I cannot," Jacob emphasized, not without compassion, "I cannot accept the fact that his Jesus is my Messiah!"

There are moments that hang in time like the twinkling ornaments Jerry had seen on the Christmas trees he had helped decorate in the Palmer's home. Some were beautiful and bejeweled, while others lacked even the refinement of taste, crude and plain. Yet, each had its place, and each was a part of what made up the bright and vital being that drew its smiles and even tears from each viewer. Take one small trinket, the least significant or meaningful, and remove it from the tree or change its place with another, or knock out one single light bulb, and the tree is never quite the same again. Whatever it may turn out to be, that one change has altered its shape, its design, and its meaning...forever.

That's the way it was at this frozen moment of time. Jerry Westfield was keenly aware that what he was about to say could...no...would change his relationship with Jacob forever. Still, Jerry had always been a "straight shooter," and that was one of the reasons Jacob loved him.

With his heart booming in his chest, he leaned closer to Jacob and said plainly, "I do, Jacob."

"You do what?" asked Jacob, knowing the answer but needing and wanting Jerry to repeat it.

"I accept Him as Messiah. I…I guess I've known that for a while, but I didn't want to admit it. Strapollos is the Antichrist, not the Messiah. It makes perfect sense to me…now.

"I feel so different, Jacob. I feel clean and free. I read a little more in Jeremy's Bible this morning, and I can understand it now! I tell you, it took everything I had not to shout all this to Ruth last night, but I wanted to tell you, first."

Jacob was close to being in shock. Certainly, he was stunned, and his breath was coming in quicker and quicker gulps. This man before him who absolutely refused to pray just a few days ago was now telling him about the Messiah? He didn't know what to say.

Jacob rose and began to walk the perimeter of the room, finally wheeling about to face Jerry.

"You are a Jew," Jacob said. "You are a son of Abraham. How can you say such things?"

Jerry's heart felt the pain of Jacob's question. Jerry wished he could just reach out and somehow end Jacob's doubt; take that look from Jacob's face and the knot of suffering from his heart.

"Jacob," Jerry said at last, "you have served the Lord God faithfully since you were a young boy. I know I have no right to speak to you about spiritual matters. All I ask is that you read some of this book before you decide.

"I will respect whatever decision you make.

"I have to meet with some people from CNN this morning. They called me a couple days ago to see if I'd be interested in hosting a series of news shows. So, I'll just leave this Bible right here, on this table. I'll leave you alone, because I know you don't like interruptions while you're thinking…and praying."

As he began to leave the room, Jerry Westfield turned back and said, "Please, Jacob, just…just look at it."

Still in awe and unbelief over the change in his friend, Jacob sighed and muttered, "Jerry, if this book had that much effect on you – on you of all people -- then I think I *must* take a look at it. I must admit I have many questions concerning all I've seen over this past year."

Jacob took a step toward Jerry and held his eyes with total depth and honesty.

"I know my God hears my prayers," Jacob said. "So, you are correct. I must go talk with Him about this…in private."

To Jacob's surprise, Jerry all but leaped on him, giving him a huge hug before disappearing up the staircase without a further word.

Jacob just stood there, still completely amazed. A minute later, he, too, went upstairs and changed his own clothes. Returning to the room, he scribbled a short note to Sarah, explaining that he would be back late, very late, that night.

Then, Jacob Klausman picked up Jeremy Palmer's red-covered Bible, placed it under his arm, and headed out to a place where he could read it alone, really alone, with his God.

He headed for the hills of Judea.

* * *

The FAX from Vatican City arrived just seconds after it was sent to the office of Demetrius Strapollos in Brussels. The secretary who received it got up from her desk and walked it directly to her employer's door and knocked.

"Enter."

"Excuse me, Mr. Strapollos," the young woman said pleasantly, with a smile. "This FAX just came in, and I thought you would want to see it right away. It's from the Vatican, sir."

"The Vatican? Bring it here!" Strapollos ordered, his black eyes flashing.

He scanned the paper quickly and said, "Well done...yes...you may go."

When the secretary had left the room, closing the door behind her, Demetrius Strapollos lay the paper flat on his desk and proceeded to read every word very carefully. As his eyes traveled down the sheet, he began to smile. By the time he reached the bottom, it was all he could do not to shout out loud for joy.

Instead, he picked up the phone and punched in Rabbi Michael Eissen's personal number.

"Yes Demetrius," came the low, somber tone Strapollos had grown used to.

Strapollos could not hide a touch of smugness in his voice. "I have something you might be rather interested in seeing. It's a FAX...a letter – from the Vatican."

"The Vatican, you say?" came the reply from Rabbi Eissen. "Is it what we expected?"

"More than what we expected; much more than we expected! It's from the Vatican Secretariat of State. They would like to meet with me."

"A very good sign! The Vatican Secretariat of State represents the Holy See in diplomatic relations with all foreign powers."

"Excellent," Strapollos sighed. "I will need you to fill me in on a few things, however. This is not my forte."

"Let me give you a brief rundown right now on how it all works;" Eissen said, "Vatican City is governed by the Pope, who holds absolute executive, legislative, and judicial powers. The executive powers are delegated to a governor, who is responsible directly to the Pope. In exercising his legislative powers, the Pope is advised and assisted by the Sacred College of Cardinals and by the various Sacred Congregations.

"In 1994, Israel established diplomatic relations with the Vatican while announcing an exchange of liaison offices with Morocco and Tunisia. Relations between the two have been vacillating ever since – sometimes good; sometimes indifferent.

"Most of those who held to those old principles that kept them apart are gone now. The new leadership under Pope Domitian I, elected at the end of last year you may recall, when his predecessor left one night with millions of others, holds to the belief that all faiths should be united under one rule – namely, his.

"But, with all the changes that have taken place over the last year, especially the building of the Temple, the new currency, and you being proclaimed everywhere as the new Messiah, well – let us be quite frank -- he knows he cannot do it alone.

"Now, keep in mind as you may know, that Vatican City has its own postal system and a currency equal to the Italian Lira. It also has a railroad station and its own radio facilities, and it manages its own telephone and telegraph services. I say this because their Annual expenditures have risen to $135.2 million, while their income has dropped almost fifty percent over recent years and now, to even new lows over the last year.

"Of course, I don't have to spell it out to you, for you see the problem, I am certain…and the opportunity it affords us.

"I believe now is the perfect time to meet with them. We can sort of help each other reach our respective goals, don't you think?"

There was a second's pause, and when Demetrius Strapollos roared with laughter, Rabbi Eissen was quick to join him.

"We will discuss this in detail at our Monday meeting, if you wish," Eissen said. "Things are moving faster than we ever dreamed they would!"

"Monday will be fine, Michael," Demetrius Strapollos answered, "I'll talk to you then."

He hung up the phone and settled back in his oversized black leather chair, filled with a delightful feeling of self-gratification.

Power, he thought. *More than sex; more than money; more than the purest of designer narcotics -- power is still the most intoxicating drug of all!*

CHAPTER TWENTY-FOUR

The Understanding

WHEN JERRY WESTFIELD ARRIVED AT THE APARTMENT of Ruth Cowen, he carried a package under his arm. Immediately, it occurred to Ruth that he had brought her candy or another gift to add to the many with which he had showered her since the 'brunch' when she had agreed to be his wife.

"I hate to sound like a cliché," she smiled, indicating the package, "but you really shouldn't have. I mean, really shouldn't have. Or, if it's more chocolates, maybe you prefer a 300 pound wife?"

"What? I'm sorry..." Jerry stammered. Then, following her gaze to the package, he suddenly understood.

"This," he said, removing the videotape from the plastic bag in which he had transported it. "Well, it is a gift, I guess you could say, but not in the way you mean. This is a tape I got this afternoon. Bob Lewis sent it to me. It's what I was waiting for. It's...it's..."

"From Jeremy?" she half asked, half stated, placing her hand on his.

"Yes."

A silence ensued that wrapped around them in Ruth's quiet living room.

"Jerry, do you want me to see it? Is that why you brought it?"

Jerry nodded his head and took a step closer.

"Yes, I'd like that very much. Only, after you've seen it, we're going to have to talk, and...we might be late for our dinner reservation."

"So?" Ruth smiled warmly. "With all the candy you insist on bringing me, I could afford to skip a meal here and there."

Then, still smiling, she took his hand in hers and led him to the VCR.

256

*　　*　　*

The tape made by Jeremy Palmer the day before he left this earth with millions like him played on to its conclusion.

Goodbye, my friend...till I see you again...

Jerry Westfield pushed the *PAUSE* button on the remote and Jeremy Palmer's gentle and concerned face froze on the TV monitor.

Ruth Cowen sat on the sofa, her chest heaving rapidly, her eyes wide, her cheeks painted with a moisture that gleamed in the room's subdued light.

"Oh, Jerry," she sighed, "no wonder you miss him so..."

Jerry, whose emotions were honed to a razor's edge by all that had taken place so far this day, simply melted into her arms, and they sat on the edge of the couch rocking back and forth...back and forth.

"Jerry," Ruth was saying as she held him and swayed with his body, "I've never seen anything that...that...strong! Jeremy's faith is incredible, and Jerry...his love for you is obvious as well.

"I...just...I don't know what to say...about what he said. I'm positive he believes it, but with all that's going on in this world, all that we know...I mean, can *you* believe it?"

There was no answer.

"Jerry? Can you?"

His eyes rose to meet hers, and beyond the wet edges and the softness and the love she had come to know and expect, there was something new...something strong and positive and unmovable.

"Yes," he said simply and softly, "I can...I do."

She let him go, drawing back a bit that she might see his face all the clearer.

"I...I don't...Please, Jerry, this is hard for me!"

"I know..."

"I mean, I'm a Jew. So are Sarah and Jacob! And you, Jerry... you're a Jew as well!"

Jerry Westfield's eyes never wavered as he answered.

"I am still a Jew. Only now, I am a Jew who has found the true Messiah. A Jew who knows a Messiah not born of evil and desire for power like Strapollos, but a Messiah who comes in peace and love to save His people. I am a Jew rejoicing in his heritage who now knows in his heart that Jesus is the 'Christ,' or as we say, the Messiah, and that knowledge just fills me with a peace and joy I don't think I have ever known before."

He drew closed, and his hands closed around hers.

"When I last saw Jacob," Jerry continued, "he had Jeremy's Bible and was going somewhere out in the desert to read and pray and think about it. I decided that I would respect whatever decision he made, and I meant that.

"I...I'd like to ask you the same thing. I love you, Ruth, and that love can never just disappear – here one moment and gone the next. Do you see that it's because I love you that I want to ask you to read some of the references Jeremy makes in the tape...to think and meditate on them... to seek...

"Well...whatever knowledge or decision you come to, I will love you...I will love you...I will love you..."

They embraced and he held her for a long time, sharing silently all he hoped to dream and dared to fear.

"Of course," she whispered close to his ear. "If this is going to be a part of you, then I want to understand; I want to be a part of it. Tell me what to read, and let's see the tape again. No promises; we'll just see what happens, OK?"

Jerry kissed her then, his lips seeking hers; his entire being tingling with an ache that was uniquely his since their first embrace; a thrill that had not lessened with time, but grown stronger.

"I'm so glad," Jerry managed to get out of a throat choked with a million words he wanted to say but simply could not get started.

"Let's see the tape again," Ruth said with a hand on his cheek.

"Sure," Jerry replied, "but first, there's something I have to show you..."

He paused.

"Something important."

*   *   *

Demetrius Strapollos stood before his desk and stared at the man occupying the armchair before him.

"If his newspaper calls him home to cover the mess in California, that might be the proper time and place to have it done. In America, muggings happen with regularity, and if one results in a death, well... *qu'elle domage.*

"I would prefer it that way. If it can be avoided, I would like him to be killed outside of Israel, so there will be not even the slightest hint of a connection.

"Am I making myself clear?"

"Quite clear, Demetri," the man in the chair answered as he absent-mindedly toyed with one of his thick, dark braids of hair.

"We cannot, however, afford to have him around much longer, especially not now that everything is falling into place so wonderfully and precisely. All the players are now 'on stage,' and it will soon be time for the curtain to rise. The time rapidly approaches when we can no longer afford his opinion of us."

"Assuredly," Michael Eissen smiled.

"Therefore," Demetrius Strapollos declared, "however you manage to get it done, it must get done – and fairly soon."

Strapollos leaned forward until his eyes were even with those of his companion.

"I want Jerry Westfield, and...

"I want him dead!"

*   *   *

Jerry Westfield picked up the remote and aimed it in the general direction of the TV which bore the frozen image of Jeremy Palmer.

"When I first played the tape," he told Ruth, "I was so overcome, I stopped it immediately, rewound, and watched it again, and again, and again. About the fourth time through, I was thinking about something Jeremy had said, and I was paging through the Bible. Anyhow, I didn't shut it off; I let the tape just play on. That's when I saw it."

"Saw what?" Ruth asked.

"Well, I think Jeremy did this tape for me in a hurry," Jerry continued without answering. "Maybe he had run out of blank tapes, or maybe he just grabbed the first tape that came to his hand. I don't know, but he loaded a used tape and recorded over what was there. His message to me takes what? – six minutes? – and after that what he had recorded previously would begin to play."

"Is that what you want to show me?"

"Yes. Kathy and Jeremy were talented in a number of ways, and one of them was music. Kathy had a lovely voice, and Jeremy's was passable. He played a guitar, and they often composed their own songs. I think they used them in church."

"I say again, no wonder you liked them," Ruth smiled.

"That's what was on the tape," Jerry continued. "They were practicing or maybe just recording a song they had written, but that's what I want you to see."

"Sound's interesting."

"I…I want you to do more than listen to it, Ruth. I'd like you to feel it. I'd like you to know what kind of people can write a song such as you're going to hear. I want you to understand what they're saying. I want…"

"Jerry…"

"Yes."

"Do you know I love you?"

"Of course…"

"Then Jerry…"

"Yes."

"Shut up and push the *PLAY* button!"

*   *   *

Jeremy and Kathy Palmer were smiling at each other as he adjusted his guitar, and she arranged her hair and cleared her throat.

"You ready, Honey," Jeremy asked.

"About as ready as you," Kathy smiled.

"OK, then, we go on four…"

With a smile, Jeremy Palmer began to mouth the numbers silently but with enough animation for Kathy to see – ONE, TWO, THREE, FOUR…

His fingers moved over the guitar, and the silver, lilting notes surrounded them. Kathy Palmer closed her eyes for a moment, then looked across at her husband and began to sing.

I searched for you where midnight met the morning;
I searched for you where laughter met despair;
Beyond my life; beyond my time;
Beyond the maze that was my mind;
I never knew that you were waiting there.

Now Jeremy turned to face Kathy, and his smile was warm and deep as he continued the song.

I never knew what waited in forever;
I never looked beyond what could be seen;
I never knew what it meant to be
A part of Love's great symphony
In worlds I never dared to dream!

They took a step closer to each other and turned to face the camera, their heads lifted, and their voices exultant as they sang together.

I never knew, I never knew
Without your touch…
I never knew, I never knew
Just how much…

I never knew, I never knew
How much I needed you.

Now, Jeremy and Kathy Palmer turned to look into each other's eyes. Ruth knew at once that even the most jaded and cynical of critics could tell that this was not something rehearsed and calculated. This was spontaneous and real.

They sang now to each other.
That Love of yours pours out and overflows me
Like water to a dry and thirsty land,
And like a seed that's finally grown,
This shaken reed had found a home,
I never knew until I took your hand!

I never knew, I never knew...

On the screen, the Palmers continued with the chorus of the song, while a separate melody played within the mind of Ruth Cowen.

Her own eyes wide and brimming with tears, she fixed upon the faces of the man and woman on the tape. Since they had begun the song with its lyrics of love, Ruth could sense that same love sparkling between them in a special, living, vibrant way. And, she could sense something else as well; something that filled her and embraced her and wrapped her as one might wrap a precious infant in a clean white sheet.

The way Jeremy looks at Kathy, she thought, *that's the way...that's the way Jerry looks at me!*

"Now," Jerry whispered, bringing her back to the living room and the tape, "listen to this part..."

The Palmers continued their song.
In all my living dreams you stand before me,
You offer me your nail-scarred hands,
And now I see who stood by me;
Who took my hand and helped me stand;
Who paid the cost for all I'd lost;
Who filled my cup and raised me up –
Truly, You are the Lamb of God!

I never knew, I never knew...

It came upon her in a great wash of insight that pounded in the open recesses of her heart and mind and echoed through the halls of her understanding.

They're...they're talking about God! They're talking about Jesus!

Of course they sang about their love for each other and out of that love as well, but there was more. Their love was cavernous, all inclusive, unconditional

– all because it was a reflection of a love that could never die, that poured itself out on all creation, that was a love that had conquered death!

Was this what Jerry had seen in them? Was this what affected him at this moment? She had always thought in terms of the here and now – been trained that way. Was their something more—something, perhaps, she had only guessed at in her dreams? Was there an answer to all the reaching out she had done in the dark time of sleepless nights and ravaging days?

Was her meeting Jerry a chance happening? Was this entire world the product of…of chance? Or…was there something else?

And…and Jerry looked at her the same way Jeremy looked at Kathy, and the both of them looked at…

Her eyes returned to the screen.

That Love of Yours pours out and overflows me,
Like water to a dry and thirsty land,
And like a seed that's finally grown,
This shaken reed has found a home;
I never knew until I took Your hand…

I never knew, I never knew
Without Your touch…
I never knew, I never knew,
Just how much…
I never knew, I never knew
How much I needed You…
I needed You…

Jerry pushed the button, and the screen faded to gray squiggles. Another button, and it died completely, leaving them in a silence that was punctuated only by Ruth's audible, wet breathing.

"Jerry," she said at length, "help me."

He was in her arms at once, holding her close, loving her, pouring out that love, and doing one other thing beside that was completely new to him this day…praying.

"Jerry," Ruth said again, "I love you; I love you so much…

"Help me to learn."

262

CHAPTER TWENTY-FIVE

The Voice in the Thunder

IT WAS SLIGHTLY PAST SEVEN IN THE EVENING, and Sarah Klausman was working in her kitchen, setting the table for dinner. She always felt that she got so much more done when Jacob was out of the house, but, now, she glanced at the clock and knew Jacob would be home soon from his travels, and the though made her glad.

Sarah ran her home with the efficiency of a corporate executive. Jacob always told her that she could do anything she put her mind to, and they had talked about her having a small interior decorating business someday. Right now, she smiled in the knowledge that she was taking care of her family – something that pleased her greatly; something she really wanted to do.

She heard the Jeep pull up to the house and recognized Jacob's step as he approached the door. He walked in with a book under one arm that Sarah recognized as the one Jerry was always carrying around; the one with the red cover from his missing friend.

"Hello, my sweet Sarah. Is everybody OK?" Jacob asked.

"Yes, everybody's fine. I got your note. Are *you* all right?"

Jacob walked over to Sarah and kissed her warmly.

"I'm going to skip dinner," he said quietly, "at least for now. Maybe I'll have something a little later, all right?"

She looked at Jacob with her soft, brown eyes and told him, "I'll feed the kids and wait for you. I had a late lunch with one of the girls at the Community Help Center, so I'm not that hungry myself."

Jacob Klausman, filled with a rush of warm love for Sarah, kissed his wife once more and said, "I'm going upstairs for a while to read...and pray."

*   *   *

Two hours crept by and then half an hour more inched its way through the universe. Jacob Klausman had still not returned from the roof of his home. With only her lips moving as slightly as a leaf might move in a gentle spring breeze, Sarah Klausman waited for her husband – waited for her best friend.

*   *   *

When Jacob had climbed the stairs to the roof of his house to spend time in prayer, he brought with him a small square of well-worn red carpet that he used as a kneeling pad. He knew you didn't need to kneel in order to pray to your God, but for Jacob, he simply felt better doing it that way.

Unlike many people he knew who liked reading formal, written prayers out of a book, Jacob preferred to pray in his own words, as if speaking to someone who sat next to him. He thought that God would rather hear exactly what he was thinking rather than what someone else had said, no matter how holy or devout or beautiful the words.

Therefore, when he had read all the references from Jeremy Palmer's Bible and then even more for almost two hours, he knelt on the square of carpet and began to pray before his God.

At this time of the year, rain was infrequent, but not unheard of, and off in the distance, Jacob could make out a heavy blackness creeping against the deep blue of Israel's night sky. Flashes of light, with the rumble of thunder so far off as to be barely perceived at all, dotted the horizon. The wind began to pick up.

Jacob began to pray the way he did so often; the way he loved to do, pouring out his thanks to God for his family, his friends, and for the Nation of Israel. He always felt very close to God under Israel's lofty skies, even if it were, as now it seemed, preparing for rain.

He had been there for a while, how long exactly he did not know, when he became aware of something or, more precisely, of someone. Someone was with him on the roof, of that he was sure! He could feel it.!

Jacob turned quickly, his body low to the ground; his practiced eyes sweeping the entire area.

There was no one there. He was quite alone with the wind and the rain that moved across the Mediterranean Sea towards Jaffa.

Perhaps, Lord, Jacob thought, *I am getting older than I think?*

264

* * *

Downstairs, Sarah heard the thunder, and she began to rock back and forth in her chair and pray. The children were in bed, and Jerry, she had been told, was out to dinner with Ruth, so she was alone. Sarah knew her husband very well, and she realized that Jacob would not come down for thunder or anything else – not until he had finished talking to his God.

* * *

Jacob Klausman resumed his prayer.

"Oh, Lord God Almighty, I am humbled in Your presence. I come to You tonight to ask for wisdom. You, Almighty God, You see the world and all who walk upon it. There are no secrets or hidden places that You cannot see. Share with me, oh Lord, Your great and holy knowledge.

"Tell me, Oh God, what I should do. I desire to see Your glory. I desire to see Your salvation brought to Your people, Israel. Forgive my sins and the sins of Your people. I do not make this request because I am righteous, but because You are merciful. Oh, Lord, hear and act! Hear and act not for me only, but for Your sake and the sake of the people who bear Your name!"

The rain began to fall harder now as blue-white lightning split the skies above Jaffa, and the thunder was a twisting, living thing that Jacob could feel rumbling through his bones.

"You have delivered me from the hands of my enemies so many times," Jacob continued, raising his voice and undaunted by the conditions about him. "When I fought against the enemies of Israel, I felt your hand upon me; when I was surrounded, you covered me. You kept me and strengthened me that I might do Your will.

"Now, Oh Lord, I must know who You are, for many have come in your name and are saying You are here, and You are there, and many have followed. Prophets roam the streets declaring your judgement, while others proclaim your coming. Come and touch me once more, that I might know your will."

There was a huge flash of almost pure white light, followed almost immediately by a splitting burst of thunder that seemed as if it would rip apart the very place where Jacob knelt.

The thunder faded…but the light…the light.

The light remained.

It had to come from somewhere, but Jacob could not tell where. Nor could he tell what it was, but it was there. The light, the bright warm and glowing light grew around him, took him in, encompassed his very being. He could see the wind-blown rain all around, but below him and in a circle about him, all was calm. Moreover, in his heart, in his mind, in every muscle of his body, Jacob felt a flowing sense of peace, deep and real. Had he the words of a thousand poets he could not have begun to describe that which flowed so freely through him now; what had wrapped itself so firmly around his soul.

In the light, there was a figure, a man. Jacob could not see his face clearly because of the radiant brightness that surrounded it, but he saw the figure move, and Jacob Klausman, in his heart and mind and down to the tips of his fingers, knew something – knew it urgently, immediately, and without question.

It was the ANGEL OF THE LORD!

Jacob didn't know if he were looking up or down or to either side. Indeed, time and space seemed to have lost their meaning. Jacob was and the LORD was, and that was sufficient…extremely sufficient.

Now, the figure bent forward, toward Jacob, and the lips smiled and spoke.

"I am the one you seek, Jacob. I am the Alpha and the Omega; who is and who was, and who is to come; the Almighty.

"Do not be afraid, Jacob, for I have heard your prayers. I heard how you sought Me with tears and a humble heart. My prophet, Joel, spoke of this day when he said, 'I will pour out My Spirit on all people. Your sons and daughters will prophesy, your old men will dream dreams, your young men will see visions.

" 'Even on My servants, both men and women, I will pour out My Spirit in those days. I will show wonders in the heavens and on the earth, blood and fire and billows of smoke. The sun will be turned to darkness and the moon to blood before the coming of the great and dreadful day of the Lord. And everyone who calls on the Name of the Lord will be saved; for on Mount Zion and in Jerusalem there will be deliverance, as the Lord has said, among the survivors whom the Lord calls.'

"Jacob, I am about to purge My people, Israel. I am sending My two olive branches to you. They will tell you what you must do.

"Remember that I love you, Jacob. Be of good courage, for I am with you and all those who call upon My Name."

The face and the words that burned so deeply into Jacob's heart began to fade, to fold in upon itself, although the smile and the peace somehow remained.

"Lord!" Jacob called after the light, "What shall I call Your name?"

The light continued to fade, but the voice was as strong as ever, resonating deep within Jacob's mind.

"Call Me, Y'shua; call me, Jesus...I am HE who saves His people."

Then, as it had come from nowhere and everywhere, the light returned to those places and was gone into the raging, wind-swept sky.

In the howling wind, the driving rain, and the splintering thunder, Jacob Klausman bowed to the ground and wept as he had never done before.

He bundled himself into as small a package as he could, rocking back and forth, marveling and praising and replaying the vision over and over in his mind.

* * *

Almost an hour later, Jerry and Ruth, having skipped dinner but caring not the least for food, came through the door, and Sarah noticed that the storm was over, and the skies were clearing once more. She sat at the kitchen table, sipping a cup of tea.

"Hi, Sarah," Jerry said pleasantly, "where's Jacob?"

"He's praying."

Jerry realized where that meant, and his eyes shot upward. He asked, "Through the storm?"

"Through the storm," Sarah affirmed with a nod.

"Is he all right?" Ruth asked. "I mean, did you check on him?"

Sarah answered firmly, "You know better than that, Ruth. Jacob is not the kind of man who can be chased by a storm."

"Wait a minute," Jerry said, turning toward the stairway. "I think that's him. I think I hear him coming now."

Indeed, it was Jacob Klausman, and he walked slowly down the steps and into the kitchen with everyone staring at him. Ruth gasped and took a step backward, blinking in wonder at the glow that seemed to radiate from Jacob's face. It was as if, somehow, a light was shinning on his face. Sarah noticed it as well, and she took a breath sharply, acutely aware that something had happened – and it was something wonderful.

Jerry Westfield saw it too, but always the observant reporter, he saw something else besides. He exclaimed, "Jacob, you're dry! Where were you? We thought you were on the roof."

"I was," Jacob smiled.

Then, Jacob Klausman turned to Sarah and said, "Go and wake the children. There is something they must see."

Without a word, without a protest, Sarah left the room. Ruth and Jerry waited in silence, as Jacob stood by a window, his head lifted to the sky.

When the children came in, wrapped in bathrobes and wearing slippers, sleep still clinging to their eyelashes, Jacob knelt to them and gently said, "We are going up to the roof, because I want you to see something; something I want you to remember for the rest of your lives. Now come."

Jacob took Sarah's hand and they all followed him up the stairs.

Toward the top, the steps became damp and slick, wet by the rain that had flowed in through the door the wind had opened. From their vantage point, they could see the roofs of the city reflect the night lights from their rain-slick surfaces. On the streets, the headlights of a hundred cars reflected from the water that still clung in shimmering puddles.

"That," Jacob said as he pointed, "is where I prayed tonight, during the storm."

The square of red carpet upon which Jacob had knelt was almost dead center on the roof. It was totally and completely dry, as was a circle about six feet in diameter that seemed to radiate out from his kneeling pad. The edges and corners of the roof were soaked, sodden with cold, black rain, but the circle into which they all now stepped remained warm and dry.

"There is something I want to tell you," Jacob stated. "It is something Jerry already knows, but now, all of you whom I love dearer than life, I must tell you as well,"

And, holding hands, Jacob Klausman told his wife and family and best friends about the light and the figure in the light and the peace and safety in the middle of the storm.

*   *   *

When the children had been returned to bed with hugs and kisses, and Jacob had held Sarah close to him for perhaps eight or nine minutes without saying a word, the four of them climbed the stairs once more in silent agreement.

They stood, side by side, facing the night that now had a decided chill to it following the rain.

Before them stretched the streets of Jaffa, and beyond that the Mediterranean, then Europe and the World.

Jerry Westfield took a step forward and swept an arm outward to encompass all that they could and could not see. Inside, his mind was racing, and he felt the words forming almost of their own volition. They were not his words, and yet they were. They boiled up within him, and he was acutely aware that they came from afar, born of a Spirit he was just learning to trust. When they poured out, it was in a tumult of love and fire, glory and the ice of a million stars.

"Can you sense it?" he asked. "Do you feel the storm?"

"Storm?" Ruth questioned. "Jerry, the storm has passed; it's clearing up..."

"No, Ruth, not that kind of storm. Not a storm of Nature and Nature's God. Not a storm that cleanses and cools and washes away the dirt of a thousand footsteps. That's not the storm I mean.

"The storm I'm talking about has already begun. It's rain burns like fire; its winds cut like polished razors. Those it touches are smeared with its grime, and the streets are clogged with the mud and blood that he carries within him. This storm will rage inside buildings; inside homes; inside the hearts or all mankind. There will be no one who will not be drenched by it; no one it will not touch or batter.

"It's roar will be heard to the ends of the earth; its screech will drive madness before it, eating its way into the skin and mind and soul. In the end, there will be no place to hide, and even death will be desired above all else, yet even that will not ease the pain.

"The boiling clouds will carry one message; one name that will be glorified before it is cursed by all – the name Strapollos...Strapollos... Strapollos...

"And we...the four of us standing here at the place of this miracle this night...we will be a part of it all. I don't know how, and I don't know why...but as God lives, we are bound up one with another."

"But how?" Sarah said softly.

"If what you say is true," Ruth began, "then how can we..."

"One way," Jacob stated with strength and conviction. "There is just one way."

He held out both hands palm upwards, and they were immediately taken by Sarah and Ruth who, in turn, took Jerry's hands in theirs.

"Exactly," Jerry Westfield agreed.

He bowed his head.

"Shall we begin," he said.

As they all lowered their heads and the words began, what clouds were left fled swiftly away, and a beautiful night sky surrounded them.

It was a sky none of them would ever see in the same way again.

End of Part Four

EPILOGUE:

The Travelers

And I will give power to my two witnesses,
and they will prophesy for 1,280 days,
clothed in sackcloth. These are the
two olive trees and the two
lampstands that stand
before the Lord
of the earth.
Revelation 11:3-4

A BRILLIANT MOON ROSE HIGH, its pale blue light flooding the desert hills. The plain stretched out in the moonlight, beautiful and cool, pastel and distant.

On the top of Mitzpe-Ramon, on the edge of the Negev, the two men stood quietly, without moving. As the Klausman family and Ruth and Jerry held hands and began to pray on a rooftop miles away to the north in Jaffa, the moonlight glinted off the dark wooden staffs these two men held in their hands. It highlighted the loose flow of their robes, and bathed the leather of their sandals in its glow.

Together, their dark eyes stared out at the expanse of desert that flowed below and before them. Then, their beards glinting silver in the moonlight, they tightened their grips on the staffs they held.

Glancing up at the moon and beyond to the stars, they began their journey.

END

BEGINNING OF SORROWS
by
Russ Scalzo and Steve Mamchak
BOOK ONE of the *Chronicles of the End Times* SERIES

About the Authors

RUSS SCALZO: Whether as a musician, composer, and founder of a Christian Rock Band or as a Deacon and frequent lecturer in Biblical Prophecy, Russ brings a lifetime of technical expertise to a story he believes may well be the substance of tomorrow's headlines.

STEVE MAMCHAK: Long-time educator and author of a number of books on teaching methodology, Steve holds ministerial credentials and heads a drama ministry aimed at presenting Biblical truth in a timely and powerful manner.

RUSS SCALZO and STEVE MAMCHAK have united their expertise and their talents to write a trilogy of the 'End Times' that they feel is both Biblically accurate as well as dramatically powerful, hitting at the essence of our lives now, and during the time that may soon be upon us.